For all who have encouraged me

and helped me with my work

and especially

for my family

Contents

Prologue

Ghost Writer

When my father is in his nineties, he tells me the story of a difficult day in my maternal grandfather's life. He is a boy working the fields in Puglia with his parents, and his small hands are covered with scratches from the wheat stalks he is binding after his parents cut them. He looks up to the road high above the field and sees a small boy about his age walking along the road carrying a book bag.

It is at the end of the nineteenth century, well after 1860, the year that marks the great divide in southern Italian history. Thereafter, the peasantry become increasingly poor, increasingly despised, increasingly unable to extricate themselves from debt. It is a time when there is never money enough or food enough, though families toil from before dawn until after dusk and live lives of virtual indentured servitude.

"Papa, where is that boy going?" my grandfather asks, looking at the boy walking alone on the road, for a boy walking alone on a road without carrying wheat in this part of Italy is an unusual and wondrous thing.

"That boy," his father says, "is going to school."

"Papa," my grandfather says, "I would like to do that. I would like to go to school."

"*Figlio mio,*" his father says, "you cannot do that, you cannot go to school."

"But why can't I go to school, Papa?" my grandfather asks.

"You cannot go to school," his father answers, "because you are a farm worker and your lot in life is to work the fields."

"But Papa," my grandfather says, "what about my children?"

"Your children," his father answers, "cannot go to school for they, too, will be farm workers and they will work in the fields like you."

In my father's retelling of the story, my grandfather pauses for a moment, looks again at the boy on the road, and says, "But Papa, my children's children. My children's children, they will go to school."

According to my father, though poverty was an impelling cause for my grandfather's leaving Puglia and coming to America to work on the railroad, wanting his descendants to be able to go to school, like that boy on the road, was the major reason he emigrated to the United States—so that his children's children could go to school.

I am the eldest daughter of my grandfather's only child, a daughter, and I have gone to school, and I have become a teacher and a writer. And although I am certain my grandfather would have been proud of my having become a teacher and a writer, I am quite certain that he would not have wanted me to write about my family. For there were, and would be, secrets in our family— that my mother's mother had died; that the grandmother I knew was her stepmother; that after her birth mother's death, my mother was abused by caregivers; that she had been institutionalized and shock treated; that my grandfather drank too much; that my father was violent; that my sister killed herself; that I was sexually abused by someone known to the family. These subjects were never discussed, much less written about.

Still, my maternal grandparents and my father were storytellers. And schooling was encouraged in my family. My mother went to high school and didn't attend college only because her family needed her income during the Depression. From when I was small, everyone took pride in my academic accomplishments, the men in my family as well as the women (unusual at that time in my culture). That I would become educated was encouraged and assumed. That I would become a writer was never imagined. Or was it?

⌣

Among my father's many (and not altogether endearing) nicknames for me was "the storyteller."

When we move from Hoboken to Ridgefield, New Jersey, my father makes me a special desk that fits into a small, triangular space at the top of a flight of stairs. He takes time and trouble with this desk, made of plywood, because it is what he can afford. He sands, stains, buffs, and polishes it; he buys a special pull for its one small drawer.

"This is where you can write your homework assignments," my parents announce when the desk is finished and installed in its place. My mother has bought an expensive desk lamp secondhand, for next to no money, she says, so I can work at night, too.

My retreat to my desk in my troubled household is encouraged, even sanctioned. In part it might have been my parents' way of giving their difficult child something to do, someplace to be other than where they were, annoying them. Often, I make up fake homework so I can stay there and escape from chores or taking care of my sister.

Most of the writing I do at this desk is schoolwork. It includes essays like "Safety in the Home, Street, and School" that win me a prize, that tell me my words might be worth something, and research projects like "The Shakespeare Controversy," in which I conclude that Christopher Marlowe has written Shakespeare's works.

Here, too, when I was younger, I'd penned elaborate schemes for a club a friend and I have organized, a club of two, she and I, the only members, and we called it "The Elms Club," a name combining our initials. It is a club of two because no one else wants to play with us, though I am not altogether aware of this. That we are only two seems fitting and right: It means that we are never excluded from any activities we plan; it means that we can lead often; it means that each of us stands a good chance of getting her way.

Our club activities (that, as I recall, consisted of doing things with dolls, with old clothes in my friend's attic, with the rubble we collected on the street that we fashioned into assemblages, with paper and pens and crayons), important as I deemed them, didn't interest me as much as our being together. Still, it was my job as the club's historian to record what we did and when we did it and why.

It was at that desk my father made that I first experienced a realm that did not heretofore exist in my life—a place where I recorded two girls' doing seemingly insignificant things that enriched their lives and made them exciting. It is at that desk that I learned the power of the imagination, the power of language to create a world, the power of language to forge a bond between people, the power of language to record experience and to reflect upon its significance, the power of language to make us feel as if what we do has meaning. And so it is at this desk that I did my first important writing, encouraged and sanctioned by my parents, with whom I had a contentious relationship.

But that I might become a writer, I never dream. I am destined for more practical matters: a career in teaching, or, perhaps the law, because, as my father says, I love to argue.

⌣

It is 1983 and I am on a very small airplane, flying from Boston to Maine to give a series of talks at Colby College about my work on Virginia Woolf. The flight has been thrilling. The pilot has hugged the magnificent coast, flown low enough so we can see the waves pounding the rocks and the salt spray pluming in the air. Soon, the plane banks, heads inland, descends.

"Below," the pilot announces, "is the Maine Central Railroad." And I burst into tears. For these are the tracks that my maternal grandfather, Salvatore Calabrese, worked on at the beginning of the twentieth century.

The richness and sorrow of this moment, the unlikely story of my life's journey, are evident to me immediately. For it is my grandfather's coming to the United States and his hard manual labor that have made my work as a teacher and writer possible. Without his emigrating, without his dream of educating his children and his children's children, without his grueling work on the railroad to support his family, without his devotion to a small girl, without his storytelling, I surely wouldn't be here on an airplane, flying below the clouds, and above the rails, on my way to give a lecture about the life of a famous privileged woman writer. Without his emigrating, where would I be? In the South of Italy, close to the village he left, poor as he was, uneducated in all likelihood, and working the fields like him.

⌣

I never would have left Virginia Woolf scholarship and started writing memoir if the late Sara Ruddick, co-editor of the landmark *Working It Out: 23 Women Writers, Artists, Scientists, and Scholars Talk About Their Lives and Work*, hadn't invited me to contribute to a book of essays she was collecting about a woman's relationship to her biographical subject and how that work changed her life. She thought a narrative about how the Italian American granddaughter of a farm worker in poverty-stricken Puglia and the daughter of working-class parents came to write about Virginia Woolf would be a meaningful contribution to her book. Writing this essay (titled "A Portrait of the *Puttana* as a Middle-Aged Woolf Scholar" and included, here, in revised form as "V and I") is a turning point in my life. For I can never approach writing again without being aware that I am not just any writer, but an Italian American writer, and not just an Italian American writer, but a southern Italian American writer. But even as I am shifting my identity and realizing I am a child of the children of immigrants, I am still unaware of what this means and I am completely unaware of the history of persecution, racism, and exile that has shaped my people and my personal history, in part because my mother has tried so hard to assimilate. I haven't yet learned about the historical circumstances of my grandparents' lives in Italy.

Writing "*Puttana*" in my own voice was not difficult; it was exhilarating. Contemplating its publication, though, was terrifying. So terrifying that I tore up the only copy of the essay when I reread it (and this was before computers, so this ripping and tearing meant I'd destroyed my work). For how could I publish an essay that spoke of my family's past, my father's violence, my husband's adultery? How could I reveal these things?

When I tell my husband I've ripped up my work, he tells me to dig the pieces of the essay out of the garbage. He knows I've written about how he almost left our small child and me. Even so, this man has become the man who tells me that what we have is a jigsaw puzzle situation on our hands and that, although I detest puzzles, I had better get to work and piece the damn thing together. Which is what I begin to do while he makes dinner.

⌒

My writing life has been a series of breakings and mendings, a shattering of the writing self that was, a repairing, through writing, of something in my life that warranted understanding and that needed fixing. I found an image to describe what I do in Luigi Pirandello's *La Giara*. In that work, a pottery mender climbs into a broken olive oil jar to glue it together, only to discover that to get out, he must break the jar and begin the process again.

This metaphor, to me, is a very Italian way of describing the creative process, as a never-ending breaking and mending. I especially like that it is an oil jar which is being repaired, for olive oil is considered sacred, the jar's inside a sacral space.

Because my father was a handyman, a man who made and fixed things, and because my mother was a seamstress and a mender—of clothes, of dishes—a woman who threw nothing away but repaired it for everyday use, and because my sister was a fine potter, and because my grandmother was a "super" in our tenement and so responsible for making small repairs, and because my grandfather built and repaired railroad lines, seeing my writing work as that of symbolic repair, of fixing a broken piece of pottery, has important personal meaning for me. And, like my father before me, I carry what I need to ply my trade—portable computer, paper, pen, books, glasses—in my writer's version of a toolbox.

The essays in this collection illustrate the breakings and mendings of my writing life. Many are versions of pieces someone invited me to write. (Their original titles and publication information are provided in the Acknowledgments.) "Can you write about how an Italian American woman like you became a Virginia Woolf scholar?" "Your husband's adultery?" "Your relationship with your sister?" "The impact of illness in your life?" "Your family's relationship to food?" "Living in New Jersey during wartime?" "What you see when you look in the mirror?" "Your relationship to your ethnicity?" "Your grandmother's needlework?" "How you would describe your work?" "How water figured in your family's history?"

Whenever I begin work, I remind myself I am only writing an essay—a trial, an attempt, a test, an exploration, an examination, an experiment, a way to learn something I didn't know before. I am trying to see if I have anything to say. And because the subject matter is defined, and the word limit set, and the editor available to help me trim and shape (as, for example, Kathryn Harrison did with "Old Flame," insisting that the last words of the piece be hopeful, not lugubrious), I find that I sail along unimpeded, even as I initially have no idea of what I'm doing, of where the writing will take me, of what the essay will say, of what the language will sound like, of how it will be organized.

But then I often discover I have more to say on a subject than I anticipated (the twenty-page invited essay on illness that became sixty, then a hundred, then a book), and so one essay leads to a longer version of it, and then to another, and another, and after a time, there are a string of related essays that might become a book, that then become a book. This collection illustrates how I begin to work; it gathers those essays on subjects I couldn't let go of and that propelled me to consider or write book-length works.

It is through writing these essays that I learned what memoir can do, and learned, too, how I want to write within the memoir form: to use it as a means of self-discovery, to fix something in my life that was broken, to record the self in the process of changing and becoming, to witness my ancestors' lives and to re-create and imagine them and to understand how their lives shaped mine, to reflect upon the significance of the lived life in the context of history, to find a form appropriate to recounting how we remember our past and make sense of it (one that insists upon associative, fragmentary, incomplete, piecemeal narratives).

In assembling the essays in this book, I have learned that, taken together, they constitute a story significantly different from my other memoirs, where, in many cases, the starkness of their meaning became blunted by material surrounding them. And here I have also restored material I'd written and then deleted—or rather, censored—experiences I was too reticent to reveal before, in writing about my sister's suicide or about my husband's adultery, for example. And here, too, I have not resisted the impulse to tinker, to add new material, to shift the ballast of an essay because my life has changed significantly as I have aged.

⌒

Virginia Woolf committed herself to writing about the lives of the obscure, for she believed these lives revealed more about the history of a culture than the lives of the great and famous. Most of us are ordinary, are no heroes. And so committing myself to writing about the obscure—my parents, my grandparents, the members of my family—instead of continuing to write about Virginia Woolf and other famous writers marked a significant turning point in my writing life. The form would have to be memoir, but a kind of memoir that permitted imagining what the lives of the members of my family might have been like based upon research into the papers (not many) and the artifacts they left behind, upon the stories they told me or that I was told about them. I came to believe this form of memoir that honors our forebears by reimagining their lives but without romanticizing them is especially necessary during a time when ordinary people are being robbed of their ability to lead a dignified life, when their past stands in danger of being erased, when in a nation of supposed promise, the future is bleak for those, like my forebears, who work hard and long, yet try to continue, against all obstacles, to hope, to dream.

The questions *Who were these people who were my forebears? What happened to them? Who am I because of what happened to them? And how can I understand us all in the context of the times during which they lived?* are questions I asked myself in writing the pieces in this collection. They have led me further and deeper than any other pursuit.

But how do you tell the story of a people who don't want to remember, who don't often tell you what they recall or, if they do, speak in puzzles, riddles, enigmas, stories that seem to be about others but that are really about themselves? How do you find their stories? And you must find them. Because the stories people try to forget are the most important stories, the ones that must be recorded, the ones history has buried or ignored or erased, the ones memoirists must tell. Memoir, then, is a corrective to history.

All a memoirist of people who led "obscure lives" can do, all I can do, is try to *imagine* their lives from the few shreds of evidence left behind, to represent them, to re-present them to readers. To imagine what their lives might have been like given the little that is known about them. To try to ascertain the significance of their lives. To accord them a little gift of time, remembrance, respect, and, yes, to try to ensure that their deaths do not erase the meaning and significance of their lives.

I am the only one of my family who is still alive. The only one left. And so the only one who can do this work of remembering. Yes, others could. But who would want to? Who else would want to spend time writing about a man who worked on the railroad, who left behind him when he died nothing more than a box filled with long underwear, a pass allowing him to ride the railroad free on certain lines at certain times, his naturalization papers, a wife, a daughter, a granddaughter who loved him, and little more? To some, an insignificant man, and so not worthy of having his life recounted. Who would want to spend time writing about a woman who was superintendent of a tenement in Hoboken, New Jersey, who, when she was forced to move to the suburbs, spent the rest of her life sitting in a corner knitting and crocheting and protecting her granddaughter from her father's rages? Who else would write about a woman with dreams of being a writer, so often felled by depression and despair, who sold shoes at W. T. Grant's in Hoboken? Of a man who was no hero and yet torn asunder by war, who had grand dreams but who was forced to abandon them? Of a sister, a postwar child, whose parents had so little to give her after the war that, years later, for this and other reasons, she killed herself?

The work of understanding the lives of my family is, as Paul Auster has said, condemned to futility. Still, I must try. And though I try to understand people who cannot be understood, not to try to understand them would be far more futile than the futile act of trying. And to try to understand their lives is to begin to understand the lives of so many others like them.

As a memoirist, I write about what was, what might have been, what could have been, for memoir must also be about desires unfulfilled in a culture that does not seem to honor, but instead often deliberately attempts to squelch, the aspirations of the poor and the outsider. I write about people now long dead who can no longer share the facts of their lives or their memories with me. Memoir writes what has vanished and will never return. And perhaps the memoirist engages in this futile task to try to bring that time back, to try to understand it, and through that understanding, to give meaning to what was heretofore inchoate, and through giving meaning to other people's lives, to give meaning to our own. Still, memoir writes what has vanished and will never return. So in this sense, every memoirist is a ghost writer, a writer who chases ghosts.

The House of
Early Sorrows

LIFEBOAT

"Gather courage."

This is what my father tells me as I cling to the gunwale of an ashen rowboat somewhere in the middle of Lake George. I'm sixteen years old; I'm swimming across Lake George; it's 1959; my family is vacationing at a cabin in Bolton Landing on the shore of Lake George; the cabin we're renting comes with this old boat my father rows beside me as I swim. (I'd wanted to rent a new one, but he insisted on this old one. "You can count on old boats," my father said, "trusty, tried, and true.")

"Pace yourself," my father reminds me as I enter the lake from the dock. "A mile on water isn't a mile on land. A mile on water," he says, "is longer, far longer."

The swimsuit I'm wearing is baby blue with a balloon bottom, all the rage this year but entirely unsuited for long-distance swimming. My mother hated it when I chose it, thought it impractical, tried to dissuade me from buying it, but it was my odd-job money, so I bought it anyway. It's the only suit I own, so it's the one I wear to swim Lake George. The balloon bottom of the suit fills with water as I swim, and when it does, it drags me down, down, down with every stroke I take. I surface, gasp for air, slap the water out of my suit, start to stroke, start to swim again.

No matter how afraid I am, what I mustn't do, I know, is hyperventilate. So I'm paying close attention to my breathing. In, out, in, out. One, two, one, two. Slow the breathing down. If I hyperventilate, my father has told me, I will black out. Shallow water blackout, it's called, even though I'm not in shallow water, for now I am near the middle of Lake George, swimming in the deep.

I remember my father's voice reminding me that swimming in deep water is the same as swimming in shallow water. Still, I know that if I black out, I'll drown, I'll die, and I can't count on my father to save me. So I'm trying to control my breathing, trying to slow it down, counting my strokes, one, two, one, two, counting my breaths, one, two, one, two, trying to plow my way through choppy water, trying to swim Lake George.

I've been doing the American crawl, the stroke my father swears by for long distances. But today the lake isn't calm, so when I turn my head to breathe, I'm smacked in the face with a wall of water. I'm struggling to keep the water out of my nose, out of my mouth, out of my lungs. There are foot-high swells in the middle of the lake. Not high enough to swamp a rowboat, not dangerous enough to drag it down to the swampy, weed-infested bottom of the lake. But high enough to make a rough swim even rougher.

When the American crawl tires me, I switch to sidestroke, then to the elementary backstroke. I can't see the opposite shoreline so I can't pinpoint an object to focus upon. Because I can't see where I'm going, I can't be sure I'm swimming straight and true, so I'm worried that I've been zigzagging across the lake, adding even more distance to an already long swim.

The best stroke for this swim would be the breaststroke. The breaststroke would let me see where I'm going every time I surface to breathe. But it's the only stroke I've never learned, the only stroke my father couldn't teach me. I'd tried hard to imitate him the many times he'd demonstrated it to me, but I fatigued easily when using this stroke. If I'd been born a boy, he said, I'd have the upper-body strength the stroke required. If I'd been a boy, he'd have had no trouble teaching me the breaststroke. But I'm not a boy, so it's a hard stroke for me, the breaststroke, with its whiplike kick, requiring the kind of musculature and endurance I've never developed. So I gave up learning it even though my father warned me that one day I'd need to see ahead of me while I'm swimming. And that day is now.

I've been treading water, choking, gasping, spitting out water for the past few minutes. I'm spent. I'm angry. What am I doing here? I see a purple stain on the surface of the lake just beyond my reach. Is it an oil slick? A gathering of tangled sea grass I must avoid? A darkening that indicates a deepening of the lake?

"Full fathom five my father lies"—those lines I studied from Shakespeare announce themselves. I try to remember the rest of the lines—bones, eyes, something about coral.

"You're halfway there," my father says. I can barely hear him over the slap of the water against the bow. Yet reaching the dead center of the lake unnerves me. I know the lake is 200 feet deep here, maybe more. If I go down, underwater currents will take my body through falls and chutes and rapids into Lake Champlain. Weeks, maybe months from when I disappear, a local boy will cast a fishing line into the lake, snag my bathing suit, and reel in my bloated body long after my family has given up hope of its ever being found.

I panic, scissor over to the rowboat, grasp the gunwale, elude my father's gaze. Holding on to the rowboat means I'm cheating, means that even if I make it to the other side and make it back, I really won't have swum across Lake George. My father doesn't like cheaters; he doesn't like quitters; he doesn't like losers. He doesn't like people who take the easy way out. The only person you're cheating when you take the easy way out, my father says, is yourself.

But my father surprises me, lets me clutch the gunwale for a moment, then tells me in his most serious voice to gather courage and move on. I keep myself from laughing. It's my father, playing to an audience, only out here the only audience he has is me.

I strike out again, away from the boat, away from him, pulling myself through water, though I still wonder what I'm doing here, still can't figure out why I've let him persuade me to undertake this swim, still wonder why I've given in to him this time, instead of resisting him as I so often do, and I hope that my giving in to him won't be my undoing.

⌣

"No, I'm busy," I tell him when he asks me to do something—take care of my sister, help my mother set the table, weed the lawn—even though this resistance costs me, even though, in the end, he makes me do what he says.

"Absolutely not," he tells me, when I want to do something he doesn't approve of, and he doesn't approve of much of what I want to do. Going to Palisades Amusement Park with my girlfriends. Going down to the Sweete Shoppe without my sister to meet my classmates. Spending a day down the shore with my older friends later this summer before I start college even though I'm almost seventeen and I've been earning real money for years.

"No," he says, "over my dead body, no." I turn my back on him, he yells, I run away, he chases me, but he doesn't catch me after I run out the door, sprint down the block, away, away, away from him.

⌣

I scissor kick away from the boat. Now I'm moving through the water more easily. The wind has veered, or backed, terms my Navy man father uses, terms he's tried to teach me, concepts I can't or won't understand. But now there is no barrier to my forward motion. Now the wind and waves urge me along as I slice a trail through water to safety on the other side.

⌣

My father taught me the American crawl a few years before in the mud hole where we used to swim on summer weekends some miles away from our house in Ridgefield, New Jersey. I already knew the sidestroke, the elementary backstroke—these he'd taught me when I was eight years old. But when I turned thirteen, my father wanted me to learn the crawl, the most important stroke, he said, the one that distinguishes good swimmers from amateurs.

"Master the crawl," he'd say. "Then you'll be a real swimmer."

My mother would pack a picnic lunch. We'd set out for the mud hole on a summer's day. My father would get into the water with me. I'd stand on the mucky bottom, and he'd show me how to move my arms, turn my head, and breathe.

"Stroke, stroke, stroke," he'd say, as I'd turn my head right, then left, then right, then left again. Then he taught me the kick, the flutter kick, he called it. He held me, first, around the waist, which I didn't like, but I had no choice, and later, after I got the gist of the kick, he'd hold me by my outstretched hands, and I'd practice until he was satisfied.

Near the end of the summer, when my father thought I was ready, he let me swim far out to the raft in the middle of the mud hole and back again to shore. Out and back. Then out and back again. He stood at the edge of the water and watched, too far away to help if I floundered. But the lifeguards were there, I told myself, and they could help me if only they were watching and not flirting the way they always did. When I emerged from the water, my father would tell me what I'd done wrong.

My hands weren't slicing into the water at the right angle.

My head was lifted too high.

My kick was throwing up too much water.

Even though my technique wasn't perfect, I'd learned something hard, something my father had wanted me to learn, maybe even pleased him by my efforts. All that summer, my father reminded me never to get cocky, never to take chances in the water.

"The water," he said, "can be your friend if you understand it, but only if you know your limitations. But it's an element you must submit to; it's one that's impossible to control."

"See," my father would say, as I emerged from the water at the end of a day, fingers wrinkled, legs aching, "see how little energy you use with the American crawl. The crawl," my father would say, "and the dead man's float could save your life."

That summer, my mother sat on a blanket, a look of misery on her face, watching my sister splashing in the water and digging in the sand at the edge of the mud hole. On these late summer days, I was my father's responsibility; one child was more than enough for my mother to handle. My sister didn't like the water. Every day we spent at the mud hole was a misery for her. She hated the sand; she hated the mucky bottom; whenever my father tried to carry her into the water, she cried.

Like my sister, my mother didn't venture into the water except to cool off. She sat on a blanket for most of the long summer's day, watching my sister during the morning, doling out sandwiches and drinks to us at lunchtime, burying her feet in the sand and flexing her toes, gazing out across the muddy water to the woods on the other side while my sister took her afternoon nap.

My mother had been a fine swimmer as a young woman, my father told me, had swum in roiling seas off the rocky coast of Rhode Island every day during summer holidays when she visited her cousin, and off the coast of Maine on her honeymoon. "The water was too cold for me, but not for her," my father said proudly.

Once, during the war, when my father was away, when she and I spent a summer with her cousin in Rhode Island, she'd ventured so far out into the ocean that her cousin, standing and waiting for her at the water's edge, couldn't be sure she would make it back to shore, and so called the lifeguard.

"Help," her cousin said. "See that girl out there? She's my cousin. She needs help."

I was playing in the sand, my back to the water, unaware of the danger my mother was in, too young to be afraid, too young to understand how dangerous the riptides were in this stretch of water. Then two lifeguards dragged a boat through the sand past me, and I turned to see what was happening.

The lifeguards rowed out to my mother, threw her a life buoy, and dragged her back to shore. When she staggered up to the beach, my mother insisted she didn't need rescuing. But her cousin said she did, and told her she was crazy, crazy to swim so far out by herself, especially because of what had happened last time.

What *had* happened last time? I wondered. But I never learned, never asked my mother, never asked her cousin. And then years later, during the many times my mother couldn't get out of bed, and, even later, when she stopped taking the pills that were keeping her alive, when she collapsed and went to the hospital where she died, I wondered whether, on the day she was rescued, and on that other day my mother's cousin alluded to, my mother had wanted to swim so far away from shore that no one would see her falter, no one would rescue her, no one would see her body sink, the undersea currents dragging her down, down, down, no one would row a boat out to her and pull her back into a life she didn't want to live.

⌣

By the end of the summer when I learned the American crawl, I could swim to the raft and back as many times as I wanted without my father watching me. This was bliss, this swimming. My head nearly underwater, my vision blurred, my ears stopped against sound, the force of my arms and legs propelling me forward. In the water, there was no father, no mother, no sister, no doors slamming, no dishes shattering against the kitchen wall, no oaths and imprecations, no tyranny, no strangling of the heart's desire.

My father taught me the dead man's float, too, that summer. And I'd practiced it, though I never intended to get myself into a situation where I might need to use it, never wanted to do more than swim to the raft in the middle of the mud hole and back in deepest summer.

"Take a deep breath," he'd say. "Float in a vertical position. Relax. Dangle your arms and legs. Raise your head a bit above the surface when you need to breathe. Move your limbs as little as possible. Don't waste your energy. Then return to the floating position." As my father taught me the dead man's float that summer, he'd told me a man could survive in the ocean for a very long time without fatiguing if he mastered this skill.

"Swim clear of a sinking ship and other survivors," he'd say. "Do the dead man's float": my father's mantra for survival. Back then, I hadn't asked him why you needed to swim clear of a sinking ship and other survivors, or whether he'd ever needed to use the dead man's float to save himself. Back then, I didn't care.

"Oh yes," my father would say, "the dead man's float can keep you alive. Unless a shark gets you. Or an enemy plane swoops down and opens fire. Or no ship comes to the rescue."

Still I thought there must have been a good reason why my father taught me how to survive in the deep. Did he think that one day I'd need his lessons? Did he imagine me jumping off a burning ship into churning water, stroking fast to get clear before a ship sank, creating a whirlpool to drag me down? Did he worry that one day I'd be alone somewhere on a vast body of water without him, and that I'd have to save myself?

Before I tried to swim Lake George, I'd never come anywhere near danger on the water; never swum in the ocean; never swum in a lake.

⌣

There had been that one time at Niagara Falls when I was seven, though, before I'd learned how to swim, when I wished I'd known how.

My father, my sister, and I took a ride on *The Maid of the Mist* to get close to the falls. My mother wouldn't go, thought it was a stupid idea, didn't believe it was safe, what with the rapids and currents and whirlpools, even though the owners of the *Maid* prided themselves on having taken scores of tourists close to the falls without incident.

"You take the kids," my mother said, just before we paid. "I'll stay back and watch." But why did she let us go with my father when she herself was so afraid? I wondered.

And so my father paid for the three of us, lifted my sister into his arms and held my hand as we made our way down to the boathouse, where we donned oilskin slickers that smelled of mildew, then walked down the slippery wooden stairs perched over rocks and rapids to the dock where we boarded the *Maid*.

The boat is underway. We're standing in the bow. The spray hits our faces.

"See why they call it *The Maid of the Mist?*" my father asks. My father is in his element, happier than I've ever seen him. "The thrill of it," he says, "to be on the water."

My father points to whirlpools, tells us they can suck a boat down, tells us about a stupid man who went over the falls in a cask and got pulled under and drowned. My sister cries.

"He drowned," my father says, ignoring her, "because the force of the falls kept his cask underwater." My sister wails some more. I clutch my father's hand, try to be brave. I wonder why he's telling us this story.

"Don't be afraid," my father says. "See how the captain steers clear of the whirlpool? You have to trust your captain."

I imagine myself falling into the water, gasping for air, drowning. I don't know how to swim. I know I can do nothing to save myself.

I back away from the railing, move behind my father for a moment. Then I shake off my father's hand, move forward, clutch the railing, stand on tiptoe, gaze at the whirlpool, and wonder whether the cask is still bobbing somewhere underwater in a vortex far below the surface, and whether that man's body, still locked inside, has turned to dust or whether it is as well preserved as the bodies of the fetal pigs in formaldehyde that I've seen on a science show on television.

Years later, when my father is very sick and I'm asking him about his life in the Navy because I want to know as much as I can about him before he dies, he tells me he learned the American crawl and the dead man's float when he was a sailor. The sidestroke, the elementary backstroke, the breaststroke, the shallow dive, too, he says. He learned to swim underwater; learned how to abandon ship; learned how to swim through and under debris, oil slicks, fire, and floating bodies.

Before he enlisted in the Navy, he couldn't swim, couldn't float, even. He'd been to Coney Island a few times with his buddies, down the Jersey Shore only once or twice, he had so little time off from work. And though he loved to wade in the water and jump the waves, he never ventured beyond where he could stand.

When you joined the Navy, though, you had to learn how to swim. But you didn't need to learn how to swim very well or very far, my father learned. Which he thought was stupid.

"Imagine," my father said, "a branch of the military where you spend most of your time on a ship in the middle of the ocean and you only have to learn how to swim fifty yards! You only have to learn how to stay afloat hoping someone will come to rescue you! No wonder we lost so many men at sea. Typical Navy bullshit, not insisting you have to know what you need to know to survive. Men in war are expendable," he said, and shook his head.

My father knew sailors who never learned advanced skills (how to jump clear of a sinking ship, how to survive in cold water, how to inflate your clothes and tie knots in shirtsleeves, in trouser legs, so you could use them to float), sailors who never bothered to become more than third-class swimmers. But my father believed it was his duty to learn everything he could to become a first-class swimmer, and he did. You couldn't count on someone else to help you in a dangerous situation. You had to be responsible for your own survival.

Out there in the ocean, once a ship is in danger, once you abandon ship, no matter what anyone says about following orders, about team spirit, it's every man for himself. A man who doesn't know how to swim well will hang on to you to survive, will push you under, and drown you. Which is why it's best to swim clear of everyone, find your own piece of debris to cling to.

"Better," my father said, "to die alone than be dragged to the bottom of the ocean by someone clawing at you because he was too lazy or too stupid to learn what he should know to take care of himself."

But in the dreams I have about my father jumping off a sinking ship, I never see him in the water alone, far from others, holding onto his own piece of flotsam. I see him rescuing someone, see him towing a limp body to a lifeboat or to shore or to a waiting ship, see him performing mouth-to-mouth resuscitation, breathing life into a drowning man's lungs. I always see him casting his eyes about, looking for someone to save, looking for someone who, without his help, wouldn't survive.

∽

I'm now more than halfway across Lake George. I tell my father I'm tired, tell him I want to give up, tell him I want him to help me climb into the boat.

"You'll make it," my father says.

"I can't," I say.

"Can't? Or won't?" he asks. "You'll have to make it."

"Why?" I ask.

"Because I'm not letting you in the boat," my father says.

∽

So what am I doing out here trying to swim across this huge body of water? Is this some kind of test? Does my father want me to succeed? Or does he want me to fail? Am I my mother's daughter? Or am I his?

This is the '50s, when few of us girls are athletes. I'm healthy, yes. I like swimming, but I wouldn't call myself a swimmer. My exercise has consisted of riding my bike, playing softball, playing basketball, taking gym, jumping waves when we visit my mother's cousin in Rhode Island, swimming out to the raft and back to shore all day long at the mud hole on a summer's day.

Still, the evening before my swim, during a cookout, my father decides I will swim from one side of Lake George to the other and back. We've helped the owners of the cabins make homemade peach ice cream; my mother's peeled and diced the peaches; my sister and I have stirred the fruit into the chilled custard; the owners have filled the ice cream machine with ice and salt;

my father's done the cranking, and he's done it vigorously, calling attention to himself as always.

We're waiting, now, for the ice cream to ripen, waiting for our very first taste of homemade peach ice cream. We're finishing our hot dogs and hamburgers. This holiday isn't as bad as I expected.

My father's telling the owner what a beautiful spot he has on the lake. The owner tells my father that, here, the lake's only a mile or so across, which is why his wife and he bought the property, because from his dock a good swimmer can easily swim to the opposite shore and back; his guests do it all the time.

"My daughter, here," my father says, "she's a fine swimmer, taught her myself, she could do it."

And now it's time for the ice cream, although my mother and my sister are still dawdling through their meals. My father scrapes the ice cream off the paddles. I help dish it out, hand it round. I settle myself into a chair to savor it. This is the moment I've been waiting for.

My father turns to me. "Tomorrow," he says, "you'll swim Lake George. It's not that far across." He doesn't ask me; he tells me.

"No," I say. "I don't want to." I have other plans for this holiday, the last one with my parents before I leave for college. I know I'll have to study hard when I get there. I've worked the whole summer up until now, up early, home late, at a hard job in an office in New York City. I want this week to rest up so I can be at my best when college starts.

"Yes," my father says, "you will."

My mother knows this is the start of one of our fights.

"For once," she says, "will the two of you please try to get along?"

She forces a smile and makes it sound like a joke because we're in the midst of a group of people, but it isn't funny. What she says doesn't help because, like always, she's not saying no to my father and I know he won't give up; I know he'll keep bringing it up until he wears me down and gets his way.

My mother looks at my father, sets her lips into that frown of disapproval when she doesn't want him to do something. Climb to the top of a mountain. Descend into a ravine. Fly a friend's plane when he doesn't have a pilot's license although he tells her he knows how to fly, that he flew planes all the time during the war to test them. She should know I don't want to do this. But she doesn't say it's a bad idea, doesn't try to stop him. She always acts as if once he's decided to do something, there's nothing she can do.

"Lou," is all she says, turning away to nibble at her hamburger.

Help, I think, *help*.

⌣

The day before my swim, we'd taken an excursion to the site of Fort William Henry at the southern tip of Lake George. My father was big on exploring historical sites, especially battlefields and forts. On their honeymoon, he'd dragged my mother across New England to see Revolutionary War sites— Lexington, Concord, Boston—on their way to the cabin they rented on the coast of Maine. Now he tells me that seeing Fort William Henry will be educational, especially for me—he reminds me that *The Last of the Mohicans*, a book I've read, is set there.

"We should go to Fort Ticonderoga, too," he said. They fired off muskets a few times a day and he'd always wanted to see a musket fired. A musket could kill accurately only at fifty yards, he said, and they took so long to load.

"The more accurate a weapon is at a distance, the quicker it is to load, the more lethal the weapon," my father said.

I'd protested. I'd wanted to sit in an Adirondack chair on the dock, soak up the sun, and read. I'd been reading Dostoyevsky, Solzhenitsyn, and Tolstoy. The Russians. I loved immersing myself in a world far away from mine. When I happened upon the Russians in the library, when I leafed through the beginning pages of a few novels, I knew I was embarked upon a grand obsession, one that would last for years. No one I knew was reading the Russians.

For my holiday, I'd chosen Mikhail Aleksandrovich Sholokhov's *And Quiet Flows the Don*, about Gregor Meckhom's life as a Red Army soldier and a Cossack nationalist. It's more than 600 pages long. Hours and hours of uninterrupted reading. Reading and doing homework are the only occupations my parents allow me to indulge in as long as I want.

And Quiet Flows the Don is another in a series of novels I've read throughout middle school and high school about war, insurrection, and rebellion, subjects that fascinate me as much as they do my father, although I never would attribute this obsession to being my father's daughter. This summer, I've read Ernest Hemingway's *A Farewell to Arms* and *For Whom the Bell Tolls*, Norman Mailer's *The Naked and the Dead*—boy's books, my best friend calls them, when she makes fun of me, and asks me what the carnage count is for the book I'm currently reading. "Too many" would be the right answer, if I deigned to give one, instead of shrugging off her disapproval.

My father gets his way as usual and we tour Fort Henry. He reads from the brochure about the battle that occurred there during August 1757—he'll add it to his collection when we get home. Wherever he goes, he asks for one, and he makes us listen to him while he reads it.

"French guns pounded the fort for days," my father reads, "and each day, they came closer to the British inside." He pauses. "Imagine what it was like knowing you were surrounded, knowing the French would overrun the fort."

My sister wanders over to a wall. She picks up a twig, squats down, begins to dig, even though she'd too old to play like this. My mother follows her. I'm left alone with my father to listen, and I do, for as much as he bothers me, I respect his knowledge of history gleaned from the many nights he's sat in his chair reading one hefty historical volume after another.

Montcalm sends Bougainville out of the fort to surrender to the French. He's holding a white flag. ("Bougainville, also the name of an important World War II battle in the South Pacific," my father says. "Remember that name when you study World War II in college." He's still irate that we never got to World War II in high school.) The French accept, but as the unarmed British leave the fort with their women and children, the Indian allies of the French attack them, scalp them, slaughter them.

Men running. Women trying to escape. Children screaming. Indians in pursuit. War whoops. People thrown to the ground. Blood, blood, and more blood. Dismembered limbs. Piles of bodies. Scalps held on high.

"Filthy fighters, the Indians," my father says, "just like the Japanese. Didn't follow the rules of war. But whether it was their idea or the French's, who can say?"

Rules of war? How absurd! I think, and look away.

"You don't know any of this about the English? About the Indians? About the French?" my father asks.

"No," I reply.

"What the hell do they teach you in school?" my father asks.

⌒

"But what if it's raining hard tomorrow?" I ask.

"It won't rain," my father says. "Look at the sky, look west. You can tell by the western sky that tomorrow will be beautiful."

I see a red-stained sky. Red sky at night, sailors' delight. Red sky in the morning, sailors take warning.

"But it might rain," I insist.

"You can do the swim even if it rains," he says. "As long as we don't hear thunder." And then he launches into a speech about how to tell how far away a storm is by counting the time between when you see lightning and hear thunder. Which doesn't help me because all I can imagine is us being in the middle of that lake, me in the water, rain, the sound of thunder at a distance, an unexpected storm coming my way.

My father estimates it should take me an hour, an hour and fifteen minutes, maybe more, to swim to the other side. Closer to an hour and a half to get back.

"On the way back you'll be tired," he says.

Over two hours. Cold water. Alone in the middle of the lake. Deep water. Arms tired, legs screaming. My father in a boat beside me, ignoring me, looking at the view or thinking about God knows what.

"But I've never swum that far before," I say.

"Oh yes you have," he says. "At the mud hole, out to the float and back, all day long. Way more than two hours. Way more than two miles."

I want to tell my father to swim the lake himself.

"Won't you feel proud if you can say you swam Lake George?" he asks. "Wouldn't you like to tell your friends you swam the lake?"

"Sure," I say, "sure." But I can't imagine being proud of something like that. Being proud isn't a feeling I'm familiar with. When I try to imagine how it feels, I think of the boy I like (the boy I love, really, the boy I have sex with, though whether he loves me or not, I don't know) pumping his fist in the air after he scores a touchdown, me in the corner of the bleachers while his girlfriend cheers for him. I think of a mother watching her child get an award for having the highest marks in the class. I think of a girl making cheerleading like I never did although I tried. And even though I get good grades in school, even though I've blocked some shots in basketball and even won a game for my team, even though I've earned a lot of money for a girl my age, I've never felt proud of these accomplishments. They're just something I've done; something I've had to do. And even if I swim Lake George, it's not something I could ever tell my friends. "Big deal," is all they'd say if I tried to brag.

I don't want to swim the lake. But I don't want to argue with my father, either, don't want to ruin this vacation. I'll be leaving for college, soon. I want to come away from this week with the memory of us as a family, enjoying ourselves, without my father ruining it with one of his outbursts, without him telling me it's all my fault. I want us to have a good time like other families.

And so I decide to swim Lake George. I tell myself it's not because he wants me to, but because *I* want to. It will seem as though my father is getting his way, but he's not.

Or maybe I *do* want to please my father. Maybe I've always wanted to please him, but don't know how. It's been a long time since I've pleased him, so long ago that I can't remember when.

I know my father is testing my mettle. That's what he wants me to have. Not courage. Mettle. He's explained the difference to me. Mettle isn't courage, isn't daring, which is foolhardiness. It's something like courage, but more. It's grit, determination, pluck, endurance. Mettle is what a good soldier, a good statesman has. So what does it have to do with me?

My father tells me about Winston Churchill's speech on "mettle."

"The only way you got through the war was if you had mettle," my father says. "Mettle. Plus a heavy dose of good luck."

Mettle, I think, *is what I need to survive having him as a father.*

⌒

I swim across Lake George. I swim back. I swim maybe two miles, maybe more. It takes over two hours. I swim the American crawl. The sidestroke. The elementary backstroke. I tread water. I use the dead man's float when I think I can't go on.

And just as my father says, I can tell everyone I swam Lake George. But I won't. Nor do I tell anyone that on the long swim back, when I cling to the gunwale of the rowboat for the second time, when I tell my father that I want to end this swim, want to climb into the boat, my father threatens to take the oar out of the oarlock and beat my fingers so I'll let go of the boat and swim free.

"That's what they did," he says, as we're pulling the boat up onto shore, "that's what they had to do when a ship went down, when one too many men wanted to climb aboard a lifeboat. Beat their hands until they slipped into the sea."

Cutting

the Bread

The Bread

My grandmother is in the kitchen cutting the Italian bread she has made. The bread my grandmother has made is a big bread, a substantial bread, one you can use for dunking, or for scraping the last bit of sauce from a bowl of pasta, or for breaking into soups or stews, or for eating with a little olive oil and a shake of salt, or with the juices of a very ripe tomato and some very green olive oil.

My grandmother's bread is a good bread, not a fine bread. One that will stay fresh, cut-side-down, on the breadboard for a few days. A thick-crusted bread. A bread my grandmother makes by hand in our kitchen, much to my mother's disgust, twice a week. A bread my mother disdains because it's everything my grandmother is, and everything my mother, in 1950s suburban New Jersey, is trying very hard not to be. Coarse. A peasant. Italian.

My grandmother's bread and the pizza she makes from her bread dough are the foods that sustain me throughout my childhood. Without them, I know I'd starve because I hate absolutely everything my mother cooks, have hated it for years. Hate it because it tastes awful because my mother burns the food she cooks or puts too much salt in it or forgets to time the chicken and brings it to the table running with blood. Hate it because it's terrible food—gristly meat, bloated bratwurst, slightly off hamburger gotten for a bargain that she tries to disguise with catsup and Worcestershire sauce. Hate it because I can taste the rage in her food, can hear it in the banging of the pots and pans in her kitchen, in the clash of metal against metal in her stirring, can feel it against my skin.

The kitchen, when my mother is cooking, is not a place I want to be.

And my mother's rage—at me for not being a "good" daughter, at my grandmother for living with us, at herself for her never-ending sorrow despite her loving my father—scares me, makes me want to hide in a closet or rush from the house. It is a thick, scorching rage that I cannot predict, cannot understand. But it is something I do not want to catch from her (although of course I do).

And so. I do not eat her food if I can help it. Do not enter the kitchen when she cooks. Do not help her cook, for she prefers when I am not near her, when no one is near her. Do not help her clean up after we eat. And I leave the table as soon as I can.

My eating my grandmother's bread and my not eating my mother's food is another reason my mother screams at me, another reason my mother hates my grandmother, her stepmother, not her "real" mother who died when she was a baby. A mother, she laments, who would have taken care of her, not resented her, as this woman does.

And so. My mother doesn't know how to be a mother to me. No cookie baking in the kitchen. No lessons in how to make sauce. No cuddles. No intimate chats at bedtime. No very much of anything.

The Other Bread

My mother does not eat the bread my grandmother bakes. My mother eats the bread she buys from the Dugan's man, who comes round in his truck to our neighborhood a few times a week. This bread, unlike my grandmother's, has preservatives, a long shelf life, my mother boasts.

This bread my mother buys is white bread, sliced bread, American bread. A bread my grandmother would never eat even if she were starving. Maybe my mother thinks eating this bread will change her, will erase this embarrassment of a stepmother, all black dresses and headscarves and guttural dialect and superstitions and flurries of flour that ruin her spotless kitchen and tentacled things cooking in pots, this woman from the South of Italy who, my mother swears, never bathes, who treats water as something to pray to, not something to wash in. Maybe my mother thinks that if she eats enough of this American bread she will stop being Italian American. And that she will become American American.

My mother's bread is whiter than my grandmother's, as white, as soft and spongy as the cotton balls I use to take off my nail polish and the Kotex pads I shove into my underpants.

My sister and I like having this bread in our house, not because we like its taste, but because you can do many things with it. You can take a piece, pull off the crust, smash it down, roll it into a little ball. You can play marbles with this bread. You can pull the middle out of a slice and hang it over your nose or twirl it around your finger.

You can also eat this bread. But it sticks to the roof of your mouth and you have to pry it off with your finger. Then you get yelled at for your horrible table manners.

My grandmother's bread doesn't stick to the roof of your mouth. Which is why my father likes it. Which is why I like it. That my father likes my grandmother's bread makes my mother angry.

From the Dugan's man, my mother also buys apple pies, blueberry pies, chocolate-covered donuts, crullers, to satisfy my father's sweet tooth when she is too depressed to make a dessert, and she usually is.

"*Merda,*" my grandmother calls everything that my mother buys from the Dugan's man. Sometimes, unsure that my grandmother is correct, I take a tentative bite of something and conclude that, yes, it is *merda*, it tastes like cardboard, and the canned stew my mother feeds us because she is too depressed to cook is also *merda*, and the canned spaghetti and ravioli, too.

Kneading the Bread

My grandmother makes her bread by hand in my mother's kitchen, much to my mother's disgust, at least twice a week, sometimes more. Making it takes a lot of time. To make it, my grandmother dumps flour on my mother's kitchen table, makes a well in the middle, and into it pours warm water in which she has dissolved some yeast. She flicks the flour into the yeasty water with her fingertips a little at a time, until the shaggy mass comes together into a ball. Then my grandmother starts kneading.

When my grandmother kneads the bread, she takes off her dress because kneading the dough is such hard work. She stands in the kitchen in her underwear. Coarse, unbleached white undershirt. Coarse, unbleached white pantaloons (these, she makes herself because you can't buy them here). Black stockings. When she strips down, my mother huffs and leaves the room. When my grandmother kneads the dough, she gives me a small batch to knead. Then she shows me how to shape the dough into a little crown, which she bakes for me after it has risen.

While our bread bakes, my grandmother takes some scraps and shapes them into little figures that she fries for my sister and me. This is my lunch on baking days. My mother violently disapproves but lets us eat them anyway because, as usual, she hasn't thought about lunch.

My mother is always angry when my grandmother bakes her bread. "There's flour all over the place, even on the floor. Jesus Christ Almighty," she says, "how much more of this can I take?" My grandmother cleans up but not the way my mother wants her to: clean enough so you can eat off the floor, although we don't eat off the floor.

My mother's face is red with rage. She re-scrubs everything with Ajax. She curses. She spills water on the floor, makes a bigger mess. It's impossible to ignore her while we eat our *zeppoli*, yet we try.

The Knife

My mother was afraid of knives. Before she went to bed at night, she would gather up all the knives in our kitchen and put them in a drawer. "This way," she said, "if a burglar comes into the house in the night, they'll have to look for them. This way," my mother said, "we'll have a fighting chance."

The knife that my grandmother uses to cut the bread is not a bread knife, not a serrated knife like every well-equipped American kitchen now has. No. The knife that my grandmother uses to cut the bread is a butcher knife, the kind that figures in nightmares, in movies like *Psycho*. The same knife, incidentally, that my father uses when I am a teenager when he threatens to kill me. (Years later, I bring up the subject, of how he came at me, how I got away because my grandmother put her body between us. "I never meant to hurt you," he said. "I was just trying to make myself clear.")

My grandmother would take the gigantic loaf of bread she'd made and pull the knife toward the center of her chest where her heart was located, as if she were trying to commit an Italian form of *hara-kiri*.

"Stop that," my mother would shout, half-fearing, half-hoping, I think, that this stepmother who didn't love her would pull the knife toward her breast just a fraction of an inch too far, so that we would finally have bloodshed in our very own kitchen, finally have a real mess on our hands that would take my mother a very long time to clean.

"Stop that, for Christ's sake," my mother would shout. And she would pull the bread away from my grandmother and often she would cut herself in the process, not much, but just enough to bleed onto the bread. And she would throw the bread down onto the counter and say, "Why can't you cut that goddamned bread like a normal human being?" And my grandmother would make the sign of the cross over the bread and kiss her fingertips and bend over the bread that she had made, weeping. My grandmother would weep because to her the bread was sacred and to her the only way to cut the bread was to pull the knife through the bread toward your heart.

Slicing Onions

When I was a girl, my mother cried every time she sliced an onion. Not cry the way everyone cries when they slice onions—you, me, the stinging, unbidden tears annoying the corners of the eyes. No. When my mother sliced an onion, she really cried, her chest heaved, her eyes bled huge tears that dropped onto the scarred Formica counter where she did all her cutting.

She wouldn't use cutting boards, my mother. She thought they were unnecessary, an extravagance, like raincoats and rainboots. And besides, she didn't need one often. When she moved to the suburbs, she abandoned the preparation of Italian food that required chopping, mincing, in favor of American food, convenience foods or things that were easy to prepare—hamburgers, meatloaf, hot dogs, toasted cheese sandwiches (though for

Christmas or New Year's she might still make a lasagna or some meatballs and spaghetti).

My mother would rub her eyes with the backs of her hands to try to stanch the flow of tears, which only made the situation worse. And although my mother had a lot to cry about—that her mother died when she was a baby, that she was neglected by the people who took care of her, that my stepgrandmother never loved her, that her beloved father had died, that her husband had come home from the war an angry man—the only time I ever saw her cry ("Having a good cry," she called it) was when she was peeling and slicing onions, and I often thought she sometimes cooked dishes containing sautéed onions (liver, meatloaf) because making them gave her an opportunity to cry.

Oh yes, my mother had a lot to cry about, but I didn't know it then. But I believed that if I ate her dinner, I would eat those tears, and I was afraid I would be as unhappy as she was. And I didn't want that. I wanted a quiet, ordinary, peaceful life. Not the commotion, the bitterness, the unhappiness of her life.

Sometimes when she cried, I ventured into the kitchen to see if I could cheer her because I worried the crying would turn to something worse than crying, and she would enter the world of her deep depression again, as she so often did, a place where she was inaccessible even to herself. Then my sister and I would be hauled off to relatives where we were cooked for, but not cared for.

"Your mother had a hard life," my father would say. But why her life was hard, he never told us. What he said was, "All your mother wants from you is a little love." And that was something I couldn't give.

Scars

When I was growing up, my mother was always cutting herself, always burning herself, because when she cooked, my mother was depressed or distracted or shouting at my grandmother. Whenever they were in the kitchen together, they shouted at each other. Screaming: the condiment that sauced our food.

My mother yelled about how my grandmother had used up all the flour. About what a pig she was. About how she stank up the kitchen. About how she ruined the pots and pans. My grandmother yelled about how my mother showed her no respect. About how my mother had forced her to live with her. About how she stole her money. About how my mother would have died if it weren't for her. About how my mother wasn't even her blood.

And because they were always yelling, my mother wouldn't pay attention to what she was doing.

And so. She'd slice a piece off her finger. Or peel her hand instead of peeling the vegetables. Or she'd pour the boiling water off the potatoes too fast and scald herself. Or she'd bang into the side of a cupboard and get a black and blue. Or she'd stick her head too far into the oven and get a blast of steam on her face and it would be red for days. "Battle scars," my mother called them. And they were.

While my mother and grandmother were in the kitchen together I kept my distance. And so I never learned to cook from them.

When I got married, I even needed a cookbook to boil water. I learned to cook Italian from Italian cookbooks, not from my grandmother, and certainly not from my mother. So the kind of Italian cooking that I cook is nothing like the Italian cooking that was cooked in my parents' house. I learned nothing in my mother's kitchen about food that can sustain the soul. In my mother's kitchen I learned about violence, about rage. I learned about using food and the implements used to cook food as weapons. Against others. And against yourself.

And after my mother died, and I found her recipe box, and went through it, the only recipe I wanted was one for pumpkin pie. She made a good pumpkin pie, my mother.

Wiping the Bowl

Just after my grandmother fell out of bed one morning, tore her nightdress off, and crawled around the floor naked, my mother decided it was time for her to go to a nursing home, that final stop on the railroad of life's journey.

So they took her there and she went unwillingly, strapped onto a stretcher and raving in an Italian no one could understand.

The nursing home was not a fancy one with private rooms and a solarium but a bare-bones piss-smelling nursing home run by the county where the very poor and the very unwanted came to die in giant wards cared for as well as the overworked, underpaid nurses could care for them, which is to say they were not cared for very much at all.

My mother went to see her stepmother almost ever day and came home crying because my grandmother wouldn't eat. My mother believed she wouldn't eat to spite her.

"Go see her," my mother said, exhausted, terrified. "Maybe she'll eat for you."

And so I went to see my grandmother on a day when the maple tree outside the window of her ward blazed red. And on that day, I fed my grandmother applesauce. She didn't eat much, a teaspoon or two, from the small quantity I dished into a little bowl.

I could tell she was near dying because she couldn't pick up her head from the pillow, could barely lift her arm, and couldn't speak. Still, she looked at me and her eyes teared and I told myself that coming here to feed her was a good thing, and necessary; told myself that these few spoonfuls of nourishment would, perhaps, prolong her life; told myself, who hadn't yet been to see her, who wouldn't see her alive again, that it was the least I could do for her after all she had done for me.

When she was finished eating, weak as she was, she reached for the bowl. It took much effort, this reaching, and I could not understand what she wanted, what she needed to do. And she took the napkin I had tucked under her chin to keep her clean. And she wiped the inside of the bowl. She cleaned the bowl as best she could.

In dying, as in living, she tidied up after herself, this southern Italian woman who wanted no other woman to clean what she'd messed. This is what I think about when I remember my grandmother. How she baked her bread. And how she wiped the bowl.

No More Cooking, No More Food

In the final autumn of her life, my mother could not move. Could not move her arms, her hands, or her fingers. Could not move her legs, her feet, her toes, her head. Could not speak, could not say anything. Could not move, could not chew, could not swallow. Hence, could not cook, could not eat.

A feeding tube inserted into her body, now her only means of sustenance. I looked at my mother, through those dying days, wanting conversation, which I would never have again, for she had long since ceased to speak. Wanting what I had never had, really: normal talks, ordinary talks, ones like other people have, about what we did during the day, what we cooked for dinner, what we felt about our lives.

"Come closer," I said to her, once, as she lay dying, although she couldn't hear me, couldn't come closer. "Come closer," I wanted to say, but didn't, "and I'll tell you something wonderful, something you've been wanting me to tell you for a long time."

I wanted to speak to her, for she was moving into the land of death, a place I didn't know about, didn't want to know about, though a place where I will one day follow her, but not, I hope, too soon.

Would she remember me after she died? I wondered. Would she remember light? Music? The taste of grapefruit? What I wanted to say was "I love you," although I wasn't sure I did. I thought that if I said the words, words I'd never said to her before, words she'd never said to me, then the feeling might follow. I wanted to love my mother before she died.

Tearing the Bread

My mother died in autumn, like my grandmother. Though these two could agree on nothing in living, they agreed that autumn, with its leaves all dry and sere and red and bronze and gold and falling to the ground, was a fitting time to die.

As my mother lay dying, I wanted to tell her a story to ease her, as she used to tell me stories so very many years ago when my father was away at war.

"Imagine we are together. And imagine that, just once, we aren't fighting, we don't hate each other, you aren't disappointed in me, and I'm not disappointed in you. Imagine we know it will come to this; imagine that because we know that it will come to this, we have learned to love each other.

"Imagine us having a picnic. There is a cloth laid upon the ground and on it are simple things: some cheese—the smoked mozzarella from Dante's you liked so much—and roasted peppers (I might have made them myself);

some mortadella, because neither of us likes prosciutto. And bread, yes, bread. Not my homemade bread, for today; I was too busy to bake bread. But good bread, sturdy Italian bread.

"About the bread there would have been some disagreement. You would have wanted a fat, crusty load without sesame seeds. (You had, by now, given up your taste for American bread.) I would have wanted them—the seeds, that is—for the flavor they impart to the loaf. But we decided that at this time in our lives, we could buy two breads and enjoy them both: the one you wanted (without the seeds), and the one I wanted (with).

"Today, we sit together on a cloth in a grove of almond trees in full blossom, this place that we return to where we have never been before, and we eat. How beautiful the trees are, you say, their flowers, so silver-pink, the searing eyes of the individual blossoms seeing that we are together. They are, I say, a transfiguration, a predilection, and a blessing, and I tell you that I am so happy that you have chosen this place for us to be together.

"And, finally, we eat, and drink the milk of almonds. And we talk. We have an ordinary, normal talk, about our day. Mine was filled with writing, reading (books about the South of Italy and the life your parents lived there and, yes, they are helping me at last understand you, understand how you were between two worlds, how both despised who you were, so that you had to become 'American,' had to bury the Italian in you, had to hate your stepmother for what she was so you would not hate yourself for what you were). Your day, you told me, was full. You'd changed the lining in all the cupboards in the kitchen, made a soup for dinner, a nice *minestra*, and sat down in the afternoon to embroider: primulas, roses, poppies on a beige ground for the pillows that now decorate my bed.

"Today we do not cut the bread, for we have forgotten to bring our knives. Today, we tear the bread with our hands. It is hard, this tearing of the bread, this partaking of it. It is hard because the loaves have been well baked and because they have a thick, nearly impenetrable crust. Yes, it is hard, we both agree, to break the bread, to tear into it, to get at the tenderness inside. Yes, it is hard to break the bread. But it is not impossible."

Playing the Bowl

On Fridays, I take my granddaughter, Julia, to her toddler music class. She calls the class "Oh my" because they are the first words of her favorite song, "Oh my, no more pie." When Julia sings, I hear a young voice, but there is something old about the voice, just as there is something old about the child. She is one of those children who look as if they are older people locked in childlike bodies.

On this day, the teacher shows how to improvise musical instruments at home. "See," she says, picking up a cheese grater and playing it with a spoon, "you don't need to buy musical instruments to make music." She's smiling; she's making music seem like so much fun.

Preoccupied with a piece of writing that has not been fun in the making, I am cranky. I think that this is the wrong message. Writing, art, music, I think, aren't just fun. They're essential. They're bone, flesh, blood, sinew, soul, spirit. And music can be hard. To hear; to make; to play.

But these are kids, after all.

The teacher dumps little plastic bowls and wooden spoons onto the floor. "Just watch the children; see what they do," she says. She turns on a recording of African drums, the rhythms insistent, intricate, energizing. The children start moving. I start moving.

One little boy picks up a bowl, a spoon, turns the bowl over, starts beating it with the spoon. Soon, all the children are beating on their improvised instruments. All but Julia.

Julia sits in the center of the circle, flips her bowl, takes her spoon, starts stirring. She's stirring as quickly as the other children are drumming. She's shaking her head and stirring. She's stirring and tasting. She's closing her eyes, lost in the stirring. She's pretending to cook as if cooking were all that mattered, as if her life depended upon it, as if the gods cared.

And she's making waffles, sauce, biscotti, scones, she's making pudding, she's making pie, and she's calling out the names of what she's making, and she's tasting what she's making.

So here is this little child with the wise face, who seems to have seen all things, this child with her mother's face, and my face, and my mother's face and my father's mother's face, and her other grandmother's face and her mother's grandmother's face, and the face of every woman in the world, and this child is stirring and cooking and singing through the celebrations, through the pogroms, invasions, bombings, evacuations, emigrations. She's stirring in Russia and in Austria-Hungary, in Puglia and in Sicily, and she's singing, this child who sees the future, who sees sorrow, sees joy, this wise, wise child.

She stirs and tastes and cooks and tastes and sings, and she sings, "Oh my no more pie; oh my, no more pie; oh my, no more pie. No more pie. No more pie."

Dark White

My father calls to tell me he's been cleaning out his files. He's found some documents I might want, he says, because I've recently asked him about my immigrant Italian grandparents. I ask what they are.

"Oh, naturalization papers, visas, some birth records, death certificates," he says. "Nothing really important."

I tell him to bring them over right away, for to me they *are* important. I know that if I don't claim them immediately, they'll wind up in the trash like other family mementos my father jettisoned when he remarried after my mother's death, for my father likes to get rid of what he considers to be the detritus of his former life.

My father lives in the present, considers his past a burden, an obstacle that he overcame unconnected to the person he has chosen to become: an American. That he once lived in Italy in Scafati, a small village near Naples, that his heritage is southern Italian, that he grew up poor in Hudson County, New Jersey, that he was taunted as a boy for being Italian and short and scrawny, that he was savaged by a superior in the Navy during World War II for the same reasons, he shrugs off as insignificant, or if not insignificant, then a part of his education—"the school of hard knocks" he called it—that made him who he is but that he does not dwell upon. So that, in the 1940s and 1950s, I did not grow up with romanticized stories of "life in the old country" or with a sense that I was from a family newly arrived in the United States, as others did.

The way my father (and mother, too) dealt with their Italian heritage was to not discuss it. Nor did they discuss *anyone's* ethnicity. They didn't use ethnic or racial labels when talking about the world or national affairs or about anyone we knew. And anytime I mentioned that a friend was this or that (for I began, in high school, to think in terms of ethnic and racial categories, as I listened to my friends' conversations about who could or could not date whom), my parents would shrug and say, "So what? Underneath, everyone's the same" or "You can't tell a book by its cover"—their way of saying that when you know someone's ethnicity or race, you know nothing at all about them. So anyone's ancestry seemed unimportant to my parents, even though they were both extremely interested in history. But this was so they could understand what puzzled them: why, for example, prejudice existed; why people were persecuted; why wars happened.

⌣

My father is eighty-six, and I am afraid that everything he knows about my grandparents will die with him. As I edge toward my sixtieth year, I want to urge from my father all the stories he knows about my grandparents that can nourish and sustain me in this phase of my life. I want them, too, so I can tell my children and grandchildren so that our forebears, these people, their lives, our past, will not be forgotten. So that they can learn, earlier in their lives than I did, who these people were.

My father's ancestry as a *southern* Italian, and my mother's, too, is something I learned about only recently. He has always been interested in Italian culture—the works of Michelangelo and Da Vinci, and Italian opera, and this was what he told me about, not the poverty-stricken Italy his parents and my mother's parents left under desperate circumstances. An Italy I myself did not learn about until I was in my fifties. And not from my father but from books like Richard Gambino's *Blood of My Blood*.

My interest in my grandparents and in how they and other Italian immigrants were regarded and treated when they came to this country is recent and urgent. In the 1940s and 1950s in the United States, some Italian Americans, like my parents, buried the past, tried to assimilate. It was, in part, because of the war—Italy was the enemy. But it was also the ethos of the times: Racial and ethnic differences were not valued but, instead, condemned and ridiculed. And there was (and still is) always a peculiar silence in the United States about the Italian diaspora and the injustice inflicted here upon Italian Americans.

I knew nothing about my grandparents' lives in Italy. I certainly did not know about the horrific mistreatment, exploitation, and enforced starvation of CONTADINI (peasants) and farm laborers in the Mezzogiorno that appears, now, to have been a form of "ethnic cleansing." And what I learned in my fifties about that history, and about their lives in the United States upon arrival, about how they were treated because they were Italian (how policemen invaded their Italian neighborhood in Hoboken, New Jersey; that Sacco and Vanzetti were assumed to be guilty despite evidence to the contrary; that Italian Americans were lynched in the South; that they were incarcerated during World War II) by reading works like Gambino's was painful.

What I knew as a child was very little: that none of my grandparents spoke English; that they (and we) lived in a working-class Italian neighborhood until we moved to the suburbs when I was seven; that they cooked foods I didn't like until I was older; that my grandfather worked on the railroad; that my grandmother was our tenement's superintendent. Which is to say I knew almost nothing at all.

I later learned from Dominic T. Ciolli's essay "The 'Wop' in the Track Gang" that Italian men who worked on the railroad earned less for their work than "whites." And that my paternal grandmother worked for meager wages as a garment worker, and that she took my father to work into the factory when he was a small child, and hid him under her sewing machine because she had no one to care for him, and that when the boss discovered him, my father was put to work—he was four or five years old.

My father, like his parents before him, is disinclined to talk about how he was treated because his family was Italian. I think this is because he is, and they were, products of *contadina* culture: proud, accepting, and fatalistic. Because they were proud, they got on with what had to be done, considered talk a waste of time and energy, and didn't like to admit they were mistreated even though they were. They called what happened to them, when they talked about it, *la miseria*, as if their plight were something that happened to them rather than something that was done to them. Because they were accepting of whatever circumstances they encountered, they didn't regard exploitation or abuse as abnormal. And because they were fatalistic, they believed prejudice against them was in the scheme of things.

So they didn't complain about this, although they complained about other things—my behavior, for example. And because lamentation is essential for an oral history to exist, and because they didn't recount their grievances but instead buried them, I have few stories to share about these grandparents; little has come down to me about how my grandparents and their parents lived in Italy or when they came to the United States; nothing about how they were treated or the difficulties they encountered. What little I learned about them came through story, only I was too young to know that the stories they told—about the ferocious sun, the unforgiving sea, the empty bellies—weren't stories at all. And because, unlike other migrants, these people were often illiterate, they left very few written accounts with which we can write their history. And their grandchildren are just beginning to write their stories, cobbling them together, as I have, from anecdote, research, speculation.

But this silence is cultural, too. To recount that you were mistreated and to see this as significant demands that you can imagine a world in which people are treated (or should be treated) humanely. My grandparents, it seems, could not imagine such a world. Though my parents (especially my mother) could.

So now it has come to me to eke out what I can about who they were from the very little I have. And the documents my father gives me help me immeasurably.

⁓

The next time we meet, my father presents me with a manila envelope. On the front, in my mother's hand, the words *FAMILY PAPERS* are printed. The letters waver, so I know she gathered them together near the end of her life to make sure (I surmise) that they wouldn't be lost or destroyed after her death. That my father saved these records seems a small miracle, for he threw or gave away almost everything else before starting a new marriage and a new life after my mother's death.

When he gives me the envelope, my father tells me a few things. That my maternal grandparents came from a small village near Bari; he didn't remember the name. And that my grandfather had come to America to work on the railroad. About the location of the village he was wrong. My grandfather, I learned, came from Vieste and my grandmother from Rodi Garganico, both in Puglia but at some distance from Bari.

"When he came to America," my father says, "your grandfather didn't know what he was getting himself into. It took him a long time to pay back his passage.

"The grandmother you knew, the woman you've called your grandmother, he sent for to care for your mother after her birth mother died. Really, there was no love between your grandfather and her. She was a 'mail order bride.' And although she had a hard life there, she had a hard life here, and she managed to find work as a super in the tenement where we all lived.

"Your grandfather, though, was never sorry he came. He had wanted an education in Italy, which was out of the question. The happiest day of his life was the first day your mother went to school."

⌣

I wait until my father leaves to read these papers. Any show of emotion makes him uncomfortable, and as I approach my sixtieth birthday, any relic from my family's past provokes tears. For I am aware of the press of time and my own eventual death. Preserving and recording whatever I can of our family's past has become urgent. Yet I sense I will discover something disquieting and unnerving here: Official documents often reveal truths one has never known.

I unfold the first paper carefully. It is my maternal stepgrandmother's certificate of naturalization. Affixed to the document is her "official" photograph, which brings back memories—how she protected me from my father's rages; helped me endure my mother's depressions; taught me to knit; gave me money from her small pension; called me *figlia mia*; sang me Italian songs (one that scared me, about a wolf devouring children); told me stories I could barely understand; made me pizza for supper and *zeppoli* for Sunday breakfast.

But the photograph also reminds me how her appearance (black dress, black sweater, black cotton stockings, black headscarf knotted on her chin when she went to church) after we moved out of Hoboken to the suburb of Ridgefield, New Jersey, marked me, because I was related to her, as different, as not quite American.

A friend: "Where does your grandmother come from? She looks like a witch. How did she get here? On a broom stick? Ha. Ha." A boyfriend: "My mother says I could never marry you, should stop seeing you. Your grandmother. Can you imagine her at the wedding?"

My grandmother was a God-sent protector in my house of anger and sorrow. But she was also someone I was ashamed of, that I made fun of to my friends so my friends wouldn't make fun of me because of her. As if in repudiating her I could leach out the Italian in me and become what I then thought was important. Being American, whatever that was.

But in the 1950s when I was growing up in suburban New Jersey (where we moved after my grandfather's death), being American didn't include having such a grandmother. And so, in public, I mocked her, scorned her. In private, I ran to her, buried my head in her lap, and secretly begged her forgiveness.

⌒

In her photograph, my grandmother is dressed in black (as she always was, her life, one of perpetual mourning, even before my grandfather died). Double-chinned (not a fat woman, but well nourished). Light-skinned (her skin burned unless she was careful during the summers she farmed with relatives in the country; but by autumn, she was tanned because of her work outdoors). Dark-haired, though graying at the temples, hair pulled back from her face, though not austerely, one wave dipping over each temple (its lustrous length braided and fashioned into a neat circlet at the nape of the neck, though this does not show in the photograph). Smile playing at the corners of her mouth (and she could be wickedly insightful in describing people's foibles, this grandmother, and merciless in mocking my father's bravura, my mother's rigidity, the incomprehensible ways of her adopted land, but never of me, and I can imagine her telling herself something wickedly accurate about the person photographing her, and smiling to herself about it).

On the document, my grandmother has inscribed her signature carefully— *Libera Maria Calabrese*—because she does not often write her name and never, never her middle name, and because she understands the importance of this moment of becoming a U.S. citizen. It is wartime, and being Italian is dangerous. (When the United States declares war on Italy, thousands of Italian Americans are arrested. This news sends shockwaves through the country's Little Italys. Though relatives here, including my father, are fighting the war against fascism, against family and *paisani* in Italy, thereby demonstrating loyalty to the new land, still Italians and Italian Americans are suspect.)

Still, being Italian, my grandmother is eligible for naturalization because she's legally considered Caucasian, although in the 1890s Italians weren't popularly considered white. (Until 1952, people not legally considered white were not eligible for naturalization.)

Not pledging allegiance to the United States, not becoming a U.S. citizen at this time, would have been dangerous for my grandparents. Italians were warily regarded, risked being prosecuted as "enemy aliens"—and my grandfather worked on the piers in New York City where warships docked. Until the United States declared war on Italy, my grandparents had sent nonperishable food, money, and clothing to relatives "back home" in Italy. And until Mussolini's abuses became known, they had supported him and followed the progress of the war because he addressed the needs of the people of the South, usually ignored or persecuted by politicians. After the United States joined the war, they desperately wanted to know the fate of their people—parents, brothers, sisters, uncles, aunts, cousins, nieces, nephews—but this concern was suspect.

Renouncing their Italian citizenship was fraught with difficulty. For although they knew they had opportunities here that would have been foreclosed to them in Italy (such as working for a wage that could sustain them, albeit modestly), still it meant disavowing allegiance to their homeland. And though they were deeply suspicious of government, this constituted a betrayal of what they valued most highly: loyalty to their families. To become a U.S. citizen was the single most difficult and significant act of their lives in this country.

Becoming a naturalized citizen granted my grandmother (some) rights and privileges of a native-born American but neither the privilege of being completely accepted nor absorbed into the mainstream of North American life. Still, my grandmother's naturalization papers remained precious to her always, I know, for she kept the document in a locked box that held her visa, her transport ticket for coming to the United States (listing every meal, like *Riso o pasta asciutta al sugo* or *Carne e ragu con piselli*, that would be served in transit), a lock of my grandfather's hair (after his death), and a set of crystal rosary beads that are now in my possession. She showed her special papers to me on one occasion: when I brought home a certificate of my own—my grammar school diploma and a commendation for my good behavior. Now each of us had important papers.

⌐

I am a toddler when my grandmother becomes naturalized and my father is somewhere in the Pacific. My mother and I live next door to my grandparents in a tenement on Fourth and Adams Streets in an Italian American neighborhood in Hoboken, New Jersey. And although I do not remember the event, I know that I attended this ceremony, for there is a picture in our family album commemorating the occasion.

I am in my good tweed winter coat, leggings, and hat, and I am standing on the steps of the courthouse next to my grandparents, who are soberly attired in their black winter coats, and my grandfather is holding my hand. Though I am not then aware of it, this is a defining moment in my life. For the person I am is, at that moment, not quite Italian, not quite American. But when I am an adult, and I hold my grandmother's naturalization papers in my hand, I become aware of inequities faced by Italian Americans in a country that has not yet fully equated the Italian American experience with the human experience and that prefers depictions of Italian Americans as gangsters, thugs, or ill spoken in movies and on television rather than as a people with as complex a historical and cultural past as that of others from far-off homelands).

Naturalization

1. The act of admitting an alien to the position and privileges of a native-born subject or citizen. (Well, not always, and not really.)

2. The act of introducing plants or animals or humans to places where they are not indigenous, but where they can thrive freely under ordinary conditions. (This, says the Oxford English Dictionary, is Charles Darwin's meaning of the term, he who coined the term "favored races"; he who in The Descent of Man said, "I would as soon be descended from

that heroic little monkey . . . ; or from that old baboon . . .—as from a savage who knows no decency.")

But what, may we ask, are "ordinary conditions"? And what does it mean to "thrive freely"? And it can't have escaped you that according to this definition, the people making laws about who was allowed to enter the United States and who was not were/are not native but Naturalized. But that non-indigenous peoples should decide what other non-indigenous people should have a legal right to be "naturalized" seems somewhat peculiar.

3. The action of making natural. (Which, of course, means that what you were—Italian, in this case—was unnatural.)

4. The act of becoming settled or established in a new place. (All those Italian Americans who feel settled, established, accepted, and completely at home in this place, kindly raise your hands. Or have you ever, like me, been told that you were "an embarrassment," "irrational," "too emotional," "too noisy," or "too shiny"—these last words were those of a former employer of mine, and on that day, I wasn't even wearing my plaid taffeta blouse, pink stockings, and patent leather shoes.)

5. The act of becoming naturalized, of settling down in a natural manner. (If settling down in a "natural manner" means doing things the way things are supposed to be done in the United States, then neither I nor my parents nor my grandparents ever became fully naturalized. I remember reading Ralph Waldo Emerson's "Self-Reliance" in high school, and not understanding how anyone could consider that a virtue. I remember arguing in college that not wanting to move away from your family, that calling your parents daily, was not necessarily neurotic. I remember arguing against a twenty-three-minute lunch period when I taught high school. This, I hear, has been reduced to something like seventeen minutes. Recently, in Liguria, my husband and I saw the student body of a rural school having a leisurely three-course lunch in a celebrated local restaurant. We learned that they dined there three times a week at the government's expense. The kids served and cleared. The only difference between our table and theirs was that ours was covered with a white linen tablecloth, theirs with plastic. I am certain that students do not dine like this anywhere in the United States. Now that, I thought, looking at those children eating their pasta, is civilized.)

Libera Maria Calabrese. My grandmother has signed her name beneath her picture on the line of the document that calls for the *complete and true signature of this holder*, and she has no doubt signed slowly, for this writing of her name, I know, took much effort and much concentration.

(I remember her, years later, watching *Sesame Street* with my children, still trying to learn how to read and write English. And I remember her signing the back of her Social Security check; remember, too, it was the only time I saw her write her name. And I wonder now, what it was/is like to live a life where you almost never had/have an occasion to sign your name; wonder what it meant/means not to be able to use the act of writing to tell people about yourself and who you were and are and where you came from; wonder what it meant/means not to be able to participate in the creation of your identity on paper, for you did/do not have the language to do so.)

And I can imagine the clerks waiting impatiently for this small and soberly dressed foreign woman to finish signing, before they scrawled their names (illegibly, of course) at the bottom of the document. (Who were these people? What were their names? And why did they write their names in a way that makes it impossible to read what they have written and so identify them? But I have noticed this: that people with authority rarely sign their names so that we can read their signatures; but poor people, foreign people, people without power, usually sign their names carefully, in the perhaps false hope that someone will recognize who they are.)

⌒

But no matter how much my grandmother cherished it, this is a strange and terrible document.

After the clerk recorded the petition number (84413) s/he typed a *personal description of the holder as of date of naturalization*. Please note that the *personal description* was not altogether my grandmother's personal description. A written portrait of my grandmother by a paid functionary who inspected my grandmother's documents, took her testimony (about, for example, how much she weighed) and filled in this information, but who also wrote down what s/he observed. Much like the secretary who worked in the psychiatric ward of the hospital where my husband was an intern: After listening to a discussion among the doctors about a diagnosis, she preempted their decision by writing, say, *Paranoid Schizophrenic* on the form before her. Those who have the power to fill out forms have the power to define us, to tell us, to tell the world, who and what we are. And so it was with my grandmother.

⌒

I make my living analyzing texts, mulling over the nuances of words, asking people, asking myself, whether a particular configuration of words means precisely what the writer wants it to mean, wondering why something is phrased one way and not another, teasing out innuendos. And when I study this document, I realize that there is something very fishy going on here. There is what Virginia Woolf would call "an aroma" about the page.

The physical description of my grandmother, which she must swear to as true for naturalization to occur, reads: *Age 57 years; sex Female; color White; complexion Dark; color of eyes Brown; color of hair Gr. Black; height 5 feet 0 inches* (she was short, my grandmother), *weight 120 pounds; visible distinctive marks Mole on forehead; Marital status Married; former nationality Italian.*

I can understand that some of what is recorded is significant—age, color of eyes, color of hair, height, weight, distinctive marks—so that no one else could use this document. And I know that stating that my grandmother's "color" was "White" at this time in the history of the United States was significant, for it meant that at this time (although not always) Italians were deemed Caucasian, hence White (although, in fact, people who are white are, of course, not really white but, as an anthropology professor of mine once remarked, Pinko-Grey), hence eligible for naturalization. And so I can understand why this was recorded, although I do not agree with what that signified (that race exists; that it can be determined; that those deemed members of certain races are superior to those of others; that those deemed members of certain races should be permitted privileges, and others not, etc., etc., etc.).

But why was it important to record my grandmother's complexion as dark? What was so significant about complexion? There was, after all, a picture of my grandmother attached to the document that clearly showed what she looked like. And, as anyone could see, her complexion was fair though the document insists that it was *Dark.*

⌒

The description above given. Now, what does this mean exactly? Does it mean *The description given above?* But if that were the meaning, then the *description above* was *given* by someone, and it would be important to know by whom it was *given.*

So which is it? *The description that the person named above* (my grandmother) *has given to the clerk?* Or *The description that has been given to the above-named person by the clerk?* Or *The description that in part the person named above* (my grandmother) *has given to the clerk and in part has been given by the clerk to the person named above?*

Well, I have learned that when things are unclear, they are unclear for a reason. Especially on government documents.

Now, imagine the scene. Imagine the official asking my grandmother to present her birth certificate that would signify how old she was and that she was, in fact, Italian, and so was, in fact, Caucasian; asking her how tall she was and how much she weighed; asking her to present her marriage license to testify to the fact that she was married.

And now imagine the official asking my grandmother to describe her complexion. Would she call herself fair? Would she call herself dark? Would she call herself ruddy? But this, of course, did not happen, could not have happened. For at this point, the official exercised the right to declare what s/he saw when s/he saw my grandmother.

That my grandmother testified that she was fifty-seven years old, and a female, and that she was exactly five feet tall, and that she weighed 120 pounds, I can imagine (although I can also hear her mocking voice later telling my grandfather about this clerk, surely he was a *cretino* to make her sign a document to testify that she was a woman when anyone with an eye to see could look at her and learn that for him- or herself).

But that my grandmother told the clerk that her complexion was *Dark* I am absolutely certain never happened. For there is no way that in March, in the dead of winter, my grandmother would have described herself as dark or could have been considered dark by anyone who looked at her, who truly witnessed her face on that day. In March, my grandmother was not dark. In March, as in her photograph, my grandmother was most certainly fair.

Whatever else my grandmother was—a peasant, poor, irreverent, an Italian from a small village in Puglia—she was not stupid and she was no liar.

My grandmother either spoke the truth or, when the truth could not be told because telling the truth was dangerous, she remained silent and shrugged her shoulders, or she told a story. And although she disrespected and distrusted all authority, and with good reason, given that those in authority in the South of Italy had enslaved her people, driven them from land that had been held in common for cultivation for centuries, paid them poorly for their work or not at all, lent them money they didn't have at usurious rates so they could feed their families less than the amount of food that could sustain them, nonetheless when it came to this official form, my grandmother would have been scrupulously honest about the answer to any question put to her, for she was wary of the consequences of misrepresenting herself on official sheets of paper that were stamped and that had official seals. This was wartime, after all.

And so my grandmother of course did not answer the question "What is your complexion?" with the answer "My complexion is dark." Because, had she been asked, my grandmother would have said, "Sometimes fair; sometimes dark," and then she would have told a story. She would have told the clerk (if she imagined s/he would have listened) how, in Puglia, she was very fair, for her work as a seamstress kept her indoors all day and well into the night; how she had to tie her scarf in a special way to protect her face from the sun; how she had to cover her arms while working in the vegetable garden in Rhode Island when she visited relatives during the summer so that her skin wouldn't burn; and then she would have digressed and talked about the beauty of vegetables, the miracle of their growing from seeds, but also the wrenching pain in the back at day's end during harvest; she would have described how, by autumn, if she was careful, her skin wouldn't burn but would become a nice shade of *bruno*, like the color of a toasted pignoli.

But my grandmother could not be fair, not to the clerk who inscribed this document, and therefore not to the United States, because my grandmother was not only Italian, she was from the South of Italy, a peasant, a *terrone*—a creature of the earth, and so the color of the earth, and because of this, she had to be dark, not fair.

Here, then, on a document that my grandmother kept until she died, and that my mother kept until she died, and that I will keep until I die, is evidence that my people's whiteness was provisional, that agents of the government were using their power to *create* rather than *record* difference in physical appearance.

⌣

One of the clerks decided, perhaps without looking too closely (for who would want to look closely at a poor Italian peasant woman?), that my grandmother's complexion was *Dark*, and if my grandmother wanted citizenship, she had no choice but to sign her name on the line. She had to attest that though she was *White*, she was not completely *White*, for she was also *Dark*. There was not one white race; there were several, and some were not as good as others.

Because my grandmother was not quite white, she was also thought to be not quite (or not very) smart, not quite (or not very) reliable, not quite capable of self-government, not quite (or not very) capable of self-control, not quite capable of manifesting the traits of duty and obligation, not quite adaptable to organized and civilized society, not quite clean enough, not quite (or not at all) law-abiding (remember the Mafia). But at this time her (my) people were believed able to build the nation's railroads, its subways, its buildings; fight its wars; mill its fabric; sew its clothing; mine its coal; stow and unload its cargo; farm its fruits and vegetables; organize its crime; play its baseball; and, of course, make its pizza, its ravioli, and its spaghetti and meatballs.

⌣

Notice, please, that the clerk did not write *wretched refuse, human flotsam or jetsam*. The words *WOP, Dago, greaser, guinea, Mafioso* do not appear anywhere on the form, and for this, I should, perhaps, be grateful, even though it is what the clerk might have thought as the word *Dark* was written and this is what my people were then called (and often are still called, in Italy, where the area south of Rome is often referred to as *Africa*). But the law had provided a category—complexion—whereby clerks of the U.S. government (thank God) could insinuate what they thought about the person standing before their gaze. Notice, please: There was no space on the form for my grandmother to describe what the clerk looked like to her. *Dark* made its implicit meaning clear: My grandmother had become "racialized."

To become a citizen, my grandmother had to perjure herself. She had to admit that she manifested an attribute she did not have, but that someone else insisted she possessed. She had to sign her name, *Libera Maria Calabrese*, verifying that, yes, she was dark, not fair. She had to *certify that the description above given is true.*

And, on the form, there is the picture of a hand pointing to the line where my grandmother was to sign her name. Upon which my grandmother signed her name and thereby testified that what had been written was true. That her complexion was dark although her complexion was fair.

⌒

The picture of the hand, you must understand, is completely unnecessary. For the blank line would have been sufficient to tell petitioners where they must sign their names. But the hand is there. And it is not there for the purposes of decorating the document or for pointing to the line, you see, for it is the hand of authority, and it has dressed itself very formally for this occasion, in white shirt and dark suit, and there can be no mistaking that it is a white hand, and that the white hand is a man's hand, and that the complexion of the white man's hand is not dark, like my grandmother's is supposed to be, but fair. It is the fairest hand of all.

My grandmother had to be made to understand that though she was privileged enough to become a U.S. citizen, she was not that privileged. She had to learn that just as there are several grades of hamburger, there were (are) several shades of whiteness. She was chuck, with lots of fat and gristle; she was not sirloin; she was not even ground round. And signing this document where the white man's light hand pointed meant she agreed she was offered a citizenship that was provisional, that certainly did not confer upon her all the rights and privileges of someone whose color was white and whose complexion was fair, very fair.

My grandmother, then, became a "Dark White" citizen of the United States of America. Someone not truly white. Someone Italian American.

Passing the Saint

A Knock on the Door

It would happen like this: A knock on the crackled glass of the door to our tenement apartment in Hoboken, New Jersey. My mother, not expecting a visitor, opening it as she would for anyone who troubled to climb the four steep flights of stairs. She had nothing to fear, not now. She knew that if the visitor were a stranger, if he got to our door, he would have been stopped, thoroughly checked out, and granted passage up to our apartment by one of the young men hanging out on the corner of Fourth and Adams in front of Albini's Drugstore, by the old woman leaning out the window on the first floor of our building, or by the old man sitting in the sun on our front stoop. No one got into our apartment house unless they could prove they had some business there.

So because there was nothing to fear from a knock on the door (World War II was over, my father back home unharmed, thank goodness, at work a few blocks away, unlike the father of the children upstairs, and so many, many others), my mother would put down her mending, or turn away from her ironing board, or pull a pot off the coal stove, and open the door, thinking it was the vegetable man delivering what she'd ordered, or Argie from down the block—the only friend who could lure my mother away from the punishing rounds of her daily household chores.

44

Outside the door, not the vegetable man, or Argie, but an old Italian man. Short, stooped, ruddy-faced from years of work in the sun, wearing a cap like my grandfather's. Hands clasped in front of him. Surprise on his face. Then, shame. A slight bow as he took off his cap.

"*Mi dispiace proprio*," he'd say. "I am very sorry." He hadn't expected a woman to open the door. "'*Mbriago?*" he'd ask. '*Mbriago*, the drunk. My grandfather's nickname. The old man had come to see him. He might be a distant relative from Vieste, my grandfather's village in Puglia, or a crony from his railroad days in Maine or upstate New York, or a pal from his years of working on the docks in New York City. And he would be needing a loan.

Ours was a neighborhood of nasty nicknames—"Joey the Fat," "Jimmy Goose Face," "Bobby Snot Eater." (Even mine—"Miss Prim," "Miss-too-big-for-your-britches," or "Miss Smarty Pants"—given me by my father, were far from endearing, revealing his disgust at what he called my holier-than-thou attitude.) So my mother never recoiled at her father's being called '*Mbriago*, though I did, for I never connected what my grandfather did—sit at his kitchen table with a flask of wine in front of him—with the word "drunk."

My grandfather drank; that was a fact. All the old Italian men I knew drank. Some took a shot with breakfast; others took wine with lunch; all took wine, and lots of it, with supper. They drank wine to fortify themselves for the day's work, or against the night's exhaustion. But to me my grandfather wasn't a drunk. There were many other old Italian men who worked all day, and drank wine all day, who staggered home, who washed themselves at the sink in the kitchen, there being no bathrooms in their tenement apartments, who changed their clothes and then poured themselves a little glass of wine to restore their spirits while they waited for their suppers, who poured themselves a large tumbler of wine to accompany their meals, who poured themselves a little glass of digestif so they could sleep all night. They, too, were called '*Mbriago*. And even the ones who weren't called '*Mbriago* drank much of the time. But although my grandfather drank, my grandfather didn't stagger, and he was never mean, and he never hit anyone, and so I didn't understand why he was called that name.

"Next door," my mother tells the visitor, pointing. She knows that anyone who comes to see her father comes for a loan, the contract, sealed by a few glasses of my grandfather's homemade wine. My mother, worrying about how my grandfather will support himself when he retires if he gives money to everyone who comes to his door, and because she embraces the American doctrine of self-reliance, slams the door on the old man, shakes her head, and grumbles her way back to work. Although she doesn't try to stop him from visiting my grandfather, there will be a discussion later that day, after supper, he, chiding her about an impoliteness that never would have been tolerated in the old country; she, imploring him to be more prudent with the small bit of money he has.

"Pa," my mother will say to him in dialect, "you can't keep giving your money away. Who do you think will support you when there's no money left?"

"My child," my grandfather will say, "don't worry about me," assuming that if he needs help, she will, of course, deliver it.

But my mother *does* worry. She's seen my grandfather sitting at the breakfast table going over his accounts using the rudimentary system he's devised because he can't read, can't do arithmetic. A column for money coming in; a column (a longer one) for money going out; a tic for this amount; an x for that one. He's told my mother that if he doesn't lend money to these people, no one will. He's reminded her that when he came to America, people he barely knew lent him money to get by until he got on his feet.

"But the people you lend to, Pa," she says, "they never seem to get on their feet."

"The world's a hard place, my child," my grandfather says. "You have to help people oil their wheels."

So far, my father guesses, my grandfather is out about $3,000. Most of it to my grandmother's relatives in Rhode Island, whom my father can't stand because he's sure they'll never make good on their debt. "They're just using the old man," he tells my mother. The rest of the money he's given away, to old men like the one at the door, men just barely making it on their pensions, and if it weren't for my grandfather's working far beyond when he should have retired, and my grandmother's being the superintendent of our building, which enables them to live in their apartment rent-free, my grandparents wouldn't be making it on their own, either.

"The Lord helps those who help themselves," my mother tells her father. He looks back at her and says, "*Your* Lord. You think He helps anybody?

Show me one person your Lord has helped." And then he lets go a volley of dialect, and I'm lost in a language I barely know, barely can understand.

The Table

In all the photographs, in all the moving pictures of my grandparents' table, there is always bread, just enough food for satiety, and always a flask of wine. But there is never water. Not a pitcher of water, not a glass of water. My grandfather never drank water. Nor did my grandmother. A little glass of water for each of them on the hottest of days is all I can remember.

When I am young, just a toddler, my grandfather's drinking wine instead of water when he was thirsty was not something I questioned or remarked upon. It was as natural to me as the green of the trees in the park around the corner in springtime, the sweat of summer, the melancholy falling leaves of autumn, or the death of the soul in winter. Nor did I drink water when I was my grandfather's responsibility. If I was thirsty, my grandfather gave me wine. Until my mother found out when she came home earlier than she was supposed to one afternoon and found me with my little glass of wine, sitting at the table, drinking with my grandfather.

"A little wine will never hurt her," is all my grandfather says after my mother tears the glass from my hands, shatters it in the sink, and carries me back to our apartment next door.

Home Movie

In one motion picture, taken by my father, my grandfather is standing behind his kitchen table, miming drinking down an entire flask of wine. My grandmother paces, looks annoyed, then tries to take the flask from him. He pulls it away from her, mimes drinking the entire flask of wine again. She grabs his arm, tries to take it away again. But he turns away from her. He's the hero in his son-in-law's home movie. He's enjoying playing the drunk he will become.

My mother sits at the table, looks away, cups her face in her hand, a gesture indicating her displeasure at what's going on. There's antipasto on the table. Another flask of wine. A cup of milk for me. A cup of coffee for my mother, another for my father. But no water. Never any water.

Water, Water

My grandfather began to work in the fields of Puglia in the South of Italy when he was seven years old. When he worked in the fields, he was not given water to drink by the landowners or their overseers. Water was scarce; water was needed for crops; water was needed for the animals that were viewed as more valuable than farmworkers, for it was far easier to replace farmworkers if they sickened and died than it was to replace animals.

In the fields of Puglia, as in fields all across the South, farmworkers drank wine to quench their thirst, not water. Wine was abundant; wine was cheaper; wine was safer to drink, that's what farmworkers believed, and they were right. Even now, if you travel to the South as I have, if you see a group of farmworkers stopping their work for a few moments to rest, you will see them passing a flask of wine among them, you will see each man or woman wiping the mouth of the flask before passing it on to a comrade. "Passing the saint," they call it. Wine, "the saint," conferring the blessing of a few moment's respite, or, perhaps, oblivion for those whose work is unceasing, for those whose bodies ache because they work long and hard.

And so, my grandfather began "passing the saint" each day when he was seven years old as he worked in the fields; he "passed the saint" each day of his farm work in Puglia until he left for America. And the reason he left for America—the reason many people from the South left for America— was that the South was arid, drought-stricken, so farmworkers couldn't earn enough to support themselves. So, at the beginning of the twentieth century, when there were a series of droughts that left many unemployed, America beckoned. And by the time my grandfather left Puglia, the habit of drinking wine, not water, to quench his thirst was ingrained. Safe water was scarce; available water was potentially dangerous, he believed (and it often was); wine was safe (even though drinking wine long-term could kill you, but this he did not know or perhaps did not believe).

If my grandfather had remained in Puglia, he would have witnessed the completion of the great aqueduct that now delivers water there, albeit inadequately. Begun in 1906, completed in 1939, it comprised 213 kilometers of subterranean tunnels built by 11,000 workmen. During the Roman Empire, eleven aqueducts served the imperial city. But the Pugliese people had to wait until the twentieth century for water to be transported to their arid land.

My grandfather lived in Puglia when safe water was scarce; when whatever potable water that was available was sold to the poor at exorbitant prices; when much of the water of Puglia was tainted and undrinkable; when there was much standing water that bred mosquitoes, which gave the Pugliese malaria, which killed the Pugliese in astonishing numbers, especially children and the old and the weak, all of whom were especially vulnerable. But the death of the Pugliese didn't much matter to the landowners. There were too many of the poor. They bred like rabbits. They were lazy, shiftless, good for nothing. They got what they deserved.

But the South of Italy wasn't always arid. The aridity and unsafe drinking water when my grandfather lived there had been caused by human beings and rooted in the history of conquest, exploitation of the land and its people, and the governments of the North failing to protect the environment of the South and to provide the South with the water it needed.

The Englishman Norman Douglas traveled through Puglia and Calabria in 1922 to compare the landscape with descriptions in ancient texts, such as the odes of Horace, who was born in Puglia, and the *Iter Venusinum* of Lupoli, and the texts of Virgil, Martial, Statius, Propertius, Strabo, Pliny, Varro, and Columella. Douglas wrote in *Old Calabria*, originally published in 1915, about what he witnessed. Everywhere he traveled, he sought rivers, streams, or springs mentioned in those texts, and he discovered that almost all had disappeared. He remarked upon how waterless the South was. Unlike the North, rains in the South came during winter when no crops could grow; in spring and summer, instead of rain, there was hot, dry air, which made it necessary for the government to develop a system to collect water when it was plentiful and distribute it when it wasn't, only this wasn't done. He described how the only available water was bottled from mineral springs and sold by vendors; how peasants and farmworkers drank wine, not water; how they were often drunk by mid-day.

But in Horace's time, the South was "covered with forests" full of "hares, rabbits, foxes, roe deer, wild boars, martens, porcupines, hedgehogs, tortoises, and wolves." These species were now found only in a few remote areas because the forests had been burned by invading armies or cut down. Douglas attributed the poverty and diseases that plagued the South—cholera and malaria—to its despoiled landscape and how little the government had done to drain the mosquito-infested swamplands. He wrote about how taking quinine was necessary to prevent malaria, but that the poor couldn't afford it.

"I dare say," wrote Douglas, "the deforestation of the country, which prevented the downflow of the rivers—choking up their beds with detritus and producing stagnant pools favourable to the breeding of the mosquito— has helped to spread the plague [of malaria]." He wrote that cholera was increasing, and that the government's not providing adequate sanitation in the South had made the spread of cholera inevitable. He told how there were more frequent landslides because of deforestation and that after landslides the threat of cholera increased.

During centuries of invasion, Turks burned everything they encountered— towns, cities, forests—as they rampaged through the South; Spanish viceroys and Bourbons and Arab invaders destroyed the land. The Adriatic seacoast was depopulated during the Arab invasion; villages and towns were destroyed; everything in the path of the invading army was burned to the ground, and, according to Douglas, the formerly "richly cultivated land became a desert."

And what the foreign invaders began, Douglas said, the government in the North completed. Northern Italian and German industrialists acquired rights to the South's timber, and the slopes of existing forests were being denuded during his journey. To cut down trees on hillsides in a country with insufficient rainfall was "the beginning of the end." Douglas believed that politicians and industrialists were greedy, unconcerned that their practices would lead to disaster for the South's economy. Once a hillside's trees were cut down, rainfall washed the soil away, exposing the rocks beneath, making reforestation impossible. But why should they care? They didn't live there. The immense profits gained from these destructive practices went to the North, or out of the country, and most of the lumberjacks were foreign so the local people didn't even earn wages and profit, even minimally, from their land's exploitation.

Centuries of conquest, coupled with the ravages of exploitative capitalism, left the South devoid of two important natural resources—forests and water—and turned the South into the arid land my grandfather left. Douglas believed this led to the "bestialization" and "anguished poverty" of the people—until the 1880s, the poor could sell their children by officially sanctioned contracts.

Douglas told how haggard the people were, and how "distraught" from hunger and thirst. The land could not feed its people, could not provide employment for its people, could not quench the thirst of its people, prompting the great emigration of the people of the South to America.

Later in the twentieth century, Carlo Levi's conclusions about the ecological damage inflicted upon the region were the same as Douglas's. Levi spent time as a political prisoner in Lucania, the desolate region between Puglia and Calabria. In *Christ Stopped at Eboli*, Levi recounts his observation that clay hills were the most prevalent geographic feature of the region. When he asked a local how they'd been formed, he learned that the trees and topsoil had long since disappeared. Because there were no trees to hold the clay during winter rainfalls, there were frequent landslides.

His local informant described the destructive process: "When it rains, the ground gives way and starts to slide, and the houses fall down . . . . There are no trees and no rocks; the clay simply melts and pours down like a rushing stream, carrying everything with it."

Because the earth couldn't support agriculture, many men from Lucania emigrated to America to work, destroying the region's family structure. "For a year, or even two," Levi observed, her husband "writes to her, then he drops out of her ken . . . in any case he disappears and never comes back." Women formed new attachments but couldn't divorce, so many children were illegitimate and they often died young, or "turn[ed] yellow and melancholy with malaria."

Levi believed the South's grinding poverty could be attributed to one cause: "[T]he land has been gradually impoverished: the forests have been cut down, the rivers have been reduced to mountain streams that often run dry, and livestock has become scarce. Instead of cultivating trees and pasture lands there has been an unfortunate attempt to raise wheat in soil that does not favor it . . . . [M]alaria is everywhere." For Levi, chronic malaria robbed the South's people of their ability to work and to find pleasure in the world.

The Hudson River

When I am a baby and my father is away at war, my grandfather takes care of me on Saturday mornings to give my mother some time alone, although instead of going out, she stays home and cleans our already clean apartment.

My grandfather puts me in my stroller and pushes me up to a parapet overlooking the Hudson River. We go to see the river every time he takes me for a walk. In springtime, when leaves are budding. In summer, when they're luxuriant and green. In autumn, when they're yellow, red, rust, and gold. In winter, when they're long gone.

On our way to the parapet, there's a street paved with bricks the color of gold. Here, my grandfather takes me out of my stroller so I can walk on them. I am fascinated by their color, how they glint in the sunlight.

"See, my child," my grandfather says. "The streets of America *are* paved with gold." And then he laughs. "Maybe this is why I came here. Because the streets are paved with gold."

When we get to the parapet, my grandfather holds me up so I can see the river.

"So much water," my grandfather says, as if he's never before seen water, although I know he has. The Atlantic Ocean when we go to visit my mother's relatives in Rhode Island. The sea off the coast of his village in Puglia. The ocean on his long voyage to America.

My grandfather stands and looks at the water for a long time. Down on the docks where he worked, he didn't have time to gaze at the river for he was working hard, offloading bales of goods from ships from before dawn until late afternoon.

Luxury Travel

When I take my husband to Sicily for his sixtieth birthday, we stay in a fancy hotel in Agrigento, overlooking the famous Greek temples.

In early evening, before supper, I walk into the nearby village and hear old women complaining about how, for yet another day, there has been no water.

After my walk, I take a long, hot bath. It is the time of the winds that blow sand up from the Sahara. There is reddish grit on my body, in my hair, on my clothes. My favorite white cotton sweater will be stained pink after I wash it, a souvenir of this holiday.

A thousand yards down the road from the village, in our hotel, there is an ocean of water, enough to fill a deep and wide bathtub for me, for anyone who's journeyed here and who can afford the cost of a room. But there, where people live and carry on their lives, no water. Why?

When I return home, I ask a Sicilian friend, who laughs at my ignorance. "The Mafia," he says. "They control the water." He tells me to read Mary Taylor Simeti's *On Persephone's Island*, and I learn that in Sicily's interior, there is very often water only once every five or ten days. This is not nature's fault, says Simeti. Sicily is "rich in water that flows to the sea unexploited" because of government neglect, and because the Mafia "controls the major wells and springs that tap subterranean water layers, and . . . sells its water at high prices," and interferes (such an innocuous word for the mob's brutality) with any attempts to provide a cheap, safe water supply for the people.

Working on the Railroad

My grandfather came to America when he was young. He came for a better life for himself and his children, yes. But he also came because he was afraid if he stayed in Puglia he would die. Die from a bullet to the chest during the workers' rebellions. Die from thirst. Die from starvation. Die from malaria. Die from cholera. Die from the evil eye. Or die for no reason at all.

And I believe it was terror, more than anything else, which propelled my grandfather (and scores of others like him) up the gangplank to the ship that would take him to America. Terror, and yes, a job promised him by a boss recruiting men from his village to build a railroad line in upper New York state. The deal was simple. If you put your mark on a piece of paper, you'd get free passage to America. When you got there, you worked until you paid off your passage. Until then, the railroad would take care of you and there would be nothing for you to worry about.

And so my grandfather came to America, and worked on the railroad, and slept in his filthy work clothes—there was no place to wash, no water to wash with—on vermin-infested bags of straw, covering himself with a discarded horse blanket, eight men to a roach-infested, windowless boxcar.

He awakened at three in the morning, just as in Italy, and walked the line to the day's worksite, and worked from five to twelve without stopping. For lunch, there was bread, and sometimes water, but not always, because fresh water was in short supply. (In a 1916 essay called "The 'Wop' in the Track Gang," Dominic T. Ciolli reported how the *padrone* of a gang like my grandfather's complained to him because the laborers complained they had no fresh water, that they'd had no fresh water to drink or to wash with for weeks, and how the *padrone* said, "These dagoes are never satisfied . . . . They should be starved to death . . . . They don't belong here.")

But, as in Italy, there was wine, always wine for the workers to drink. Wine: antidote to rebellion. Wine: pacifier of those plagued by injustice. Wine: quencher of rage. By the time my grandfather paid back his passage and moved to Hoboken to work on the docks, he was an alcoholic. But that word doesn't describe the man my grandfather had become: a wounded man who'd lost hope, yet a proud and dignified man who continued to work hard and save little and who loved his daughter and his grandchildren more than anything in the world.

When my grandfather talked about his days on the railroad, there was a rage in his eyes, a rage that could pummel a wife, start a riot, burn down a building, kill a *padrone*, but did not. And so. He'd take a glass, pour himself some wine, and then a little more. After his third glass, he'd look for the rage, but it wasn't there. After his third glass, he'd miss *paisani*, and his mother and his father, both now dead, neither of whom he'd ever seen after he left Puglia.

Last Supper

"The day your grandfather dies," my father says, "he's digging out the basement in the house of one of your grandmother's relatives. And it's hot down there, and it's hard work because he's got to put all the dirt he digs into a sack, and carry it up the stairs, and out to the back yard, and your grandfather is doing this to make a few extra bucks because his pension isn't enough to live on and because he's always giving money away to anyone who comes to his door, and this pisses off your mother and your grandmother, but they can't do anything to stop it.

"And this day, he isn't feeling so good. He's tired and dizzy even before he starts working, and after a couple of hours, he wants to stop, but they tell him a deal's a deal, and that he has to keep on working until the cellar is dug out. And to keep him working, those bastards give your grandfather wine to drink. And, you know your grandfather, there wasn't a glass of wine he would refuse. So he takes the wine, quenches his thirst, forgets he's tired, and keeps right on working until mid-afternoon when the job is done. Keeps working through the heat of the day. Keeps working even though he's hot and tired and dizzy and feels like he can't breathe."

My father thinks the rest of the day goes like this:

My grandfather comes home, washes himself at the sink, changes into a clean set of clothes, has a glass of wine and a little lunch with my grandmother. After he finishes his meal, she leaves to do a little shopping for their supper, he pours himself another glass of wine, gets the spiral notebook listing money that people owe him, sits down at the kitchen table, starts tallying his accounts using that system of his own devising because he's never gone to school, never learned arithmetic, though he's told me he hopes some day I'll learn everything he hasn't. He's scribbling away, getting angry, because it's a year later, and his wife's relatives in Rhode Island still haven't paid their debt, and he's tallying how much they owe him when he falls to the floor. He's had a massive heart attack. No one is home to help him. And so my grandfather dies alone.

A few hours later, my mother, my sister, and I come back home. My mother knocks on her father's door to ask for help. We've been shopping; she's tired of being with my sister and me; she wants him to take care of us while she puts her groceries away.

My grandfather doesn't answer. My mother panics: He's supposed to be home. Where could he be at this hour? She struggles my sister and me into our apartment. Tells me to climb through the open window out onto our fire escape. Tells me to climb through my grandparents' open window next door, tells me to unlock their door.

I do as I'm told. I've done this before when my grandfather's forgotten his keys. So this is why I'm the one who finds my grandfather dead.

Transubstantiation

In Pier Paolo Pasolini's film *Uccellacci e Uccellini* (*The Hawks and the Sparrows*, 1966), a contemporary Italian father and his son travel into the past, to the time of Saint Francis of Assisi, and they become monks. The father, Brother Ciccillo, prays for a miracle, that all the wine in the world will be transformed into water, that there is no more wine in Italy. He prays there will be enough water in Italy so those who've become drunks because they've had no water to drink will now drink only water.

I read about Pasolini. Learn of his belief that the workers of the world, like my grandfather, will save the world. Learn that his father, like my grandfather, was an alcoholic. Learn that his father, like my grandfather, died because he drank.

Brother Ciccillo's hoped-for miracle: wine into water, not water into wine.

Last Rites

At the wake, I go up to the casket to see my grandfather's body. He is wearing his one good suit, the one he wore to my First Communion. There is the smell of flowers from the few commemorative wreaths surrounding him, the smell of mothballs emanating from his suit, the smell of death.

"That doesn't look like grandpa," I say. "And it doesn't smell like him, either." A neighbor stands behind me. She is watching me, listening to me, awaiting her turn to view my grandfather's body.

I am kneeling down, as I have been told to kneel by my father. I am supposed to be paying my last respects to my grandfather, as he has told me I must do. I don't know what last respects are, just as I don't know what first respects are, so I don't know what I'm supposed to do. But I have watched the stream of visitors go up to the coffin, kneel down, touch my grandfather's hands frozen in prayer, make a hasty Sign of the Cross, kiss their fingers, and move on, but I will not do this. My mother kneels in silence next to me. She hasn't said much since the day her father died; she will say even less in the months to come. Sometimes it will seem she has followed him to wherever he has gone.

Everyone in the funeral parlor talks about how badly she's "taking it." No one asks how my sister and I are "taking it." My grandfather, the man who took care of me whenever he could, who sang me songs, who told me stories I could barely comprehend of a land where wild seas drowned fishermen, where rainfalls were so powerful they made the land slide away, rainfalls so relentless they washed away all the good earth and made it impossible to grow anything to eat; of a land where wolves ruled the night and invaded dwellings and carried babies away, and men and women walked to the fields in the dark and worked in the blaze of day without a tree to shade them during their precious few moments of rest.

"And what did your grandpa smell like?" my neighbor asks.

I remember my grandfather, at his kitchen table, drinking wine. I remember my grandfather at our kitchen table, drinking wine. I remember my grandfather crushing grapes in the basement, stomping on them in the autumn with feet that would stay purple until winter. I remember my grandfather drinking wine when he took care of me, drinking it, sometimes, right out of the bottle. I remember my grandfather giving me watered wine to drink when he took care of me when I told him I was thirsty. I remember my mother's anger at my grandfather when she came home and found me drinking at the table or drunk, asleep on my grandparents' bed under the giant cross on the wall with Jesus Christ bleeding.

(In high school, I'm the girl who drinks too much at parties. The girl who drinks so much she can't remember how she gets home. The girl who drinks so much she passes out on the way home.)

"And what did your grandfather smell like?" the woman asks again, for I have not answered her.

"Like wine," I say.

The woman laughs. "*Mbriago*," she says. "That's who your grandfather was: *Mbriago*."

"No," I say. "That isn't who he was. He was my grandfather."

WHITE ON BLACK

Most days, as I was growing into young womanhood, my old Italian grandmother used to sit silently all day long, very close to the radiator in a corner of the dining room of our house in Ridgefield, New Jersey, her old black shawl covering her shoulders, as she crocheted white tablecloths and knit sweaters or afghans from wool she'd unraveled from sweaters we'd outgrown, outworn, or despised, or from wool she'd unraveled from sweaters she'd scavenged from dustbins or bought from second-hand stores.

During winter, the radiator hissed and clanked, creating more noise than heat, although it was still one of the warmest places in our drafty old house. But sitting close to the radiator in the corner of the dining room meant my grandmother never sat in the sunlight that filtered through the sheer dining room curtains so she could barely see her work. That corner of the dining room was forever in shadow, and the economies of our household forbade the use of artificial light during the day. Still, it seemed as if her fingers knew what to do no matter how dark it was in the corner that had become the greater part of her world.

I could count on my grandmother's being there, always there, for she had nowhere else to go, nothing else to do, but crochet and knit. Here in Ridgefield, she had no friends, no acquaintances, so far was she from Hoboken where she'd lived for so many years, so far from a meaningful life, earning her own living as the superintendent of the tenement where we all lived until my grandfather died, complaining with her cronies on the stoop of our building at the end of a long workday, walking to the market to buy vegetables for her and my grandfather's simple supper, going around the corner to church on weekends to light a candle (but not to pray) for the relatives in Puglia she'd never see again. Still, as I went about my self-absorbed life, I often forgot she was always sitting in that corner of the dining room near the radiator.

> *Her old Italian grandmother used to sit very close to the radiator to keep herself warm, she used to say, all through the long northern winters, the heat of the southern Italian sun having long since abandoned her. Her old Italian grandmother used to sit in her straight-backed chair, all in black, mourning her husband as she crocheted the white lace tablecloths she'd give the girl, her granddaughter, when she became a bride, and as she reused old wool for sweaters no one in this house wanted, sweaters no one would ever wear.*

It was more than seven years since my grandfather had died, seven years since my parents had taken her to this place where she didn't want to be, and she wore black still, although I could remember the two of them, husband and wife, grandfather and grandmother, scowling at each other across the kitchen table, him swearing in the harsh accents of Puglia where they'd both come from.

She was his second wife. His first had been much more beautiful. And there are two photographs, now crumbling, of him as bridegroom, twice decked out in the black suit that he would be buried in, twice newly shod, twice with boutonniere (the first, a single rose; the second, a sprig of lily of the valley), twice holding the pose for the photographer, he, so unused to finery, who'd laid the rails of the Delaware, Lackawanna, and Western Railroad single-handedly (if one were to believe his granddaughter's stories), who'd come all the way from Italy to do that, who later brought over his first wife, his girlish wife, who took in washing during her pregnancy, who died, from influenza, like so many others, when their baby, my mother, was but three months old.

Soon after, through a local priest, he worked out an arrangement with a woman from Puglia who was looking for a situation. He needed a woman to care for his child; she needed a husband so she could come to America. And I imagine her, on the boat, on the way over, knitting him a sweater from finely spun wool that she'd secured by bartering a linen tablecloth her mother had embroidered for her trousseau, for she was inclined neither to finery nor extravagance, although her mother believed that this cloth, adorning her daughter's table on Sundays and feast days, would prove she'd come from a proud family and so deserved respect.

The local Italian priest had written to Italy on behalf of my grandfather (for he could neither read nor write) to tell his wife-to-be that it was sometimes very cold in this new land, even cold indoors, and that the tenement they would live in would have only a coal stove in the kitchen to heat their living quarters, and it would be inadequate to the task, and that it was colder, even, where her husband-to-be labored outdoors on the railroad for many months of the year, up north near a big lake, far bigger than the one near her small village, and that it was colder than she could ever imagine, and so she knit this sweater to please him, to show concern for him, although she did not yet know she would never please him, that since his first wife had died no one could please him but his tiny undernourished daughter.

And she crocheted herself a shawl, too, on the voyage over, for she was quick with her needles, and the wool was thick, and the work went fast, for she had nothing else to do but knit and crochet, and she was unused to inactivity. The shawl was black, for although she would wear white for their wedding (borrowed finery from her relatives), he was in mourning, would always be in mourning, and so black was what she used for her work, and black was what she would wear to honor her husband's dead wife for some time to come and, perhaps, for the rest of her life, although she had heard it said that the women in this new land, even older women, even women from the old country, sometimes wore colorful garments of reds or blues or greens, and there was something within her that would have liked to have worn those colors too, although she'd never dare wear them.

Yes, the black shawl was something she'd wear around her shoulders to keep herself warm in this strange new land with an inhospitable climate, and she was happy at her knitting and crocheting, although it was a difficult passage, and it satisfied her to crochet this shawl that she knew she would need. But she'd decided that, no, she wouldn't knit the child (my mother) a thing, not now, perhaps not ever, because, although she would care for her because that was the bargain she'd struck, and so, it would be her duty and her responsibility, the child was his child, not her child, not their child. The child was not her blood.

Why my grandmother sat close to the radiator during winter, I could well understand, for although it threw off very little heat, this place was one of the warmest parts of our old, poorly heated house. Her body, born to southern Italian sunshine, never got used to the cold, although she lived here longer than she had lived there.

By the end of November each year, she would be wearing her long underwear, two or three dresses (one atop another), two or three handmade wool sweaters (one atop another) knit from fanciful lace patterns, out of keeping with her otherwise austere appearance, and her old black shawl. Everything except her long underwear—dresses, sweaters, shawl—was black, everything was frayed and worn, everything was poorly mended, for she was no seamstress like her mother, like my mother, and she now had no patience for the needle.

Often, my father would yell to my mother, so loudly that my grandmother could hear him, and in dialect, so that she could understand him, although he rarely communicated with her directly, for he resented her presence in his household, hated her intrusion into our lives, although what could he do, she had nowhere to go.

"Tell her to buy some new clothes, some warm clothes, goddamn it. Tell her she's a disgrace. Tell her people will think we aren't taking care of her. Tell her to take a bath. Tell her she stinks."

My grandmother would manipulate another very complicated stitch on the white tablecloth resting in her lap, or she'd tug at another seam in the sweater she was unraveling, and she would ignore his yelling, ignore what he was saying, and defeat him, as always, and for this, if for nothing else, I loved her, for to us both, he was the enemy, and I could not count the times that she'd thrown her needlework to the ground, stitches slipping off her needles, ball of wool or cotton unwinding across the floor, to put her body between his and mine, I could not count the times she'd taken the blow that was meant for me.

But, of course, although she pretended to ignore him, she could not. Just as although I pretended to ignore him, I could not. He would get the better of us both, and this, perhaps more than anything else, was the unspoken bond that connected us.

So, my grandmother would continue to buy nothing new, nothing American, nothing warm enough for winter, even though wearing more than one dress and all those sweaters and her black shawl and no coat on frigid winter mornings when she went to Mass marked her as a peasant, disgraced my parents, and embarrassed me—embarrassed me so much that I betrayed her by laughing with my friends rather than silencing them when they called her "the old witch" (for, by now, she had but a single tooth in her rotting gums), when they called her "the garlic eater," and held their noses and said "Puew, puew," when they said she ate babies for breakfast.

On the rare occasions my mother would come home with a new dress for her—black, surely, but with a pattern of delicate white flowers, or a store-bought sweater (solid black, of course), or an overcoat (black, again)—my grandmother, knowing it was better to yield than to resist, and knowing that yielding was the best and most potent form of resistance, would take the item, thank my mother, hold the garment out in front of her at arms' length, and put it in her bureau drawer or closet, where it stayed, unused, until she died.

⌐⌐

Why my grandmother sat inside the house close to the radiator in summertime, I could never understand, for it was stifling there. Perhaps it was from habit, or from a desire to be unobtrusive, for in our household, the only way to escape criticism or censure was to be unobserved. Yes, the radiator felt cool to the touch, but that corner of the dining room was stifling. There was the front porch with its breezes, or the back porch with its shade, but my grandmother didn't ever sit outside except perhaps in the evening, after supper, as the sun went down.

The radiator must have grown to be something like my grandmother's companion, I came to believe. Or perhaps it was that because my mother rarely bothered her when she was knitting (as my mother rarely bothered me when I was studying), my grandmother believed she could stay there without interruption, without complaint, knitting and crocheting. The radiator and her needlework and the food she cooked became her only comforts. The radiator didn't yell at her the way my parents did, nor did it mock her, as people outside the household did. The radiator didn't tell her what to do; it didn't tell her to be what she couldn't be: American. It didn't condemn her for what she couldn't not be: a southern Italian peasant. The radiator didn't betray her the way I did.

In summer, when it was chilly to the touch, it must have radiated the idea of coolness from its ugly gray mass so that, for a woman used to having so little, it might have seemed little enough. There, ignored and despised, she could carry on with the work that was the one thing, the only thing, that sustained her, that and a love for me that defied explanation, for she detested my mother, and I did nothing to deserve her love, nothing to invite it, except, perhaps, bringing her a cool glass of water now and then so she would not have to interrupt her work, and, once, thanking her for teaching me how to knit after sitting on the floor next to her for several mornings as she held my hands and guided me through the mysteries of casting on, knitting, purling, and casting off.

And so she sat, through the years in that darkened room, on the straight-backed chair, close to the radiator, crocheting the tablecloths meant to grace our dining room table on important occasions, though she herself would not sit there but, instead, would take her meager fare in the kitchen by herself.

When she did her work, my grandmother could have sat in one of the dining room chairs that my father and mother had refurbished when we moved up to Ridgefield from Hoboken, but the fact that she didn't, the fact that she dragged one of the chairs into the dining room from the kitchen, instead of sitting in one of the dining room chairs as my mother urged her to do, was another of my grandmother's small rebellions against my parents' attempt to dominate her.

My parents bought these chairs used at a flea market and they were battered but grand. Their backs were high and curved. When I first saw them, I was thrilled, for they fit into the grand fantasies I had as a child. They were, I was quite certain, the kind of chair that Queen Elizabeth I—I had read about her—might have sat upon when she was enthroned and issuing edicts to her dominions. Queen Elizabeth's chair was probably gilt. Ours, though, were oak and the worse for wear, although after my mother cleaned and polished them, the scrapes and dents in their surface all but disappeared.

When my parents brought the chairs home, I imagined my mother recovering them in cut red velvet. It was a fabric I'd never seen but had become familiar with in my reading. She could have gotten this fabric, cheap, from our relatives in the garment industry. And so I hoped our family that had once lived jammed together, too close for comfort, in three rooms without heat or hot water or a proper bathroom in a tenement in Hoboken might begin to act like the people I read about in books, might begin to act grand.

My parents, though, had another plan for these chairs. My mother wanted to create the aura of a "modern" home in the old, run-down, Christmas-tree green wreck of a house that she and my father had bought with money my grandfather had given my parents before his death. So they took the chairs, and against my pleadings, sliced off the elegant, curved, high backs of these chairs. And instead of the red plush of my imagination, my mother recovered them with something boring, sensible, and washable, reusing the old chairs' ornate brass tacks to hold down the fabric.

There they stood, these bastard chairs, so altered, so changed, that they seemed embarrassed by what they had become. And I never entered that dining room without thinking of the desecration they had endured, and without being ashamed of them.

And there my grandmother would sit on the straight-backed kitchen chair by the radiator in the corner of the dining room crocheting or knitting the sweaters we never wore, knitting the afghans that, when finished, we would throw into the bottoms of our closets, so hideously garish and ugly in their colorations were they that no one with any self-respect—this is my mother talking now—would ever use them, much less display them. There she would sit, this woman at her needlework, through the late 1940s, the '50s, the '60s, into the early '70s, until the year 1974, when she was taken to the nursing home run by the state.

There, she died, in that piss-smelling nursing home that didn't cook pasta or anything Italian, which accounted, my mother believed, for the fact that my grandmother lost so much weight so quickly. And it didn't permit knitting needles, or crochet hooks, or wool, either, for fear the patients might use the needles as weapons or the wool as a way to strangle themselves, a nursing home where the only outlet for a patient's creativity was cutting and pasting, on Fridays, but always under strict supervision, decorations appropriate for the season—snowflakes in winter, flowers in spring and summer, and autumn leaves in the autumn during which she died.

My grandmother—the Vermeer of needlework. Her handiwork, unappreciated in her time; now, family treasures after her death, after my mother's death. The sweaters are gone, and the afghans too. They were collected and thrown into giant plastic bags and dropped into a Goodwill box after her death, together with all that unused clothing my mother had bought her, and her old black shawl, which, by now, was tattered and moth-eaten.

But the tablecloths, I still have—heirlooms that adorn our family's festive tables, presents I give my sons and their wives, and that I will pass on to my grandchildren. I have many, many tablecloths to share. For you can crochet a lot of tablecloths, through all those years, when you have little else to do.

My grandmother must have known how little we valued, how little we desired what she made. Yes, we covered the dining room table with her tablecloths on Thanksgiving, Christmas, and Easter. But that is all. The afghans, we never used. The sweaters, rarely. But still, she kept crocheting, still, she kept knitting, so that, at her death, there were thirty or so tablecloths, stuffed in bureau drawers all over the house, in boxes under her bed and in the bottom of her closet. As if to crochet and to knit was what was important. As if what she made was not. As if the admiration of others did not matter.

Once, I saw her finish a tablecloth and begin a new one on the same day without stopping to admire what she had accomplished, without holding it up to the light of the window, admiringly. To crochet and to knit in the absence of anyone's desire but your own. To crochet and to knit because the very act of knitting, the very act of crocheting gives you what others do not, what others cannot give you, what this country that you came to does not give you: a sense of worth and some small scrap of human dignity.

FOURTEENTH
STREET

When my father was in his mid-twenties, he thought it was time he started looking for a wife. He was living in North Bergen, New Jersey, with his parents and four sisters, and his best friend told him about a friend of his girlfriend's, who was Italian and movie-star beautiful. She worked in the shoe department at Grant's in Hoboken and he could go there to meet her.

My father recognized her at once from his friend's description—her womanly figure, her dignified bearing, her dark hair caught in a snood at the nape of her neck. She was dusting the shoes on display, tidying the stock, adjusting price tags.

My father watched the woman who would become my mother for a few moments before she noticed him. He stood, wondering, hoping. *Could she . . . ? Would she . . . ?*

She turned, saw him looking at her. He smiled and she smiled back, a shy smile. She was even more beautiful than he'd imagined, a dead ringer for Ingrid Bergman, and he wondered why she was dusting and straightening shoes, smiling at him, when she could have been an actress in Hollywood.

She blushed, looked down, dropped a shoe. He rushed to pick it up but she got to it first. It was the blush, he told me years later, that did it. And he told himself, *She's the girl for me.*

He moved closer, but not so close to frighten her, introduced himself, told her how he'd found out about her. Asked if she'd meet him for a cup of coffee and a piece of pie at Schnackenberg's Luncheonette after work. She agreed, and he said, *So then, I'll see you, sooner rather than later.* As he walked away, he discovered what it was like to walk on air.

That weekend, they went up to Fort Lee, had root beers and deep-fried hot dogs at Hiram's. The next week, he borrowed his father's car and drove to Hiram's to buy her a hot dog to eat when he picked her up after work because she was always starving. The first time he presented her with the food, she was astonished. "For me?" she asked, as if he was the first to bestow special favors.

Each evening, they'd drive up to Hudson County Park in North Bergen and they'd park the car in a lover's lane and neck. They said very little to each other at first. She was shy. He was afraid he'd say the wrong thing, scare her off. But like all new lovers, they were shocked that they cared for someone who cared for them in return and so were satisfied with silence, gazes, timid caresses, and the flush of growing passion.

It was a cold winter and there was very little heat in the car, but it was the only place for them to have privacy, so they embraced as much from necessity as from desire. Between embraces, they wrote messages on the windows fogged with love. When he wrote that he loved her, she wrote, "Me, too," unable, yet, to write the word "love." He teased her that, because she wrote what she wrote, after he wrote what he wrote, what she wrote meant that she loved herself and not him.

She blushed. But the words he needed from her she couldn't yet give him.

He wanted her now with a fierce longing, but he knew that she was not the kind of girl you could take before marriage. He had a good job working in the surveying department at Keuffel & Esser right down from where she lived with her parents on Adams Street. If she would have him, they could build a life together.

"Two can live as cheaply as one," he'd tell her if she balked at his proposal.

One night, on impulse, he wrote the words "Will you marry me?" slowly, carefully, because he wasn't sure whether "marry" had one "r" or two. He did not want to reveal what he believed: that he was a stupid man, for he could tell by the way she spoke that she was a smart woman. And although she came from a poor immigrant family, she had a lot of class—the way she carried herself, proud and erect; the way she dressed—beautiful sweaters, tailored skirts. That he was stupid and wouldn't amount to anything, his teachers told him often throughout the few years of his schooling—you couldn't call it an education. But he'd spoken Italian at home and so spoke English haltingly as a child, been enrolled in one school after another as his family moved to satisfy some unspoken and never-realized desire of his father's. But he had to risk everything, know if she would be his, so that if she would not, he could leave her before the scar of love festered.

So there they were for her, his words, his entreaty. And then, in the next moment, just one word from her, a miracle: "Yes."

They did not yet know much about each other. She did not know of his ferocious hatred of his father, of how he started work as a toddler buttoning the shirts his mother had sewn. He did not know of her deep and abiding sorrow at the loss of her mother, of her adoration of her father. They did not think that what they did not know mattered. They loved each other, wanted to marry, and for now that was enough.

Her father wanted to meet him, couldn't wait for her to marry and start a family. She was in her mid-twenties, old by her father's Old World standards, almost too old, he thought, to find a husband. They would marry in July. She wanted to travel to Maine on her honeymoon so she could clamber down slick rocks to swim in a roiling sea. This surprised him, the danger of this desire, for she seemed so timid and fragile, so needful of his protection.

The day he met her parents, he borrowed his father's car, drove from Angelic Street in North Bergen ("I live on Angelic Street, but I'm no angel") to the tenement apartment she shared with her father and mother on Adams Street in Hoboken. He liked her father—his warm welcome, gusto, gnarled workman's hands—and believed the man might become more to him than his own father. He was nothing like his father's dandy of a father who manicured his nails, fancied himself too good for hard labor, used money he earned as a barber on himself rather than on his family, leaving them to fend for themselves on his frequent trips to Italy. Her father had been a railroad man, had come to America to work; but he was a longshoreman now, working the Lackawanna docks in New York City. He was ruddy-cheeked from hours of work in the sun, grabbing and heaving burlap bags and cotton bales from pier to railroad siding with his longshoreman's hook, red-faced from drinking (too much, my father suspected). When he came home, spent, weary, he hung his hook on a wall in the kitchen, a ready weapon to defend his home.

As a gift, my father brought her father a growler of beer—a round tin can filled with beer—because he knew longshoremen drank. The old man was grateful. "All you had to do to get him to like you," my father told me, "was give him something to drink." But it was more than the beer, of course. Her father could tell a hardworking man by the strength and roughness of his hands, and he knew this man would work hard to care for the daughter he adored, the daughter who almost died from malnutrition because the caregivers he hired to care for her while he worked on the railroad ignored her.

My father learned that he was a principled man. He worked the New York docks because he wouldn't work the Hoboken docks. In Hoboken, you couldn't get a job unless you "shaped up" each morning, paid "cumshaw" to the mob. Her father had left Italy because of his subservience to landowners there. "I'd rather starve than pay the mob," her father told him. Years later, my father told me the Hoboken docks were just as they were depicted in *On the Waterfront*. "That's why your grandfather got up before dawn and traveled to New York," he said.

Her stepmother was another story. She didn't welcome him as his mother would have, inviting a guest to sit down to take a cup of strong espresso with a few biscotti. When he arrived, her stepmother nodded, turned back to her cooking at the stove. "In time," he told himself, "she'll like me." But the old woman's affections were reserved for kin, several of whom lived in Hoboken.

The day he met her parents, the man and woman who would become my parents walked up Fourth Street to Washington Street, past Our Lady of Grace Church, Church Square Park, Demarest High School. He didn't take her hand in public, though he wanted to, for he believed she wouldn't be comfortable with a public display of their affection. They walked to the trolley station, took the trolley to Fort Lee. (I imagine him resting his arm on the seat behind her, wanting to show the world that she is his.) During the ride, he told me, and in the days to follow, as they began to know each other, sitting in the park, walking on the promenade above the Hudson, they shared stories about their lives. It was their season out of time while the great engine of war stood waiting to maul their future. They spoke of where they worked, their bosses' peculiarities; of where they'd gone to school; of where their parents had come from. Both their families were from the impoverished South, hers, from Puglia, his, from Campania. In Italy, this would have been an impediment to their marrying. But here their backgrounds were similar enough to negate the differences.

He told her about when he'd lived for a time in Scafati, his father's ancestral village. When his family moved there from the United States—his father had dreams of owning property, becoming a landlord—he took his roller skates. No one in the village had ever seen them. "They called me the devil on wheels," he said, and she laughed. What he did not say, because it was too painful, was how difficult life was there: how his parents, his four sisters, and he lived in two small unheated rooms; how his mother worked at the canning factory while his father stood on street corners with his cronies pretending to be a big shot; how his mother cooked on an outdoor brazier; how he saw his grandparents every day, how he loved them, and how he knew when his family returned to the States that he'd never see them again; how he was molested by a trumpet player in the local band.

He was happy he'd asked my mother to marry before he knew much about her, for what he learned told him she was way too good for him. She'd finished high school, won prizes and scholarships, wanted to attend college, wanted to become a writer like Edgar Allan Poe and Charles Dickens, both of whom had lived in Hoboken. But she had to work to help support her family. You'd never know by looking at her that she came from a poor family, that she lived in a flat without heat and hot water, without a bathroom—just one shared toilet to a floor.

"I want to give you the world," he thought. But he could not. He was just a workingman, and the most he could promise was a roof over her head, food to eat, and a love to last a lifetime.

He'd never gone beyond the eighth grade, wasn't good at bookish things. But he liked to read—his index finger tracing the abyss between the lines— to find out about the stars in the firmament, the strata beneath the Earth's surface, the shift and movements of the continents through time. He told her he'd gotten left back so many times, what with moving and working after school to help his mother (odd jobs, even stealing if it was that or starve), so that when he reached eighth grade, he was already sixteen years old. So

he decided to call it quits, worked a few years at one job after another—
repairing engines, making pens—then joined the Navy. By then, his father
had run through whatever money he had and they were living in housing for
the indigent. This, he was ashamed of; this, he didn't tell her.

He joined the Navy, he said, not to see the world but to get away from his
father. He thought he might get an education—that's what they promised—
become a pilot, make something of himself. (He didn't tell her that he left
because he was afraid he'd kill the bastard the next time he hit his mother.)
Leaving his mother was the hardest thing he ever did, he worried about her
all the time. But he told himself now it was his sisters' turn to take care of
her. He had to make something of his life so he could come home, get a
good enough job to help her out so she wouldn't have to work anymore.

He'd spent a few years in the Navy living better than ever before. He
had his own cot; three squares a day; hot showers. He was lucky there was
no war. What he got in the Navy was training to be a mechanic—in the
service, a poor man could learn a trade—but not the education he needed to
become a pilot. So instead of learning to fly airplanes, he became an aviation
machinist's mate and learned how to fix them. And whenever he climbed into
a cockpit to check something out, he pretended he was a pilot.

He told her about his other dream, of becoming an opera singer. He'd
pointed out the names of the composers—Verdi and Puccini—on the frieze
of the band shell in the park on Fourth as they'd walked by. On that trolley
ride, on their way back to Hoboken, he'd taken her hand, sung, "*Che gelida
mannina*" from Puccini's *La Boheme*. He had a spectacular tenor voice, he knew.
It was the first of many serenades.

She was pleased, not embarrassed. No one but her father had ever
made such a fuss over her. She loved his singing, and the other passengers
were charmed and clapped: One man even shouted, "Encore, encore!" and
for a moment my father understood what it might have been like to sing
Rodolfo at the Met, fans rising to their feet, shouting his name. But he was a
workingman, and a workingman he would be all his life, and it was best not
to think about it. (After they married, had children, they would live with the
consequences of dreams unrealized. Now, though, "what could be" had not
irrevocably turned into "what might have been.")

It was early in 1941 when my parents met and fell in love. My mother's friends assured her that the United States would never go to war, even though Hitler had taken Poland; there was the Neutrality Act to prove it, and the country was protected by vast oceans. But my mother was convinced the worst would happen. The previous spring, her father's stevedore friends working the New Jersey piers had loaded the contents of hundreds of freight cars filled with guns and ammunition into the holds of British ships. Neutrality? The United States was already involved, although we pretended not to be.

During my parents' courtship, Germany invaded Yugoslavia and Greece; my father thought Hitler wouldn't stop there, you could see it in his eyes. There'd been talk in newspapers of developing a two-ocean Navy. The Lend-Lease bill had passed, committing the United States to aid those fighting totalitarianism, short of war, and Navy ships were escorting British transports across the Atlantic. If they were attacked, wouldn't this mean war? My father had already completed one tour of duty and figured that, because of his experience, he'd be called up again. He could fix an airplane, his superior officer had said, with spit, paper clips, rubber bands, and glue.

Once, I ask my father why my mother let herself fall in love with him if she believed he would be snatched from her and put in harm's way. "I convinced her," he said, "that if she loved me, I couldn't die."

Before they married, they looked for an apartment in Hoboken; they wanted to be close to their jobs; she wanted to stay close to her father. But it wasn't easy to get a nice apartment. The city had scores of factories, scores of docks. Hoboken was the only deep-water port on the New Jersey side of the Hudson and it was the terminal for many rail lines. All the workers in these bustling facilities needed housing in this mile-square city, so vacant apartments were very hard to find. My parents had to settle for an apartment in a tenement on Fourteenth Street—it was the only one they could find. Fourteenth Street, though, wasn't a place my grandfather wanted his daughter to live. It was right down the block from one of the largest shipyards in the country. If war was declared, it would be near the dry docks working around the clock to build and repair ships and outfit them for war; near where servicemen would pour off ships for a few hours' carousing in the saloons lining the street. But this place was better than no place at all, and he knew that the young couple couldn't live with him and his wife in their three tiny rooms.

Although my parents weren't keen about the neighborhood, in some ways the apartment was better than any place they'd lived before. It was brick, not wood; it had central heating, not a coal stove; it had doors separating the rooms. For the first time in his life, my father would have a bed to sleep in; my mother, for the first time, would have privacy and a place to call her own.

They were married six months after they met in my mother's parish church, St. Francis, on Third and Jefferson. It had been erected in 1890 by Italian Catholics from Liguria. My mother loved the stained-glass window depicting St. Francis of Assisi, her favorite saint because of his kindness and gentleness. She wore an elaborate silk gown with a cathedral train, made for her by a friend. Her father, wearing his one good suit, his unruly crop of hair slicked down, walked her down the aisle with pride. All his hard work had been worthwhile.

On their way to their honeymoon cottage in Maine, my parents toured Revolutionary War battlefields in Massachusetts—my father was fascinated by the history of warfare. In their honeymoon pictures, my father is relaxed and happy, my mother, appears nervous. He didn't consider how these wartime reminders might affect my mother. In one photo, my mother looks distressed as she gazes at a statue of a musket-bearing soldier: I imagine her picturing my father being handed a gun, put in the line of fire. When they returned to Hoboken, my parents learned that the Germans were advancing upon Stalingrad. In five months, the Japanese would bomb Pearl Harbor, and the United States would be at war.

My parents returned to the apartment my mother had decorated as if it were in a posh brownstone on Castle Point Terrace. From her years as a saleswoman, she had developed a refined aesthetic taste. "She made the place beautiful," my father said, "even though it was on Fourteenth Street and you could smell the cooking from the restaurant downstairs."

My mother knew how she wanted to decorate her home. She'd pored over magazines, wanted it to be beautiful, unlike her parents' functional, austere home, marking her transition from her parents' Old World ways to the modern way of life my father and she would create together.

They'd installed a rug in the parlor—rose, with a stylized leaf design. And the furniture they'd bought at Art's in Ridgefield for their parlor was the best they could afford—a suite upholstered in deep rose; a Chinoiserie side table (all the rage); another side table that could open into a dining table for four. Their bed was graced with a quilted silk comforter and pillow shams—a bridal gift from my mother's best friend, Rose. And they'd bought from a Hoboken store catering to Italian immigrants a used Italian chifforobe to store their clothes.

Hanging the leaf-patterned wallpaper in shades of beige, soft green, and ivory in the parlor and bedroom was a nightmare because the walls weren't smooth. "In the time it took to hang that wallpaper," my father said, "I could have built the Taj Mahal." But they persevered, prepped the walls, hung the paper, transforming this place into something they could be proud of, as they listened to radio reports describing the German invasion of Minsk. My mother borrowed her stepmother's pedal-driven Singer sewing machine to run up a set of drapes in ivory and beige stripes. It was as if by laying carpet, papering walls, and hanging drapes they could shut out the war and create a space that violence could not penetrate.

But abroad, homes created with equal care were obliterated in a moment. "If it could happen there, it could happen here," my mother thought, as she pored over photographs of gutted interiors in newspapers, focusing upon images of shredded wallpaper, smashed tables, demolished mirrors, riven grand pianos, shattered crystal chandeliers. It wasn't that my mother valued material objects more than people's lives. But she deplored the destruction of those sacred spaces and the loss, not just of life, but also of the particular kind of life that had been created in these rooms once promising safety and protection.

~

On December 11, 1941, less than six months after they married and four days after Pearl Harbor, Italy declares war on the United States; the United States declares war on Italy. My parents discuss what the war will mean to them and to their parents, now declared enemy aliens; they're certain that my father with his valuable skills fixing airplanes will be drafted. It's an uncertain time.

On or about December 21, 1941, two hundred eighty days before my birth—the normal gestation period of a human being—I am conceived. It's two weeks after Pearl Harbor; ten days after my parents feel certain my father will go to war. And so I wonder, now, what kind of an act of love this was, the one that made me, performed during the first gasp of our country's involvement in that terrible war. There was love, surely. But there must also have been panic, despair, desperation, fear, terror. And I wonder how my parents, my mother and my father, knowing already that my mother could be undone for days by a pot roast inadvertently burned, could have chosen to conceive a child who would be born into war.

"We are all of us made by war," as Doris Lessing said, "twisted and warped by war, but we seem to forget it."

After they took their baby home from the Margaret Hague Maternity Hospital in Jersey City to their apartment on Fourteenth Street in Hoboken, her father was more mother to his daughter than his wife. She'd been in labor for days; it'd been a difficult birth. He'd paid extra for the best doctor and a private room so she could rest. Still, when she left the hospital, she wasn't well at all, despite the doctor's assurances that many women go through this kind of thing after giving birth, that once she got home, she'd be much better.

But she wasn't better, she was worse. She wouldn't get out of bed, wouldn't feed their child, this tiny baby who cried all the time.

"The baby's crying," he'd say.

"I know, I know," she'd answer without moving. She'd lie in bed, staring at the wallpaper, wrapped in her pink chenille bathrobe, wasted milk leaking from her breasts, drying and crusting and making her nipples bleed, which was why she said she couldn't nurse. For if she nursed the baby, she would have been drinking her mother's blood along with her mother's milk.

When my father talks about this many years later, he never says my mother was depressed. He says she was befuddled.

"At first, she never knew whether she should feed you or let you cry; whether to let you cry or comfort you; whether to hold you or put you down. Sometimes she'd stand over your crib and watch you cry, trying to figure out what to do. Then she gave up trying to figure out what to do and went to bed."

She'd never had a mother's care. Her mother died when she was a few months' old during the flu epidemic. After her mother died, her father sent her to caregivers—he was now working the railroad in upstate New York. They took his money and spent it. When he came home, his daughter was nearly dead. So he sent for a woman from his province in Italy to come marry him and raise his child. She came, but she said the child was not her blood; she fed her, yes, washed her, changed her, clothed her, but, the rest of the time, ignored her.

My father told me sometimes he'd get so angry at my mother he'd want to drag her over to my crib, force her face down to my face, so that she'd feel my hunger. But he never did. What he did was seethe, crash some pots and pans together as he cleaned, and then take care of me himself, feed me the formula the doctor warned against. What was his choice? To see his child die of starvation? And he'd remind himself that he'd loved my mother from the first moment he saw her in the shoe department at W. T. Grant's Department Store up on Washington Street; he'd tell himself this was just a phase.

Hell, he knew her life was hard. Cleaning, cooking, shopping were hard. Every surface in the apartment became covered with soot. Clothes, diapers, sheets had to be scrubbed on a washboard in the sink, wrung out, hung outside to dry. You had to lug coal up from the basement for the stove, clear out the ashes, take them down. To shop, you had to dress the baby, haul her and the carriage downstairs, walk to the market, walk back, then tote the groceries, the carriage, and the baby upstairs, hoping that whatever you left behind was there when you came back for it.

⌒

Through the difficult time after my birth, my father told himself my mother would return to her old self, the woman with the shy smile he'd fallen in love with. His job, through it all, was to keep working, take care of his daughter, not give up hope. My father never regretted marrying my mother, not when she wasn't being much of a mother, not later in her life when she became so depressed she couldn't care for their children and had to send them away to live with relatives until she recovered, not when she was hospitalized and shock treated. "Everything I am, I owe to her," he once told me after her death, wiping tears. "We made a life together. She found me better jobs. She told me I was worth something." Sometimes he thought it was his fault, that if after I was born they could have afforded a better place to live, she would have been more cheerful.

"Just let her cry and she'll go back to sleep," his wife would say in a voice more agony than statement, as she settled herself into a sleep that wasn't sleep but obliteration.

"Patience," the doctor said. "Sometimes this happens at first. But give her time, she'll come round."

"What about the baby?" my father would ask.

"Oh, they're resilient creatures," the doctor said. "Feed her some sugar water. She'll make out just fine."

"Give her time." My father didn't have much of that. The war was on. He'd finally gotten the orders he'd feared would come. Soon he'd be shipping out. But where was that maternal instinct his own mother had whose life had been much harder than his wife's?

One day he couldn't take it anymore, left the apartment, went to the drugstore, bought bottles, nipples, evaporated milk, Karo syrup, and a vitamin supplement with iron. If his wife couldn't feed his daughter, he'd feed her himself. He'd decided to petition the Navy to let him stay home until his daughter was a year old. "If I leave before she's a year, she won't make it, my wife can't take care of her." And so he stayed, and his wife became more cheerful, and his daughter reached a year, and now she was a chubby little thing with a full head of hair tottering around the apartment.

On her first birthday, he took pictures of her staggering across the parlor with hands held out towards a very large ball, smashing her birthday cake, resting her hand on her mother's cheek, his wife smiling that wan smile that spelled trouble. "Not yet, I can't leave yet." So he petitioned to stay a little while longer, was granted a bit more time.

When his daugher was fourteen months old, he couldn't put it off any longer.

He shouldn't have been going away. It wasn't that he didn't want to do his duty; he believed he could better serve his country by helping make surveying instruments that were critical in wartime. His boss at Keuffel &

Esser had given him a coincidence rangefinder used to determine distances that was confiscated from the Germans. He and an engineer had broken it down, figured out how it worked, made a working model. It was put into production, and Army scouts used it during the war. (He never told his wife about the black widow spiders they kept in the basement of K & E; their webs provided the filaments for the crosshairs of rangefinders, and there was a woman they called the "spider lady" whose job it was to tend the spiders, take the filaments, and place them into the grooves they'd cut into the glass.)

The foreman at K & E could exempt only one man from service because of war work. It should have gone to him, my father thought. Instead, it went to one of the foreman's relatives. "That's how things go," he told his wife. "Who you know is more important than what you do."

President Roosevelt had announced the United States would accept nothing less than the unconditional surrender of Germany, Italy, and Japan, which could only mean a long and protracted war. As the time for my father to ship out neared, the Battle of the Atlantic against Germany's U-boats was raging; Soviet troops were fighting 4 million Axis troops along a 2,000-mile front; and British and American troops were invading Sicily, beginning the costly Italian offensive.

My father read the newspaper account of General Patton's speech to his troops on the eve of the invasion of Sicily. Patton declared that Italian American soldiers should consider it a privilege to kill Italian soldiers, for Italian American soldiers were descended from ancestors who were free men because they had chosen to come to the United States, whereas Italian soldiers were descended from ancestors who were not free because they had chosen to remain in a homeland that despised them. "Remember," Patton said, "that these ancestors of yours so loved freedom that they gave up home and country to cross the ocean in search of liberty. The ancestors of the people we shall kill lacked the courage to make such a sacrifice and remained as slaves."

Years later, my father could still remember the impact of that speech on the Italians and Italian Americans living in Hoboken. He could still remember the fury people felt against this son of a privileged family who knew nothing of the suffering that had prompted the Great Migration, knew nothing of how the poor bore no allegiance to a government that worsened their lives, knew nothing of the sacrifices entire Italian families had made to send just one child across the ocean to earn money to be sent back home to save the family left behind, knew nothing of the wrenching emotional cost of Italian American soldiers fiercely loyal to the United States fighting and killing *paisani*, and sometimes even blood relatives.

My father always called Fourteenth Street the asshole end of Hoboken. It was near factories, docks, boarding houses where sailors stayed on shore leave. It was busy, noisy, filthy, and dangerous, no place for a wife and child to live while a man was on an island in the Pacific during wartime. On Fourteenth Street, the smell of coffee from the Maxwell House Plant up on Hudson Street, the largest coffee-roasting plant in the world, never went away; the stench of chemicals from factories nearby permeated the air; the racket from the rivet guns at the shipyards never stopped, day or night; the noise from trucks transporting wartime supplies never ceased; the shouts from drunken revelers in the saloons on every corner could be heard all night long. It was the kind of place, my father said, where if you were in the wrong place at the wrong time and the mob wanted to settle a score and shoot someone full of holes or toss a stoolie off a roof and you happened to be walking by, you might get yourself killed. "Everyone in this part of town," my father told me Frank Sinatra said, "carried a twelve-inch pipe . . . and they weren't studying to be plumbers."

And so before he shipped out, my father tried to find a better place for us to live. All day and through the night, trucks with supplies and munitions for the war rattled down Fourteenth Street to the docks where their cargo was loaded onto ships. The Todd Hoboken Division alone handled close to 8,000 ships and 34 million tons of goods during the war. And ever since Bethlehem Steel had purchased United Dry Docks and expanded their facilities, the waterfront was even busier. Would one of those trucks get into an accident and explode on our block? The docks were a target for German submarines, and if one slipped undetected into New York harbor, and if a submarine torpedoed a ship loaded with munitions, our apartment would be destroyed, we would be killed.

In 1900, there'd been an enormous fire at the piers near River Street. The *SS Bremen, SS Main, SS Kaiser Wilheld der Gosse, SS Saale,* and twenty-seven other watercraft burned, killing more than 200 people. That day the sky turned black from the smoke from fires, and the people in Hoboken, before they learned what happened, thought the world was coming to an end. If this happened once, it could happen again.

There was a saloon on the corner of Washington and Fourteenth, another on the corner of Garden and Fourteenth. Beneath the apartment was an eatery frequented by dockworkers and servicemen. All through the night, my parents heard the carousing and brawling soldier and sailors. Even during the day, Fourteenth Street bustled with servicemen on shore leave. They poured off vessels at the docks, looking for a place to drink away their pay, drink away their fears, spending their money like the drunken sailors and soldiers they were, in the saloons and dancehalls catering to servicemen for which Hoboken was famous.

Sauntering down the street, several abreast, arms locked, they hawked every woman they saw, looking for a good-bye fuck before sailing off to Europe or the Pacific, places where men like them were dying in great numbers, places from which they might never return. No, Fourteenth Street was no place for a woman and child to live without a man to protect them.

My father wanted to move us south and west, away from the piers, from the city's major thoroughfares, into one of the Italian tenement neighborhoods. My mother would be closer to her parents, closer to food shops, closer to parks, closer to the Free Public Library on Park Avenue, an Italian Renaissance structure with a beautiful interior of oak and cypress where my mother went often for a little peace and quiet and to borrow books. But my father knew finding another apartment would be almost impossible because vacant apartments were scarce, people weren't moving, especially women with husbands at war who wanted to remain in their familiar neighborhoods: there was a housing shortage—residential building had ceased when construction companies started building factories for war work like the Todd Hoboken Dry Docks slated for ship construction, conversion, and repair.

Saturdays and Sundays during those last months, my father would lug my stroller down the stairs, come back upstairs to get me, and settle me into it to begin his search for an apartment. He'd make the rounds, staying away from neighborhoods beyond his means: the mansions on Castle Point Terrace near Stevens Institute of Technology, the exclusive Eldorado Apartments, and the Yellow Flats on Washington Street where Hetty Green, one of the richest women of her day, had lived. Instead, he searched through Hoboken's working-class neighborhoods, up and down First through Tenth, then up and down Garden Street, Park Avenue, Willow Avenue, Clinton Street, Adams Street, Jefferson, Madison, Monroe, Jackson. He climbed stairs, knocked on doors, stopped people on streets, talked to women in shops. "Do you know anyone renting an apartment? I need a place for my wife and child."

When we came to my grandparents' apartment on Adams, we'd stop for a visit. When we came to Church Square Park between Garden and Willow, my father would let me crawl up and down the steps of the bandstand and drink some water from the fountain while he smoked a cigarette. Then he'd push me on the swings for a while before heading home.

As the day for his departure approached, my father, in desperation, started looking outside of Hoboken. He'd push my stroller up the steep viaduct at the west end of Fourteenth. If he found an apartment up there, my mother and I would be far from her parents. But any place would be better than where we were living.

⌒

His wife brushes a piece of lint off his uniform. It's just like her, tending to him in these last few moments before he ships out, making sure he looks his best.

"Send your money home," she says. "I'm good at scrimping. When you come back, we'll try to find another place to live. When you come home . . . ."

They both think, but don't say, "not when, if . . . ."

She turns away. The child stands between them, tugging at his trousers, looking up at him. She won't let him go. She's dressed in a sailor suit, bought for their last day together. They've taken goodbye photos: him, in his dress blues crouching next to his daughter in her snowsuit on this cold November day; him, knelling next to her, she in her sailor dress; his wife, trying to smile, holding their child who refuses to say "cheese" for the camera. They'll be sent to him enclosed in one of her daily letters.

"Five bucks a month is all I need," he says. "I don't drink or gamble. Don't worry," he says, "I'll be home sooner, rather than later, then we'll see." These were his parting words from the day they met—"I'll see you," he'd wave and say, "sooner rather than later."

But he *will* worry, though he can't tell her, for he needs to be strong. He'll worry, not about himself, but about her, about whether she's managing to take care of their daughter with him away, for she's fragile, this wife of his, breaks down easily. But she's fine now and his daughter is more than a year old, and he hopes she'll grow sturdy and strong while he's away.

⌣

Nine months after he ships out, my father receives a letter from my mother. She tells him that one night, after she puts me to bed, she's having a cup of tea in the parlor, writing her daily letter to him, and she hears a commotion on the stairs. She's used to servicemen mistaking the apartment's entrance for the restaurant's. Usually she opens her door, leans out, shouts down the stairs to set them straight. They leave, the ruckus stops.

But on this night, the voices are many and menacing. She's afraid to open the door, hoping, wishing the servicemen will discover the place they've stumbled into is not where they want to be.

The noise doesn't stop. The men don't go away. They clatter up the stairs to our landing, pound their fists on our door.

My mother has no telephone, no way of communicating with anyone, short of throwing open the parlor window and calling down to passersby below. She hopes her neighbor hears what's going on. But she's a woman with her husband away at war too, so how could she help?

The pounding gets louder; my mother's afraid the commotion will wake me. She opens the door a crack to tell them they're in the wrong place.

"There were a group of drunken sailors outside the door," she writes my father. "Five or six, I couldn't tell. Someone told them there was a whorehouse in our building." Her tone is cool, measured, contained. No need to worry, he tells himself, reading her letter at night in his Quonset hut by the light of a kerosene lamp. He's thousands of miles away on a tiny island in the Pacific when he should be home to protect her.

"I told them they were mistaken," she continues. "But they were so far gone, they thought I was a tease. There were so many of them, they pushed their way in."

My father puts down the letter. Takes a cigarette. Lights it. Draws the smoke deep into his lungs. Exhales. "She's all right," he tells himself. "She wrote me this letter."

Except for a few lines about her father's not feeling well, her stepmother's feud with the woman living next door, and her signature at the end of the letter, "Yours faithfully, Mildred," that was all.

She had written nothing about whether she was frightened, whether she'd been harmed. He wondered if she'd told him the whole story, wondered whether she was keeping something from him, wondered whether anything terrible had happened.

"If they laid a hand on her, I'll find them and kill them," he vowed. Knowing he'd never find them, knowing he'd never kill them, knowing he'd never know what really happened on that night.

(Years later, when I tell my husband about this episode in my father's war stories, he asks, "Was she raped?" I recall a pounding on the door, a table overturning, a neon light blinking through the window, a cry, and that is all.)

The next letter my father receives is devoted to my mother's plans for leaving Hoboken for an extended holiday with me to visit her stepmother's relatives on a farm in Rhode Island. She writes that it'll be fun for me— feeding chickens, harvesting vegetables, playing with animals, swimming in the ocean.

My mother's plans told my father everything she wouldn't say, everything he needed to know, but didn't want to. Something far worse than what she described had happened. Her trip made no sense. She didn't like her stepmother's relatives, didn't like visiting them. It would be a difficult trip, taking the better part of a day. She'd have to take a bus, a ferry, a taxi, a train, and then another taxi, toting luggage and a strong-willed little girl. The journey, he knew, was propelled by fear, fueled by terror.

Had one of them dragged her into their bedroom, thrown her on the bed, torn her clothing? Had she cried out, scratched his arms, bitten his face? This became real to him. The noise on the stairs. The servicemen at the door. The bed. The soldier. His wife. Her screams. His daughter's cries.

"What kind of world is this," he thought, where a man is forced to leave his wife and child, travel halfway around the world to help make the world safe, while his wife is left alone to fend for herself and their child? "What motherfucking kind of world is this?"

꙳

After my mother and I leave for Rhode Island, my grandfather, reading his daughter's mood, suspecting something, decides that when we return, it will be to another apartment nearer to him. Next door to my grandparents lives a woman my grandmother can't stand. In one version of the story, the woman is contemptuous of my grandmother, sneers at her, throws the rent money at her. She doesn't believe a poor Italian woman should be a superintendent, intimates she got the job because my grandfather's connected. She and my grandmother fight. The woman smears shit on my grandparents' door. My grandmother takes the woman to court for harassment. My grandmother wins the case. The woman moves out. My mother and I move into the vacant apartment when we come home.

But in another version, my grandmother is the instigator, bolting her neighbor's door of the shared toilet from the inside, then leaving for the day to visit relatives. All day, she sits and crochets and drinks an occasional cool glass of water until the woman, desperate, breaks down the door, which gives my grandmother cause to evict her. In this version, on the day the woman moves, she walks down the street, finds a pile of dog shit, picks it up, puts it in a bag, walks back to the tenement, climbs the stairs, goes to my grandparents' door, and smears shit all over.

On the day that my grandparents move us to Adams Street, my grandfather borrows a truck and gets some of his stevedore friends to help. There isn't much furniture—a sofa, a chair, two side tables, a lamp, a bed, my crib, a chifforobe, a kitchen table and chairs, a rocking chair.

My mother doesn't have many clothes: a few housedresses, a good tweed suit, a good silk blouse, a good dress, a good winter coat, two pairs of shoes, a few sets of underwear and stockings, some nightclothes. Nor does my father: a suit for special occasions, a few ties, a bowtie for looking dashing, a good pair of shoes, two sets of work clothes, some changes of underwear, a bathrobe. Nor do I: play clothes, a sailor dress, a pair of Mary Janes, a coat, sleepwear. In the kitchen cupboards there is very little: a set of everyday dishes, some flatware, some glassware, a few pots and pans, a colander, a washboard. Packing and loading takes just a few hours.

There is a picture in our family photograph album of my grandfather, my mother, and me, on the sidewalk of the house in Rhode Island, after he's arrived to accompany us to our new home, taken just before we leave. This picture, my mother will mail to my father to reassure him. My grandfather wears his good suit, his good pair of shoes; he grips my hand, keeps me close. In his other hand is a large suitcase. I am dressed in a shirt and overalls, and I clutch a teddy bear. My mother stands behind us, a hand on my shoulder, trying to smile, wearing a coat, even though it's August.

Through all the years we live in Hoboken, my mother avoids Fourteenth Street. Whenever we return from a holiday, or a visit to my father's parents in North Bergen, my mother insists that my father drive down Willow instead of taking a left onto Fourteenth Street to get back home.

⌒

When I reach back in memory to that Fourteenth Street apartment, I don't recall much. The blinking of the neon light from the restaurant downstairs. The sound of laughter late at night. The moan of a ship's horn. The clanging of the trolley making its turn from Fourteenth Street onto Washington. The rush of men in uniform up and down the sidewalk. A plume of smoke from a ship berthed at a dock. These memories arrest me, move me back to a time long vanished, but a time still with me, perpetually.

But there is this too.

I remember clutching at my father's trousers as he walked out the door. I remember awakening from a deep sleep, a banging at the door, the sound of men's voices, my mother's screams. I remember coming home from Rhode Island to an apartment that was entirely familiar but utterly strange. I did not know, but sensed, that we had moved because we had been exposed to great danger.

It is not until my father is ninety-three years old that he tells me how he walked me up and down the streets of Hoboken to find us a safer place to live before he left for the war, how my mother wrote him about the servicemen who blasted into our apartment, how my grandmother made life so miserable for the woman next door that she moved out and smeared shit all over my grandparents' door.

When he told me his stories, my father was weak, didn't get out much. I spent afternoons sitting with him in his sunroom in the house in Ridgefield he shared with his second wife. In the years before his death, he revisited the years he met my mother and married her, the wartime years, over and over again. I rejoin him back there, through story, learning what I have not known before: how he met my mother; how I was conceived just after the United States declared war; how he cared for me when my mother couldn't; how he wanted to move us to a safer place but couldn't; how he tried to give my mother hope when he left for the war with a dream of a safe and beautiful place they would move to after the war; how she was harmed but how he couldn't help her; and how the day he read her letter he became a man who believed that no good can come from war.

By evening, when I would call to wish him goodnight, he would not have remembered my visit. The next time I would see him, he would tell me the same stories. About how he met my mother, how she blushed in that first moment, how she was his true love, how he looked for a better apartment for us, how he'd had to leave us on Fourteenth Street even though he didn't want to, how my grandparents moved us, and how he came back to a place he'd never called home.

THE HOUSE OF
EARLY SORROWS

I

From my cot in the room that I share with my parents in the tenement on Adams Street in Hoboken, New Jersey, I can see a holy picture of Jesus Christ on the cross, tucked into a corner of the mirror opposite me.

The picture is small. Just a few inches wide, a few inches tall, and laminated, so it reflects the light. I am just a child, and each time I look to the mirror, what I see terrifies me. It's not my face I see—my attention is directly drawn to what I will one day learn is a representation of the Crucifixion. A man in pain beyond comprehension. A man unable to hold his head upright, the inclined head alone, a depiction of unimaginable suffering. A head with matted hair. A head crowned with thorns. The thorns, puncturing the flesh, bloody rivulets running from the wounds down the face. The hands, punctured, too, and oozing blood. I can see the nails, the stab wounds in the torso, the crown of thorns, the feet nailed to the cross. Blood, blood, and more blood.

I can see this man, again, but now, not in color, but carved in wood, hanging on a cross over my parents' bed, the wooden legs and wooden hands affixed to the wooden cross with real nails, the kind my father pounds into an errant board on the stairs with his hammer. And I see this same wooden

man again, hanging on an even larger wooden cross over my grandparents'
bed next door. There, atop my grandmother's bureau, there is this man, again,
but now he is lying down and painted very white, whiter than anyone I've ever
seen, even in summer, legs crossed, painted blood oozing from his hands and
side and from the wounds on his head where the crown of thorns used to be
but now isn't, lips rouged with a color something like that of my mother's
lipstick.

"Who is this man?" I wonder. "And why is he here, and here, and here,
and here?"

I am two years old, then three (and my father has gone away to war and
then come back home), then four, then five. And now I am tall enough to
see into the mirror in our bedroom when I stand on the floor next to my
cot, and now I am in Catholic school and old enough to know that this
man is no ordinary man, that this man is the Son of God, but I am not old
enough to really understand what this means although I spend a lot of time
in catechism class pretending that I do.

And now I am six, then seven. And through these years, the mirror is not
something I use, as my playmate does upstairs, to make silly faces in front
of, or to make sure that I'm brushing my hair just so, or to see the results
of a session of playing dress-up in my mother's clothing, imagining what I
will look like as a woman grown, for I do none of these things—make silly
faces, brush my hair, play dress-up—in front of the mirror or anywhere else.

2

I am seven when my grandfather dies, my sister not yet three. What I remember from this time is a darkened apartment; a chenille bedspread pulled up
around my mother's neck; the sound of my mother's weeping; the sight of
my sister sitting in the corner of her crib sucking her thumb and rocking, the
stench of her piss-filled diaper; my father's entreaties to my mother to try to
get up and get dressed; my father's anger when nothing he did helped her;
the sight of my mother, when she does get out of bed, shuffling around the
apartment in her slippers and worn bathrobe, trying to wash the dishes, trying to wash clothes, trying to bank the fire in the coal stove, trying to make a

meal, but giving up washing the dishes, washing the clothes, banking the fire in the coal stove, trying to make a meal, and retreating, once again, to bed.

During this time, there are no birthday parties, no Christmas celebration, no New Year's gathering. The year that I turn seven, brisk autumn turns to deep winter without any break in the funeral procession of our days. My grandfather is dead. My grandmother has grown silent. She and my mother never speak, never fight. My father is at work. My sister seems to have disappeared. Gone are the days when after coming home from school I crawl after her on the floor, grab her from behind, and tickle her. My mother has retreated to a place where we can't find her. My father urges me to take care of my mother, take care of my sister, while he's at work but there isn't much I can do when I come home from school besides climbing into my sister's crib and lying down beside her. When she falls asleep, I take the silk parachute my father has brought home from the war and I throw it over our kitchen table to make a private retreat where I can hide from my mother's sorrow and do my homework by the light of a lamp I take into my hideaway. During this time, I pray for homework, for more homework that I can ever finish, for, aside from homework, there is nothing for me to do.

My grandmother is in mourning, too, but there is a vigor in her sorrow that makes it seem as if widowhood is a role for which she has long prepared. The day my grandfather dies, she puts on black, her widow's weeds, and tells my mother she has made a vow that she will wear black and only black for the rest of her life. She'd come to America to marry this man, to help him raise his child. They have constructed a bulwark of Old World life inside their home against the strangeness of this place that neither of them understands. Now that is dead, despite the fact that there was no love between them; she will spend her time mourning him, doing her chores, saying her rosary, going to Mass, knitting and crocheting, and waiting to die. Whatever disputes have occurred between her husband and her, however much her arranged marriage might not have satisfied, my grandmother devotes herself to her husband's memory with a staunchness that one would have thought was preceded by a vital passion.

She installs a small shrine to his memory atop her bureau. A photograph of him in his one good suit in a cheap frame. A tiny bouquet of artificial flowers before it. A reclining statue of Jesus Christ, crowned with thorns, the wounds of his passion seeping blood, a reminder of a suffering far greater than her own. On the wall, in place of the mirror shrouded in black cloth on the day he dies, and taken down off the wall on the day of his burial, a garish portrait of the Madonna and Child, her eyes, sorrowing, anticipating the tragic loss of her beloved Son.

My grandmother moves a chair next to her bureau, and this is where she sits early in the morning and in the evenings, in the light of the candles flickering before her husband's photograph. When I go to visit her, she pays no attention to me. I see her fingering her rosary, hear her making novenas to the Virgin Mary, to Saint Jude, to Saint Lucy, whose eyeless visage will adorn my family's gravestone. *Oh Immaculate Mary, Mother of God, accept this wail of sorrow laden with suffering. Oh Saint Jude, may you help me to not despair. Oh Saint Lucy, may your sufferings let me see that my suffering is but little compared to yours.*

Still, much as my grandmother embraces widowhood, she seems less scarred by my grandfather's death than my mother. For my mother, there is no such clear-cut role. Perhaps part of my mother's inconsolable sorrow at her father's death is that her stepmother can now claim him for her own and assert her sovereignty in the matter of mourning. Widowhood is an Old World role my grandmother understands, with its strict rules about dress (black), comportment (sober, sorrowful, and suffering), and required duties (prayers both at home and in church; candles lighted in memory; frequent visits to his grave). When she puts on her black dress, black stockings, ties her black kerchief beneath her chin and walks out into the world of our Italian neighborhood, she joins a tribe of women in black like herself, some of whom have lost elderly husbands, too, but many of whom are the mothers, wives, and grandmothers of men killed during the war.

After a short time, my grandmother resumes her duties as superintendent of our building, but with a decorum she hadn't before demonstrated. She no longer engages in histrionics and the streams of invectives she has become noted for against tenants who haven't paid their rent, who don't silence their barking dogs, who don't stow their trash properly. She comes by our apartment each day to check on my sister and me, ignoring my mother and pretending she isn't there, to make sure we are fed, and to finish, however haphazardly, the chores my mother has started. At the end of the day, she prepares a simple meal of the foods she prefers—bean soups, vegetable soups, pastas, frittatas—and asks my parents, my sister, and me to join her at her table.

But the grandmother who tells me stories, who sings to me in dialect, who gives me treats at her kitchen table, who gives me coins to spend on candy, has vanished, never to return. And though, in ensuing years, she protects me, teaches me how to knit, gives me money for treats, our special bond is severed and I lose her as surely as I have lost my grandfather.

There are motion pictures from this time of my family at my grandfather's gravesite. My grandmother, dressed in black, still as a statue, kneels on the ground alone, or beside her cousin, also a widow, also in black. My mother does not kneel, does not pray. She rests her palm on the top of the gravestone of St. Lucy, her plucked-out eyes in the dish she holds in front of her, looking gravely into the distance. My sister toddles around or she plays in the dirt with a spoon. I stand erect, frozen, most often in a striped shirt and overalls, my prison's uniform, wondering what I am supposed to do.

3

My father thinks that moving away from Hoboken will help my mother. Buying a house, a fixer-upper, might give her something for the two of them to do together, might help her move on. When my family moves into the old house in Ridgefield, less than a year after my grandfather dies, instead of one bedroom for all of us, now there are three. One for my parents. One for my sister and me. One for my grandmother should she come live with us, and she does, in time. The mirror from the bedroom my family shared in the apartment gets moved into my parents' room over a new bureau, part of a suite of furniture bought used for the bedroom my mother shares with my father in our new house.

My mother decorates the room I share with my sister. Patterned wallpaper with roses. Chenille bedspread for the double bed I share with her. A lowboy for my sister against the wall closest to the window. A highboy on the wall nearest the door for me (and through the years to come, I will shove this piece of furniture against the door on the many occasions I try to prevent my father from getting into the room and reaching me). Sheer curtains, and later drapes, handmade by my mother. Comfy area rugs. My parents buy us a new mirror with a wooden frame and hang it on the wall atop my sister's dresser.

On my sister's lowboy, in front of the new mirror, but off to one side, my mother places a very large framed picture of Christ crucified, a giant-sized version of the one from before. Neither my sister nor I am consulted about this. One day, after I return from school, it has appeared. Same inclined head crowned with thorns, same matted hair, same punctured and ravaged flesh, same rivers of blood, same scene of suffering and torture as before—only much, much larger.

My mother has taken a great deal of care with this detail of our room's décor. She has shopped for the picture (but where do you go to buy a picture like this?), she has measured it, she has framed it, and she has placed it just so, so that every time my sister or I look into the mirror, we see Christ crucified counterpoised against the image of our own faces. The image was horrifying to me then, and it still is, for it reveals not that we should be grateful because of how Christ suffered for our sins, but instead how brutal people can be, and how they can harm one another, and that the world is not a safe place for any of us. And in the years to come, the constancy of this image in my life is what will propel me away from churchgoing, for by the time I am a young woman I have lived with this picture for far too long, so long, that it has become, I fear, the lens through which I have come to view the world.

Years later, when a friend from college enters my room and sees it—for the picture is still there—and sees the crucifix hanging over the bed I still share with my sister, she asks, "What is this, Crucifixion Central?" She hasn't yet seen the reclining Jesus Christ still sitting atop my grandmother's bureau in the next room, but now encased in a coffin of Plexiglas my father devised to protect it and to keep out the dust. And when my friend asks me whether this is Crucifixion Central, I suspect, for the first time, that Christ crucified is not an altogether normal embellishment for the room of two girls.

Now my mother is long dead, and so I cannot ask her why she did this. But I do know that it wasn't because she was a deeply religious woman. There were times she went to church and times she didn't. Times she went to confession and took Communion, and times she didn't. Times she told us to listen to what the nuns said, and times she said to ignore what they were teaching us because a lot of it was malarkey. Times she revered the local pastor, and times she thought him too much of a dandy man, who spent far too little time with the poor and far too much time with the ladies of the Rosary Society, one in particular, who lived around the corner from us in a beautiful house where this priest showed up during the day when the woman's husband was at work, and far too frequently, or so my mother said.

Did my mother place this horrifying image before the mirror to ensure that my sister and I would spend no more time in front of the mirror than was absolutely necessary? Did she want to prevent us from becoming narcissistic mirror gazers, hair tossers, primpers, girls more interested in appearance than in developing character? Did she want us to understand that whatever difficulties we experienced—my father's rages, her depressions, our childhood sufferings—counted for little or nothing when compared with such enormous pain? Or, instead, was this supposed to be a *momento mori*, a reminder of our mortality and life's brevity that might encourage us to seize the moment? But the latter was most assuredly not so, for my mother took little pleasure in living and was far too inclined to withdraw from whatever was happening.

4

The place before the mirror is, and always has been, an anguished place for me. I spend time in front of it only when absolutely necessary. When I am a young girl, and my father tells me to get myself in front of the mirror to comb my disheveled hair *or else.* When, as a young adolescent, I sneak on forbidden lipstick and then wipe it off. When, as an older adolescent, I put on makeup as quickly as I can before I dash out the door to meet this boy, or that one, because being with anyone someplace else is a thousand times better than being in this house. And when, as a young bride, on the day of my wedding, I adjust my veil and tell myself this is the last time I'll be standing in front of this mirror, and it's none too soon.

As a teenager, I have a habit of standing in front of the mirror and looking at myself when I am crying, when I am enraged, or when I am terrified because my father is on one of his rampages. I have a habit of standing in front of the mirror and sticking my tongue out at myself in derision after my parents have told me that, again, I have not done what I was supposed to do.

I have a habit of standing in front of the mirror to see if my last battle with my father has resulted in any bruises, and to determine whether I will have to wear, yet again, a high-necked, long-sleeved shirt to school instead of the V-necked, short-sleeved sweater that I love.

Most times, though, I avoid looking in the mirror. For when I do, I see the image of myself—sometimes happy, but more often sad, angry, or terrified—juxtaposed against that of Christ crucified.

And that I never thought to take that picture and stuff it in the bottom of a drawer under my clothing, or in the back of my closet behind the bag of hand-me-downs, or in the garbage can on trash day does not now strike me as strange, although I suspect it should. But knowing my mother as I did, I no doubt realized, then, that another image of Christ crucified just like the last one, or perhaps—heaven forbid—an even larger one, would have appeared in its place sooner rather than later, without a word uttered between us about how I had disposed of it, for, as always, my mother wouldn't want to call attention to what I had done to stir up any more trouble than there already was in our house. That portrait of Christ, as I think of it now, denied me a sense of my own image; it denied me the ability to look at myself and see who I was, who I was becoming.

But it also denied me a sense of the reality and extremity of my own pain as a child and as a young woman, for whatever I suffered seemed so much less than *that* suffering. Reflected back to me as I witnessed myself crying, or enraged, or terrified, or harmed, was only a simulacrum of that even greater suffering. Whatever pain I felt, however harmed I was, did not count. My pain could not compare with an anguish far greater than any I would ever experience.

5

And yet.

There was my father's violence. Always, my father's violence. Unpredictable. Coming without any reason, at least to me. He hit me, and worse. Came at me with a knife. Choked me. Tried to smother me. But even more fearsome were his threats of a violence greater than any I'd already experienced, in store for me in some diabolical future in which he would lose all self-control and rampage through the house, as he so often did, in search of me, only this time, I wouldn't be smart enough or fast enough or strong enough to repel him.

"If you don't shut your mouth, I'll break every bone in your body."

"If you do that again, I promise that I will kill you."

"If I get my hands on you, I'll break your neck."

"If you say that one more time, I'll rip your arm off."

"If I catch you, I'll throw you out the window."

I did not perceive these as idle threats, for I had often been at the receiving end of blows that had left their mark, and so I, like many other children, became adept at describing this welt or that black-and-blue mark as having been the result of my walking into a cabinet or falling down the stairs or bumping into the iron, and, no, I never once said, "It was my father who did this." I was the child grownups call clumsy, wearing my wounds like badges no one suspected I'd earned in the war between my father and me.

And although my father couched his threats in a way that made it seem as if I were the provocateur and so able to control my fate if only I refrained from doing the things that disturbed him—"Don't make me do this . . . ." —even back then, I knew that his rhetoric was deranged, and that he was the one at fault for what happened to me, and that I wasn't, for the offensive behavior I engaged in was merely what I saw other girls my age doing (my friend across the street, for example, to whose house I often fled to escape my own) without anyone's threatening them with harm. Wearing lipstick. Chewing gum. Going out with boys. Talking on the telephone. Tapping their fingers at the dinner table. Refusing to eat this, preferring to eat that. Staying out later than they were supposed to. Forgetting their keys. Spilling juice on a dress. Dropping bread on the floor. Having a messy room. Tracking dirt into the house. Not responding to a command the first time it was uttered.

Though I did not realize it at the time, the image of Christ crucified came to represent to me my father's brutality. It reminded me, every time I looked in the mirror, that I wasn't safe. I did not learn that the body could be cherished by those we love and those who profess to love us. That the people we love can be kind to us. I learned that the body can be harmed in so very many ways, and that being wounded is the natural order. And my mirror— reflecting back bruises, tears, scratches—told me this more often than I care, now, to remember.

6

And there was this, too.

I believe that my mother's attachment to the image of Christ crucified, and her insistence on its being in a place where we couldn't avoid seeing it, represented her own internal suffering. Hers was a primal and deep sorrow that overwhelmed our family. From this distance in time, I cannot say whether the times she withdrew into herself and could barely be roused from her stupor to go up the stairs to bed at the end of the day came just before or immediately after one of the occasions when my father had run amok, or whether it was unconnected to my father's behavior at all. But how could it not have been?

When it overcame her during summers—and she could barely clothe herself, barely shove something inedible in front of us at mealtimes, barely tend to a lacerated knee from our unsupervised, tempestuous play—my sister and I would be sent away to relatives. If it came on during the school year, we did the best we could without her care, walking to school without boots or umbrellas, eating unheated frozen turkey dinner barely defrosted, wearing our underwear outside in, then inside out, day after day.

There was no way for my mother to name what came upon her. No way for her to tell us where she vanished to during those times. No way for her to comprehend why ordinary life, or what passed for ordinary life in our household, distressed her. And her withdrawal deep into herself meant that we were left to deal with our father on our own, or with the help of our grandmother who lived with us, that specter of a woman who haunted our house, who was willing to defy him no matter what the consequences, and to whom I owe my survival, although I never told her so, and this is one of the great sorrows of my life, not to have understood what she did for me until long after she died.

And so perhaps this image was meant to tell us, in a way that my mother could not, what the essence of her agony looked like. To look in the mirror, to see Christ's image before it, was to see my mother's suffering incarnate.

7

The story my father told us to explain my mother's behavior goes like this.

When my mother was about ten months old, her mother died from influenza during the great epidemic. After her mother died, my mother, still an infant, stopped eating and almost died.

Her father, who had to travel to upstate New York for his work on building the railroad, placed her with relatives. She began to gain weight slowly and was soon out of danger. Then her care became a burden—the relatives' caring for their own children was difficult enough.

My grandfather found another woman to tend to my mother, but she was neglected, and the money this woman was given was siphoned off to feed and clothe her own children. When my grandfather unexpectedly came to see my mother, he found that she was starving.

One caregiver followed another until my grandfather sent for a woman in his native province of Puglia to marry him and to raise his daughter. This woman, though, could not, did not love my mother, and whatever care my mother got was roughly and disinterestedly provided.

My mother survived. That is, she survived corporeally. But even as a young child, she became so depressed that she was institutionalized and given shock treatments. While my mother is alive, she never speaks of her birth mother, never tells my sister or me how she almost died, and never tells us her story of suffering and of sorrow. She is, for us, only our mother, not a woman with a history, with a past that might help explain to us what happens to her. And like so many other children, we come to believe that what happens to her has something to do with us, that what happens to her is all our fault.

"You could have been nicer to her; you were never nice to her," my father tells me after I'm married and have children when my mother is once again institutionalized and shock treated. "You could have invited her to lunch every now and then."

8

In the motion pictures of my mother and me when I am a child, she never looks at me. There are no moments when she gazes into my eyes. No pictures of her gazing at me while she combs my hair. None of her smiling at me while I play dress-up with her or as we bake together (for we never played dress-up together, never baked). I have learned from a book called *No Voice Is Ever Wholly Lost* by Louise Kaplan that the loving gaze of a mother or caregiver is incorporated into self-love. The mother's gaze, the first mirror of the self.

Why could my mother not look at me? Was it because she was so depressed, so locked into herself, that she did not have the emotional energy for a child? Or was it instead that looking into my face was too painful for her and so she avoided it?

One day, when I am sorting through the memorabilia my father gave me after my mother's death, I find two large and crumbling wedding photographs. One of my grandfather and the woman I have come to know as my grandmother. And one of my grandfather and my mother's birth mother. I have never seen this photograph before, never seen what my birth grandmother looked like.

I take it into the bedroom of the house I share with my husband and two sons. Prop it up in front of the mirror. Look at her. Look at myself.

I am in my late forties when I do this, more than twenty years older than she was when she died. Still, there is a stunning resemblance. My face looks like what hers would have looked like had she grown as old as I am now. Her face looks like my face when I was twenty years old.

Was it that my mother could not look at me because I reminded her of her dead mother? Although she was just an infant when her mother died, a photograph of her remained on my grandfather's bureau. Was my face a too-painful embodiment of her loss? Or was it that her caregivers did not look at her, and so she never learned how to gaze at a child? But no, for there are many pictures of my mother looking at my sister. I know that I am the one she could not look at, I am the one she could not bear to see. And if my mother never looked at me, is it any wonder that I cannot look at myself?

9

In 1972, when I am thirty years old, I embark upon a series of paintings of faceless women. I have not yet seen the motion pictures of my childhood; I have not yet discovered the wedding portrait of my grandfather and my mother's birth mother; I do not yet recall how the image of Christ crucified dominated my childhood. I am a woman in my prime, trying to venture beyond the boundaries of a past I don't yet understand, and a significant part of this journey occurs when I stand in front of a canvas propped upon an easel, brush in hand, paint on the palette beside me.

Still. Each day, before I go into the studio, I stand in front of the mirror in my bedroom, tilt my head to the right, and look at myself. I am not looking at my features, for they do not interest me, and I am not trying to reproduce them or distort them in my work. It is only the attitude of the tilted head that I adopt when I face myself in the mirror that interests me, and that I will replicate in my work again and again.

The first paintings are of a woman, in stylized dress, against a bold ground of color. The next are abstractions of mothers who embrace children yet who are indifferent to them. The next are groups of three women, sometimes standing, sometimes sitting, each acting as if the others aren't there. Always, the women are faceless. And always, they seem, by the inclination of their heads, sorrowful.

Back then, when I was asked why I painted women in this way, I replied that I wasn't interested in the specific features of a woman's face. I said that I was interested in form, in the shape the outline of the head makes when it is tilted in this particular way. I said that I was interested in playing with the aesthetic possibilities of painting this oval shape (now black, now brown, now blue) against a flat ground of color. I said that I was interested in composition, in the problem of placing the tilted oval of the face against the rectangle or square of the canvas.

I said that I wasn't interested in the features of a specific woman's face—not mine, not anyone else's—though I knew how to capture a likeness. I said I was interested only in portraying an archetypal woman, and the shape of the tilted head was all I needed, and the specific features of the face were insignificant to and even detracted from my purpose.

I did not say—I could not have said—that I was painting faceless women because of the faceless women in my life. My mother, who had disappeared into the facelessness of despair. Her birth mother, who had been erased from our family's history. Her stepmother, who was accorded no real place in our family. And perhaps even the painter herself.

I could not have said these things because I did not know them. Even so, I saw this work as self-portraiture, or, rather, as anti-self-portraiture. By this time, I was fascinated with Rembrandt's self-portraits, with the act of a painter standing before a mirror and painting, not what he sees, but who he thinks he is. I did not have the hubris to see myself as painting in the tradition of Rembrandt, did not even see myself as a painter, but merely as someone who painted. Still, I was fascinated by the thought of a man standing in front of a mirror at various times throughout his life, to discover, and record, who he had become. There is always—at least for me—in those Rembrandt portraits, a profound sense of loss, a loss of the self that had been. My work—though I did not know it at the time—was grounded in the deep sorrow that looking into a mirror seemed to unleash in me.

Though I loved the smell of oils, the riot of color on the palette, the blank linen canvas propped upon the easel, the northern light washing the studio, the first stroke of brush on canvas, and the slow and steady work upon it, the moment of completion, this series of paintings of faceless women are my last paintings. Soon after I complete them, and for reasons I do not understand, I abandon painting and begin writing. Perhaps I suspected that language would one day help me understand the enigma of these paintings, the unsolved mystery of the women in my life.

10

At more than sixty years of age now, I could not tell you what I look like, could not say how my face has changed or stayed the same throughout the years, could not say whether I consider myself beautiful, or plain, though some (but never my parents) have said that I am beautiful. (My mother's and my father's words: "Beauty is as beauty does.")

Until I am in my fifties, I could not even tell you the color of my eyes.

Once, I have to indicate this detail, the color of my eyes, on a form.

I go into the bathroom to look in the mirror to learn their color. Greenish-brown—what some call hazel—and rimmed with black. The same as my mother's. Or so my father has told me after her death. ("Your eyes are like your mother's.")

Can a woman spend her adult life combing her hair, putting on makeup—foundation, eyeliner, eye shadow, mascara, blush, lipstick (some of which I use each day)—and not know what she looks like? I see skin that is being covered with foundation. The eye outlined. The cheek taking on the color of the rouge. The shape of the lip turning red. I see all these things. But I do not see myself.

My Sister's
Suicide

Early Summer, 1993

My basement is a complete mess, and has been for years.

When my father remarries after my mother's death, he sells the house I grew up in, and most of its furniture, except for the three pieces I take. He packs up our family's mementos and tells me if I don't want them, he'll dispose of them.

I'm furious he's chosen to bring very little from his first life—his clothes, his tools, a few photos of my mother (but none of my family or me or my sister)—into his new and happy life, though, in part, I understand. The last several years have been difficult for him. My sister's suicide. My mother's depression. Her terrible, inexplicable, terminal illness.

I sense he wants to leave anything behind that will remind him of those years. I tell him I'll take everything, go through the boxes, and decide what to keep, what to give away, what to throw away.

"My father goes off to Florida to get married," I tell my friend Kate. "And he leaves me behind to deal with all his shit." I make it sound like he's forced me into taking his discards. He hasn't. I take them because I can't bear to think of these boxes' being heaved atop a pile of trash at the town dump. I'll take what I want. Dispose of the rest. I'll take care of it right away.

But that was three years ago.

Every morning, when I go downstairs to throw in a load of laundry—a ritual that helps me think about what I'll write that day—I pass the pile of cardboard boxes. I think someday I'll make time for sorting through them, I really will, but today, I don't have the time, or the energy, or the courage.

"Clean the basement." These words have appeared on hundreds of my "To do" lists.

"Today I have to deal with what's downstairs," I tell my husband over coffee almost every morning. Using a studied irreverence to mask my fears and feelings, I've started to refer to the boxes in the basement as "my mother's death stuff."

"When I take care of my mother's death stuff," I tell him, "we can put the Lifecycle down there, get some dumbbells, put down indoor/outdoor carpeting, make the basement into an exercise room."

What has stopped me from cleaning out the basement, I know, are the three cardboard boxes marked with my sister's name, "Jill," in the barely legible handwriting of the last months of my mother's life.

It's not that I expect that when I open these boxes, I will find documents— my sister's letters or diaries—explaining the reasons for my sister's suicide some seven years before. I know my mother too well. Had they existed, she would have destroyed them.

What I know I will find, and what will be painful for me to see, are the few, seemingly trivial objects my mother has chosen to save from my sister's thirty-seven years of life. The objects that will tell me what it was about my sister my mother wanted to remember.

When I let myself remember Jill, I always see her in work clothes. In her house in the country in the Pacific Northwest. In the back yard of the tiny house she and her husband lived in for a year on Catalina Island, where the strains on their marriage had already begun to show. I see her bending over her potter's wheel, her long, honey-colored hair covering her face. I see her hands, red as raw meat from working with clay. A worker's hands. Remembering her hands is harder than remembering anything else about her. I see her arranging delicate teapots in the kiln. Preparing it for firing. Harvesting vegetables. Feeding her numerous pets—cats, dogs, and, once, a pig. She called him "Piglet," and let herself grow too fond of him, for he was being raised for slaughter. In those days, she and her husband caught or raised almost all the food they ate, and they were living frugally so he could finish his Ph.D. dissertation.

My sister is living on the West Coast. Her most recent love affair has ended and she begins "freaking out," as I phrase it in my diary. She wants to sell her house and move back east.

"I have no reason to stay here," she tells us.

I'm worried about her, and my husband and I offer help. We'll find an apartment, she can take a job in my husband's company, and take some time to get her life together.

After my sister starts coming apart, I begin noticing, and recording in my diary, disasters I read about in the newspaper or hear about on the radio.

"People hurt when the ceiling of a shopping mall fell in. People hurt when someone doused them with gasoline in a supermarket and set them on fire," I write. My children start to call me D. E. W. "Distant Early Warning."

August 1983

"Jill has moved here from the West Coast," I record, "and it isn't as bad as I thought it would be. I've been keeping her busy and helping her out."

Against my advice, and for no good reason—she has plenty of money from the sale of her house—Jill has moved back into our parents' house.

"A surefire recipe for disaster," I tell my husband.

December 1993

My life has been a shambles since soon after my sister's arrival. Several tele-phone calls a day from my mother, my father, and Jill. My mother, insisting I should include Jill in my life. Take her along when I go for a swim, have her over for lunch. My sister, complaining about my parents. About my father's condemnatory attitude—how he disapproves of her seeing this man or that one, how he lectures her on how she can improve her life. About my mother's jealousy of the time she spends with my father. My father, telling me Jill spends too much time in bed, telling me to call her, to give her a pep talk. Calling my husband for advice, and in exasperation. Watching the three of them deteriorate. Trying to help. But trying to keep my distance.

"What has come out so far," my mother tells me one day, after a family therapy session, "is how happy we were, as a family, and how close." What has not come out, I think to myself, is the violence.

I am teaching full-time at Hunter College, finishing co-editing Vita Sackville-West's letters to Virginia Woolf and *Between Women*, raising two teenage boys. *I have no time for this*, I think. I wish they would leave me alone. "I have just about been worn out by everyone's needs," I write.

I believe I have kept my sanity by keeping my distance from my family. My battle against depression has been an ongoing struggle I finally believe I'm winning with the help of a wonderful woman therapist. I don't want to be drawn back into their orbit. It's too dangerous for me. "The whole family is fucked up," I write in my diary, "and they want me to be fucked up with them."

Throughout the early part of December, my sister's moods vacillate wildly; the swings get wider and become more frequent. She is depressed and can't get out of bed. Then she has a great day. She meets a man she takes to immediately; she likes him so much she thinks she can marry him. She gets a job. She asks me how I'm doing, and seems to mean it—the first time in months. Then the man disappoints her, and she is very depressed.

In the middle of December, my mother is in very bad shape. She checks herself into the psychiatric ward of our local hospital.

My sister gives me her perspective of my mother's deterioration.

"She's doing it to get back at me."

I listen. Wonder if Jill is exaggerating. What is happening with my mother and sister seems connected in some dangerous way I don't want to understand.

"Before she decides to go crazy," my sister says, "she writes out her menu for Christmas and makes a shopping list for food. She balances her checkbook and leaves a note about the bills that will have to be paid."

She also finds, and goes through, all my sister's mail. She reads the sexy letters my sister has written to a lover during her marriage, the ones he's written to her. Then, according to my sister, she begins swallowing Valiums, goes to bed, and refuses to get up.

(Just after my mother's death, as I am selecting a piece of jewelry to pin on the lapel of the pink suit I have chosen for her wake and burial, I find an article about adultery published during the time my sister was living at home, tucked into my mother's jewelry box. Women who commit adultery, it says, tend to have husbands who don't sexually satisfy them.)

At first, the doctors try drug treatment. But it has to be stopped. My mother quickly develops a serious allergic reaction to the drugs. Shock treatment, the doctors say, is the only alternative. We find out, from my father, something we have never known: My mother was institutionalized as a young girl, and later, as a young woman, not long before their marriage. And she has received shock treatments before.

When I find this out, I'm not surprised my parents have kept it secret. Mental illness, after all, is not something anyone discussed openly when we were growing up. Still, we lived with it. Still, we knew about it, though we didn't have a name for it. Having a name for what was happening in our home might have helped. My sister is furious we haven't been told before. I wonder whether this was the reason Jill and I were so often sent to Rhode Island to spend our summers with relatives.

As my mother gets worse, my sister gets better. She seems more cheerful. Sure, now, that if she sets her mind to it, she can control her life and make it work. Craziness is a ball that is being passed back and forth between them.

My father comes to my house to spill out his sorrow and bewilderment. He tells me that finding my sister's love letters sent my mother over the edge. That, and the fact that I'm going away with my family for Christmas. His rage spills over. He bangs my kitchen table with his fists.

"All your mother ever wanted from you," he tells me, "was a little love, which you never gave her." So, I think to myself, but don't say: *Nothing has changed; whenever anything goes wrong, he blames it all on me.*

I control myself. Don't say much. My husband isn't home. My father has caught me off-guard, come over unannounced when I'm home alone.

He talks about my sister. Weeps about how rotten her life is. Tells me what she's told him about her sex life with her first husband. It's not something she's revealed to me. *This isn't right,* I think. *No father should know this much about his daughter's sex life.* I wonder when my father and my sister had such intimate conversations.

Summer, 1951

It's an interminable summer. I am nine. My sister is five. We're living in Ridgefield, New Jersey.

Down a very long hill from where we live is a summer day camp. My mother signs my sister and me up for it. Nothing much happens in this camp. The teenage counselors ignore us kids after they give us instructions on how to make lanyards, how to make papier-mâché, how to fill hideous rubber forms of gnomes and elves with plaster of Paris and then paint them when they are dry, how to finger-paint. After they dole out supplies and instructions, they sit as far away from us as they can on the top of a picnic table where they spend their time smoking and flirting. Occasionally there are games of kickball and tag. Less often, there are nature walks across a wooden footbridge into the woods on the other side of the park.

When we tire of craft projects, when we're not playing games, and not on our nature walks, there are a few rusty swings, an off-balance merry-go-round, and a filthy sandbox with a few shovels and pails where we can amuse ourselves if we're bored even though most of us are far too old for such nonsense.

Camp lasts all day long, from 9 to 4. We eat our horrible packed lunches at picnic tables under the trees. If we're thirsty, we drink water from a fountain where the water tastes like mud. Most days, it's excruciatingly hot.

Coursing through the park is a little stream. When there are heavy rains, it becomes wider and deeper. During these times, we kids break the most important rule of the camp—"Keep away from the stream"—and slide down the bank to get to it. The streambed is filled with litter, broken bottles, and cigarette packets so I know it's not a good idea to walk into the water. Still, it's forbidden, and so, alluring. The boys splash and annoy the girls. The girls stand timidly at the edge of the water. I hold my sister's hand to make sure she doesn't get wet. Once, a boy pushes a younger girl into the water. The counselors are nowhere to be found.

What I hate most about camp is that I'm responsible for taking my sister and bringing her home, and for minding her while we're there. There are no kids her age at the camp, no one for her to play with. I do know a few other campers, but no one will hang out with me when I have my sister with me, which is always. Sometimes, when they think she's out of earshot, they whisper, "She's such a leech," to one another. And that's how I feel too, and I'm not old enough to realize it's not her fault I'm stuck with her.

My sister is always with me because my mother is having one of her hard times. When she's like this, she wants us out of the house. If things get really bad, my father packs us up and spirits us to our grandmother's relatives in Rhode Island. But if things aren't really bad, but just plain bad, I become responsible for my sister all day long. This summer, things are worse than just plain bad, but for some reason, we're staying home.

"Take good care of your sister," my father intones to me each day as he leaves for work. "Do what your mother tells you."

⌣

One day when we're at camp, the boys are rowdier than usual. The counselors, like always, are sitting far away from us. One kid has a peashooter, which is absolutely forbidden. He hides it in his pants.

When he thinks the counselors aren't watching, he shoots a pea at one of the little kids, hits him in the arm.

"Cut it out," I say.

"Just try and stop me," he says.

I decide my sister and I can't stay here. It's too dangerous. I don't want anything to happen to her. Don't want anything to happen to me either. I tell her to get her stuff, we're leaving. We're leaving, but we can't go home.

I have some money on me—I always tuck into my pocket a five-dollar bill my grandmother has given me, just in case. I decide we'll walk up the very big hill to Ho-Made, an ice cream store my sister and I love that our parents rarely take us to. I figure it's not that long a walk, maybe a little longer than from our house down to camp. We'll buy ice cream and something to drink, hang out inside for a while, then walk back home.

Our parents have never forbidden us to walk up to the top of the other hill so I tell myself I'm not doing anything wrong. Still, I know they never would have allowed us to walk all the way up there.

We cross the stream, we walk through the woods, we emerge from the woods onto one of the roads close to the top of the hill.

As we're walking up the road, we see a standalone stone garage. The garage door is open. The inside of the garage is dark.

Before we can pass, a man emerges from the darkness.

"Hey, girls," he says. "Want to come inside where it's cool?"

It's been a hard climb through the woods. We don't have water. We're both perspiring so much our tee shirts are soaked through. Still I know that we shouldn't go inside.

"No, thanks," I say. "We're on our way to our aunt's, just around the corner." I tug at Jill's hand. She breaks away from me.

"I'm tired of listening to you," she says. "I'm hot. I'm going inside."

I get angry at her. I know she shouldn't be doing this. I yell at her. She ignores me. But I don't follow her inside. I stand rooted to where I am. I don't know what's happening. I will never know what happened.

Some time later, and how long, I can't say, Jill emerges. She doesn't say anything. She doesn't say anything for the rest of the day. She doesn't say anything the day after. She never mentions the garage, the man, what happened. And I don't ask her, I don't tell my parents.

If only.

If only my mother wasn't sick. If only we were taken to Rhode Island. If only I wasn't afraid of my father. If only I didn't have to take care of my sister. If only the boy with the peashooter didn't threaten us. If only the counselors were paying attention. If only I thought my sister and I could have gone back home without my being punished. If only. If only. If only.

But then again, nothing might have happened to my sister. But then again, something might have. At best, I didn't want her with me. At worst, I deserted her when she needed protection. And this is the burden I've carried, one I can't put down. Although I've told myself I had nothing to do with my sister's suicide, maybe I had everything to do with it.

Christmas, 1983

I am in the Cayman Islands with my husband and children, having the scuba-diving holiday that we'd planned for months. It's a difficult time and I shouldn't be here.

My mother has had an acute psychotic break and is in a psychiatric ward undergoing shock treatments. Every day, we make a call to see how she's doing. She isn't doing well.

My father is enraged at me for going away with my family. My husband and I have almost canceled this trip. I have almost stayed behind. But my husband has insisted that I need to get away, that *we* need to get away as a family after the strain we've been living with for months.

After my sister came east, and we all realized she couldn't live with our parents, my husband arranged for her to have a job in a business he was associated with in Florida. We all thought Jill could make a life there. She'd found an apartment; she seemed happy; the job was easy for her; she was looking forward to more responsibilities. We all felt sure this was the perfect solution.

And then. She met a man while she was sunbathing on a beach. As she told the story, they struck up a conversation, and found they had much in common. They spent the day together, went out to dinner, talked about their lives.

Like her, he was in transition. Unlike her, he didn't have a job. It seemed he didn't have enough references or good references or something like that— about this part of the story, Jill was unclear.

Anyway. She decided, after knowing him for just a day, to help him out. She wrote him a letter of recommendation on company stationery. Said he'd worked for the firm for some time. Detailed responsibilities he'd had. Commended him on his work ethic. Praised him highly. She invented a position for herself far superior to the one she had. And, of course, she never told us what she did.

A few days later, a prospective employer called my husband's office. A follow-up to the glowing letter of recommendation he'd received for this job candidate. My husband was baffled. This man never worked for the firm. Who signed the letter?

My husband calls me at home, tells me what happened.

"What should I do?" he asks.

"What would you do if she wasn't my sister?" I reply.

"I'd fire her, of course," he says.

"Then fire her," I say.

And that's why my sister comes back to live in my parents' home. And that's why, years later, my father tells me we're the reason my sister kills herself.

In Cayman Brac, my husband and I are waiting to hear how my mother's shock treatments are going. The last test report isn't good.

I try to relax, try to get some rest, but it's not easy. I walk to the end of the pier in the wind and wonder if I'll fall off or be blown away. I have a moment of exquisite pleasure watching a sunset, then panic when I see a toddler run on the pier unattended. I am happy to see my sons together in a paddleboat, but wonder if they'll run aground on the reef. And I can't enjoy my dives or swims. I know there are sharks and moray eels and barracuda and spiny sea urchins underwater. After a dive instructor tells a story of a diver swallowed by a 700-pound grouper (which everyone but me regards as apocryphal), I stop diving.

What soothes me is lying on my belly at the edge of the water, watching hermit crabs. I do this for hours, while my husband and sons dive. The sea grass is filled with them. They have red and blue bands around their legs. Their parade across the sandy bottom amuses me. Their fights don't seem territorial. I notice they sometimes hitch rides atop one another.

I see a small one, struggling under the weight of a huge shell. A large one, just barely protected by a small shell. I wonder how they select the shells they haul around on their delicate bodies for protection. Is it that they come upon an empty shell by accident? Or do they possess some aesthetic sense? Or do some feel a greater need for protection than others and, so, look for shells that are far larger than their bodies? Are there brave hermit crabs that don't mind being exposed? And timid ones who've had dangerous encounters?

I've taken my diary to Cayman Brac. Its cheerful cover of purple and white irises in bloom is out of keeping with the family tragedy I'm recording in its pages, the family history of violence and insanity I am trying to understand. Writing in my diary, as always, helps me immeasurably. It is, by now, a five-year habit—one I began in deliberate and self-conscious imitation of Virginia Woolf.

"What I see clearly," I write, "is how as a child, I was blamed for their bad times, how they expected me to make them feel good, and how unfair that was, and how impossible it would be for any young child to do what they expected." I remind myself of my mother's history of being unmothered, of its consequences in her care for my sister and me. Her mother died when she was young, and she was passed around from one inadequate (and perhaps abusive and surely negligent) caregiver to another. At times, she stopped eating (or wasn't adequately nourished) and nearly died.

I write, too, about my work. About how work, for me, is salvation. I wonder whether I have chosen to work on Virginia Woolf because of the similarities between her family's history and my own. In making out a work plan when I return home (which always makes me feel good), I write, "Think about [Virginia] Woolf and incest." This idea comes as a surprise. I had vowed never to work on Woolf again. (Six years later, I publish a book-length study about Woolf as an incest survivor.)

My father has told me in a telephone conversation I've had with him when I'm still on holiday that my sister is returning to the West Coast. He's taking her to the airport. He's afraid something terrible will happen if she leaves, but my mother, in her moments of lucidity, insists on it. She says she won't come home from the hospital if Jill is still there. And I wonder why. Is it that my mother feels left out when my father and sister spend time together? Is it that my mother has found in my sister's letters something more troubling than her sexual revelations? Has my sister written that she was sexually involved with my father? And has this, and not the fact that my sister was unfaithful, been responsible for my mother's distress?

For a time after I get my father's call I feel bad for him and for my sister and for my mother. Feel guilty that the weight of my mother's and sister's illnesses is all on his shoulders. But I am fighting to stay clear of their tragic family triangle. In my journal, I write I am fighting for my life.

January 1984

My sister is gone. My mother is home. She's not back to how she was before she was hospitalized (and will never be), but at least she's functioning. She has begun to cook, and to clean. The last report from my sister has been good. She's gotten an apartment, and a job, and a car. Everything seems to be returning to what passes for normal in my family.

One morning, I'm cutting an orange for breakfast. I am, as always now, distracted. I slice a piece off my finger, see the blood pour out, and faint. I have a history of blackouts. I've had them since childhood. They terrify me.

I'm always afraid the next one will be the last one. Afraid I'll die. My family has always called what I do "fainting," but I'm not so sure.

(As I compose this, I can write only a few words at a time before I feel like I'm going to pass out. I look away from the computer. I look out the window to the back yard. Watch the squirrels. I try to center myself. I burst into tears. This last paragraph I have struggled to write is the hardest, most personal passage I've written. I do it a few words at a time. It takes me days. But it's important for me to be able to say this.)

This one is scarier than most. My husband tells me that this time, I stop breathing for a long time, and he thinks he will have to resuscitate me. He knows that if he does, he'll break my ribs, so he waits through, one, two, three interminable seconds to see if I'll start breathing on my own. Just as he's decided not to wait any longer, he tells me I start taking deep, shuddering breaths.

The ambulance comes. My sons watch me taken away on a stretcher. The doctors, as usual, can't find anything wrong with me. "Stress," my husband says. "It's all the stress you're under."

This is a danger sign I can't ignore. I call my therapist and get back into therapy.

February 1984

A few weeks after I go to the hospital, I record in my diary, in very controlled prose, that my sister has killed herself.

"Jill killed herself at the end of January—January 29, to be exact," I write. "What to record here about it? The feeling I have, of having escaped. The distance I put between myself and my family, necessary, because it saved me. Sadness, certainly. But also . . . a sense of freedom, almost of euphoria, that I was no longer responsible for her, and that I had been responsible for her for so very, very long, as long as I can remember."

There is a family photograph of the two of us, taken when I am about thirteen, and when she is ten. I am sitting in my nightgown, in my mother's rocking chair. Jill is on my lap, pretending to be a baby. I hold a toy bottle to her lips. I pretend to feed her. My father is taking this picture and we are posing for it. I look as though I have been pressed into this against my wishes. My glassy eyes look past her, past the camera, and past my father, into the far, far distance. Jill looks straight into the lens. She wears a phony smile, pretending she's having a good time. But I can see the sadness in her, the sadness that is always there.

"Did you have to bring her?" These words I hear from one or another of my friends, or boyfriends, throughout my teenage years, whenever I arrive at a basketball game, or the park, or the Sweete Shoppe, where we all hang out. My parents don't allow me out of the house without my sister. I can't stand being in the house—a place where someone is always yelling at someone else—I need to get out of the house as often as I can. I nearly always accept my parents' condition that I take my sister with me. If I don't, I get into trouble. But I make her pay.

I race to wherever I'm going so fast that it is a terrible struggle for her to keep up with me. When we get to where we're going, I ignore her, pretend she isn't there.

She stands at the edge of the crowd. My mother hasn't wanted her home. I don't want her with me. My friends think she's a royal pain in the ass. She looks the way she always looks, like she's on the verge of tears.

⌒

The call comes, as these calls do, around midnight, while I am sleeping. The phone awakens me. My husband answers it. He's in his study, a room that adjoins our bedroom. I can hear him talking and I know, from the tone of his voice, that something is wrong. The first part of the conversation is muffled. Then I hear him say, "Yes, I'll tell Louise. I'll tell her parents. I'm sorry, so very, very sorry."

I hear my husband's footsteps. I sit up in bed. Prepare myself. I know what his news will be, though I have kidded myself into thinking that because Jill seems better, I can have some breathing space, some time to catch my breath, until the next crisis. I can get on with my own life and not worry so much about hers.

⌒

My sister has hanged herself in the basement of the house she's shared for less than a month with the woman who's called us. She's used a belt to do it. She's killed herself early in the morning. "It is a beautiful sunny morning," she has written in the note in which she tells us that she can't go on and has decided to take her life.

This is not the first time this woman has found someone dead, she's told my husband. Her brother killed himself the same way, and she's the one who found him.

When my husband tells me this, I feel so sorry for her, and furious at my sister for putting someone so vulnerable through this again. But then I think, "I'm glad she didn't do it here. I'm glad I wasn't the one who found her."

My husband calls my parents. My father answers the phone. I can hear his screams. "No! No! No! No!" Then my mother's cries.

I get on the telephone with them. I don't remember what I say. My husband takes the phone out of my hand and says we'll be in touch throughout the night. I hear him tell my father that, no, Louise can't come. He is protecting me. "She has to tell the boys," I hear him say. "She has to be here with me and with them."

When I tell my friends about my sister's death, I tell them that the belt she's used to strangle herself had been a gift from me. I don't know if this is true—I *had* given Jill the gift of a belt—but I am compelled to say it, and, at the time, I don't know why. Now, though, it seems to have been my way of taking responsibility for what happened to her, though I've never admitted to myself that I've felt guilty about her death. And there is this, too. My telling the story this way links us, binds me to her, even in death.

1 February 1984, My Sister's Birthday

Throughout my sister's wake, I remain detached and controlled. I don't cry. I store up incidents to tell my friend Kate, who comes with her husband and children the first night. It is the only way I can get through this.

When my parents, my husband, and I are brought up to the casket by the undertaker to view the body, my mother kneels down on the pew, looks at Jill, then turns to me and says, "Doesn't she look beautiful?"

"Mmmm," I say. I don't contradict her. Jill doesn't look beautiful. Her face is disfigured. Later, my husband, Ernie, who is a doctor, explains why.

My mother gets up. "See," she says to me. "She came home to us, after all. She came home to be with us on her birthday."

This is the craziest thing my mother has said so far. I can't stand it. But I tuck it away in my memory to tell Kate.

It *is* my sister's birthday, the first of February. She would have been thirty-eight years old. I think, but don't say, *Wouldn't it be better if Jill were away, and still alive?*

⁓

I remember something that happened with Jill in the autumn, soon after she came east.

She's walking away from me in the parking lot of the Y, where I've taken her swimming, toward her car. She's tossing over her shoulder something she's saying offhandedly.

It is, I recall, a beautiful October evening. The sun is setting. The sky is glowing fuchsia, orange. In less than three months she'll be dead.

I don't want to hear her; I'm really not listening; I want to drown out her crazy talk. This day, she's gone on and on and on about the new man she's met, and how they've "clicked," and how she's thrilled he has a daughter, how she's always wanted a daughter, and how, this time, she knows it's going to work, she's going to make it work. I've heard this before. I want to be alone; I wish she weren't here.

"Who wants to be forty?" she says. I'm forty-one, and think it's just a dig at me. Then she says, "Me, I'll never be forty." I think this is another crazy remark. Or that Jill is telling me she's afraid to grow old. When she's not wearing her overalls to do her pottery or her gardening, she still dresses as if she's fifteen. Cute little outfits. Foolish little-girl shoes. Proud when she's thin enough to buy her clothes in the pre-teen shop.

Jill is still talking. Now she's talking about my father, and how my mother hates them for spending so much time together alone.

"She's jealous of us," my sister says. "Jealous of how well we get along."

I don't answer. I climb into my car. Give a wave. She heads for hers. I'm relieved that, inside my car, there's silence. As she walks away from me, I see she's still talking. But now she's talking to the air.

Two dreams I have around this time. The first: The surface of my parents' house is boglike; if you go into a room, you get sucked under and can't get out. The second: I am in a house that is also a school, and someone is hitting me, and no one will come to help me.

⌣

Very few people come to my sister's wake. Mostly, our relatives. My parents' friends. My sister's life in the East ended when she moved west with her husband just after her marriage in 1968. Her ex-in-laws, who live nearby, don't come. My eldest son is not there. He's refused to come to the wake or to the funeral. Jill killed herself during the week of his final exams. He has to get good grades to get into a good college, and he's angry at her for, as he put it, "fucking everything up."

I've picked out the casket. ("Make it plain," I say to the undertaker. "She was not a pretentious woman. Lived most of her live in overalls, at her potter's wheel, or out of doors.")

I've picked out the clothes she'll be buried in. (An ordinary plaid blouse, and slacks, I decide. My parents let me have my way. They are barely functioning.)

I've chosen a few poems to read. I've said a few words about my sister's gift for working with her hands, for making pottery, and for turning humble things into works of art.

Before the undertaker closes the casket, he asks us if we want to say good-bye.

My mother takes my hand. She wants me to join her and my father at the side of my sister's casket. She wants us to say good-bye to my sister as a family. I pull my hand away.

"No," I say. "I want some time with Jill alone." My mother tries to grab my hand again but gives up when she realizes I won't give in, and that I am stronger than she is and willing to make a scene to get my way.

At last, at last, alone, I kneel down and look at Jill. I try to look beyond the misshapen face in the casket to the Jill I remember. The Jill I shared a bed with for fourteen years because my mother, who practiced economies, determined that it was far cheaper to buy a double bed for the two of us than to buy each of us a bed of our own.

Of course, Jill's not in the casket. The only place, now, that she'll ever be for me is in my memory.

I reach into my purse and pull out an envelope. In it is a picture of her and the man who left her when they were happy. They are clowning for the camera. It's Halloween, and she has carved a pumpkin. It stands beside them on the counter. As with everything my sister made, there's wonder and magic in her work. The pumpkin looks like a demon mask, the kind used to ward off danger and evil. In the envelope, too, is a card on which I've written the words "I love you," even though what I feel for Jill is more complicated than love.

I put the envelope, and one of the first pots my sister made, into the casket. I can't, I won't say good-bye.

Late Summer, 1993

I've had a good, work-filled summer. Finished a book about revenge. Finished revising my second novel, about two teenage sisters. For its epigraph I have chosen lines from Sylvia Plath's "Two Sisters of Persephone": "Two girls there are: within the house / One sits; the other, without . . . ."

I've cleared my desk. Filed away my notes and manuscripts. Sent everything off to my agent. For the first time since 1974, I have no writing to do, although I have some ideas about what I want to turn to next. This has been my plan: to give myself some breathing room.

My asthma, which has been disabling for close to a year and a half, is under control. My hard work—daily fast walking, meditation, therapy—is paying off. I feel better in every way than I have for years, though of course there are still problems. My terror of losing consciousness, of fainting while I am in my car stuck in a traffic jam and no one can get to me. It has been a year and a half since I *have* lost consciousness, though I feel as if I am on the verge often. In therapy, we chip away at this, bit by bit. We look at the similarity between this and the way my sister has chosen to die. We develop strategies for me to try when the feeling comes over me. I can see myself making progress.

And on a day like any other day I go down into the basement to do the laundry but, instead I go straight to the back, to the boxes marked with Jill's name. The ones that came into my possession after my mother's death. My friend Kate has come over, and I have excused myself for a minute to run downstairs to throw a load of laundry into the dryer.

Sooner or later, I tell myself, I have to see what's in those boxes. It might as well be now.

I call up to Kate and ask her to come downstairs. I tell her what I'm about to do and ask her if she'll stand by me while I do this.

The first box contains some clippings—an announcement of my sister's being "lady-in-waiting" to the high school prom queen, news items from her graduations, from her induction into an honorary society. The announcement of her engagement. And of her wedding. (In each picture, Kate observes, she smiles a forced smile.)

Underneath the clippings, carefully folded, and wrapped in tissue paper, are my sister's Girl Scout beret and her merit badges. We find it strange that my mother has saved them.

In the next box is my sister's collection of porcelain dolls. I take them out, and we look at them. "They're ugly," Kate says.

Under the dolls, though, is a small wooden suitcase, and inside the suitcase are the clothes my sister has made for her dolls.

I can see her, in memory, bending over my mother's Singer sewing machine, her long honey gold hair falling in front of her eyes, peering through her thick glasses, at the garment she is making. I hear the rat-a-tat-tat of the foot pedal as she stitches along. All the clothes my sister has made are dressy. Cocktail dresses with matching headbands. Evening gowns. The kind of dresses suited for a life my sister will never know.

"Of all the things to keep," Kate says. *Of all the things to treasure,* I think, *my mother has chosen these.*

But in keeping these things, I know, my mother has tried, desperately, to hold on to the memory of a once-happy child. The happy child my sister has never been.

She used to walk around the house when she was a little girl, my sister, carrying this little wooden suitcase that my father had made for her out of plywood for one Christmas. I can remember him making it with great care from a pattern he'd mailed away for in his shop down the basement where I would go to retrieve the laundry for my mother. When I clattered down the stairs, my father would hide what he was doing, and when I asked him what it was, he'd say, "A surprise for your sister; keep quiet about it."

"Would you like me to make this for you?" my father asks my sister one evening after supper when my mother has tried, and failed, to force my sister to eat something she doesn't want to eat. She's three or four years old.

My father pulls my sister onto his lap after she refuses, again, to eat my mother's cooking, after my sister refuses, again, to open her mouth so my mother can feed her just one more bite, after my sister collapses in inconsolable tears. And my mother storms out of the kitchen, red-faced with fury, as my father tries to soothe her.

My father takes her into the sunroom and shows her a picture of a little wooden suitcase in one of his handyman magazines. "Shush," he says, "shush. If you want this, I'll make it for you, and you can pack it with whatever you want and carry it wherever you want to go."

My sister nods, stops her sobbing. My sister is my father's favorite, and he dotes on her in a way he doesn't on me, which is fine, for what I want, then, more than anything, is to be left alone, and to be allowed to do whatever I want without parental interference.

My father finishes the little suitcase with a mahogany satin stain, with brass hinges, and a brass latch that she can open herself without any help from me, thank goodness. And it remains, for years, my sister's favorite present.

Before she starts sewing clothes for her dolls, she packs it with her paper dolls, the ones she plays with for hours, cutting out the clothes with a blunt scissor, dressing the dolls and undressing them, stacking them and their clothes on top of one another neatly before she locks them away in her little suitcase. Years later, she uses the suitcase to store the clothes she sews for her dolls. And whether she took the little suitcase with her when she moved back west, or whether she abandoned it at my parents' when she leaves, I don't know. But there it is, now, at the bottom of the big cardboard box marked "Jill."

When I open the little wooden suitcase, and find it stuffed with her dolls' handmade outfits, and I take them out and hold them, I start crying. I can see Jill, now, wandering the house, carrying her little wooden suitcase, on her way to nowhere.

At last, at last, I'm crying for my sister, crying for the tragedy of my sister's aborted life. I'm crying for my mother, and I'm crying for myself. I'm glad Kate is here for comfort. I know I'm ready to let my sister go. I'm ready to say good-bye.

breathless, adjective

I

I am alone, walking on my favorite beach in Sag Harbor, on the eastern end of Long Island. It is just after sunset on a warm day in late spring. I try to ignore the trouble I'm having breathing, the coughing attack that has continued, unabated, for the past two hours, the slamming inside my head, my fatigue. Tell myself that maybe this illness I've had for seven months, which no doctor can diagnose, is all in my head. If that's so, maybe it's something I can control. But even if I can't control it, maybe I can work on my attitude.

For the next few seconds, I try to ignore this body I inhabit that feels as if it has declared war on me. Try to notice the changing sky. Watch the pair of mallards davening for their evening meal. Ignore the chronic cough, the pain in my chest, the lump in my throat, the rasp in my breath. And can't. Sometimes I wonder whether I'm exaggerating how awful I've been feeling. Tell myself I'm just too sensitive. "The Princess and the Pea," my husband calls me, after the fairytale princess, so sensitive she could feel a tiny pea beneath a pile of mattresses. And he's right. I'm hypersensitive, always vigilant. Bothered by noises, smells, heat, cold.

Usually when I walk I feel better than I do the rest of the day. Sometimes even my chronic cough disappears. Today, though, I'm aware of every breath I take. Inhale. Cough. Sputter. Exhale. Inhale. Exhale.

I have learned that we take about 20,000 breaths each day. That's 834 breaths an hour, 14 breaths a minutes, one breath every four or so seconds. If I continue to be painfully aware of every breath I take, I will labor through 13,344 breaths during each day's waking hours, and 4,870,560 breaths in the next year.

Inhale. Can't get enough air into my lungs. Feel like I'm suffocating, like I have a tomcat sitting on my chest and I'm breathing against its weight. Feel like I'm drowning in mucus. Clear my throat. Cough. Clear my throat. Swallow. Clear my throat. Choke. Exhale. Inhale. Better this time; if it were always like this, I could take it. Clear. Swallow. Exhale. Inhale. Shit—Tomcat's back. Drowning. Mayday. Mayday.

I gasp, walk along, wonder how much longer I can take this, look out over the bay toward Shelter Island, now a navy blue mass against a yellow-pink sky. If I'm lucky, I'll see the pair of swans who live in this bay in flight against the evening sky. If I'm lucky, this illness will go away as quickly as it began. If I'm lucky, I won't have to kill myself. Still, I've decided that I *will* kill myself if someone can't figure out what I have and cure it, if this illness that has invaded my body and turned me into someone I don't know, and don't want to know, lasts very much longer.

When my husband asks why I'm in such despair, I can't explain how laboring through 13,344 breaths a day, coughing constantly, means I can think of little else but how the next breath will feel. It's been hard to do anything (though I've been trying to do everything)—teach, think, read, write, make love, cook, do laundry, enjoy a view—when you feel like you're suffocating, when you think that the next breath you take may be your last.

I sink down onto the pebble beach. Put my head in my hands. Last year at this time, before I got sick, I took this beauty for granted. I took everything for granted. Like breathing. Something my body did without my acknowledging it for the miracle it is. Last year, I didn't know the meaning of the word "despair."

> **breath, noun.** 1. the air inhaled and exhaled in respiration. 2. respiration, esp. as necessary to life. 3. life, vitality. 4. the ability to breathe easily and normally. 5. time to breathe, pause or respite.

breathless, adjective. 1. without breath or breathing with difficulty; gasping; panting. 2. with the breath held, as in suspense, astonishment, or fear. 3. causing loss of breath, as from excitement, anticipation, or tension. 4. dead, lifeless. 5. motionless or still.

2

This illness I have comes on suddenly. We're leaving a movie theater, and I'm walking toward our car with my husband, laughing, joking. And then, without warning, in the space of a few minutes, I become very sick. I'm feverish, shivering, my head is pounding, my throat is hurting, I start coughing, I'm feeling like I'm going to die. My husband thinks it's the flu because it's come on so suddenly.

Six months later, I'm still sick. Each morning I wake up hoping I'll be fine. By mid-morning, I start coughing. By lunchtime, I'm exhausted. By afternoon, I have to take a nap. I collapse into bed by eight and sleep though most of the night. During these six months, I've had only five symptom-free days. Various doctors have ruled out AIDS, Lyme disease, heart disease, lung cancer, emphysema, whooping cough, sinusitis. Other doctors have told me that this is the aftermath of a severe flu; that I can feel like this for a year, or more; that this is a chronic viral syndrome and incurable; that it's definitely bronchitis; that it's chronic motor rhinitis (a fancy way of saying I have a runny nose). I've spent thousands of dollars on doctors and medications, been on nine different drug regimens, and I'm still sick. And finally, and inevitably I've been told that I'm a hysteric—this from a pulmonary specialist in an emergency room who complains to me about his terrible cold and coughs in my face as he examines me.

I go to the emergency room because of a coughing attack so severe and prolonged I almost lose consciousness. "I think I have asthma," I tell the doctor. It's just an uninformed guess.

"No wheezing," he says, "it can't be asthma."

Long pause.

"Are you going through a bad time? Making yourself hyperventilate? Have you considered this might be hysterical?"

I get so enraged, though I don't say a word, that I feel an adrenaline rush. I want him dead. And my breathing eases completely, and I know that, right now, I'm fine. As I rage out of the emergency room, I think this is good to know: that whatever I have, if I get angry enough, I'll feel better.

3

I go to a health food store to buy a stash of tea that helps ease the pain in my throat. On impulse, I buy a copy of *Vegetarian Times* with an article, "A Breath of Fresh Air," by Lucy Moll.

Moll describes what it feels like to have an asthma attack—"breathing is extremely difficult . . . . the asthmatic is in terror of suffocating . . . . the amount of oxygen in the blood drops significantly . . . . the attack may be fatal if medical attention is not received immediately." She discusses possible symptoms: incessant coughing, thick mucus, difficulty breathing, a feeling of suffocation, twitchiness in the throat, tightness in the chest, cold hands and feet—the symptoms I've described to every doctor I've seen. Still, there have been breakthroughs in understanding this disease and its treatment.

Asthma, of course. Just as I've suspected. And when I finish reading Moll's article, I think, *There's hope.* I call my husband and tell him to call the doctors he knows at Columbia Presbyterian to get me an appointment with a pulmonary specialist.

⌣

"Congratulations on staying alive," the doctor says after he examines me, after he explains that undiagnosed asthma as bad as mine can kill you. I ask if it's common for a case like mine to go undiagnosed for so long. "All too common," he says.

He tells me it might take six months to a year to bring this under control; he prescribes a bronchodilator, to open the airways; a corticosteroid (used with a spacer) to treat the underlying inflammation. I'll be taking twenty-eight doses of medicine a day to start, but as I improve, I'll need less. I need to monitor my vital capacity with a meter several times a day. The major problem in treatment, he says, is compliance: Many patients don't use their medicines as directed; many ignore their symptoms until they're in crisis.

Before I leave his office, the doctor asks what I do to take care of myself. I tell him about my exercise and meditation practice. "Since it's been working," he says, "keep it up."

For months, I've been living in a nightmare. Although I'm not happy I have asthma, still, it's good to have a name for it, good to have a treatment protocol. I decide that I'll try not to let asthma rule my life. I expect, someday, to be back to normal. Still, it's important for me to learn as much about asthma as I can, and I start reading about this disease. I learn that it is likely caused by a complex interaction among several factors: genetic predisposition, exposure to allergens or triggers (smoke, exhaust, chemical fumes, pollutants), a hyperreactive nervous system due to stress, trauma, and/ or caregivers' unresponsiveness to their baby's needs. That some combination of psychotherapy, herbal remedies (ephedra, for example), homeopathy, stress reduction, relaxation techniques, meditation, yoga, conscious breathing techniques, aerobic exercise (which can also induce attacks), dietary and nutritional changes (macrobiotic or vegan diet, vitamin therapy, avoiding trigger foods), and acupuncture are often effective.

But after a few months of treatment, my asthma is nowhere near under control. I've coughed all day some days; I've been lightheaded and fatigued; I've started to feel hopeless again. Still, I haven't yet told the doctor how sick I still am. I continue to teach, try to write, cook, deal with the household. I try to exercise, talk about my feelings, get enough rest, do far less, enjoy simple pleasures, believe I'll one day be well—all strategies I've read about.

When I finally do communicate to him that I often cough hundreds of times without stopping, he decides to change my treatment. I'll need a short course of oral steroids—burst therapy—to treat the underlying inflammation that isn't responding to inhaled steroids. And soon, but not immediately, I'm somewhat, but not completely, better. That won't happen for many years.

4

I sit at my desk three hours a day, coughing and writing, writing and coughing. I set a timer for thirty minutes and stop and get up and do some breathing exercises. I'm newly aware of the limited time I have to write. Before asthma, I didn't squander my writing time, but I surely didn't treasure it. Now I cannot take this time for granted. I must do what I can to enable myself to be fit enough to work. The time I have at my desk now feels sweeter than before, yet also poignant for I am aware of the fact that there are days when I'm so sick that writing becomes impossible.

When I write, I'm usually oblivious to my body. This has changed since my illness. My body now makes me aware of itself with every stroke of my pen, with every strike of the keys. I'm writing through my body in a way I haven't before. I wonder what this will mean. Will my work change?

I miss the deep concentration of the long sojourns at my desk before my illness—writing for five or six hours straight, breaking only for a cup of tea or a quick lunch. I miss how the world dropped away. Now I will need to learn a new way of working—one that requires me to repeatedly leave and then reenter the trance of writing. I wonder how other writers with illnesses, with asthma, have managed to work under these conditions. I decide to find out, for I know that having this information will help me.

I have been writing a book about how writers used their work to get back at people in their lives who betrayed them—writing as revenge, using, among other examples, the works of D. H. Lawrence and Virginia Woolf. And, until I got sick, I didn't realize they struggled to write despite ill health, nor did I recognize their heroism in working under adverse circumstances. Now that I am ill, I want to learn how they faced illness. I go back through the letters and journals of these writers and notice what has eluded me.

Woolf, in her fifties, worked steadily to finish *The Years* despite disabling headaches and a difficult menopause that made her pulse race and her heart beat wildly and gave her anxiety attacks so severe she mistook them for insanity. In her diary, she wonders, not when she'll be well, but when she'll be well enough to work. Her diary recounts a heroic struggle, her reluctance to stop work though she is barely able to lift her head from her pillow. What I learned from Woolf's diary is that if one works when one can despite illness, and through illness, then one can restore one's sense of self-worth so deeply challenged by being incapacitated.

When I first worked on D. H. Lawrence's *Women in Love* I barely noticed that, for much of the novel's composition, Lawrence was desperately ill, often bedridden, too weak to arise. I knew that he suffered from tuberculosis, but

I ignored its consequences, as many biographers ignore (or worse, interpret as neurotic) the impact of illness on their subjects' lives and works. Lawrence moved often, from city to countryside, from country to country, continent to continent, in search of clean, untainted air he could breathe freely. I'd thought he was restless, escapist, but now I realized he was trying to care for himself and doing whatever he could to find respite from his illness.

Before my illness, I minimized Woolf's despair and criticized Lawrence. Now, like Woolf, I wanted more than anything to work, and I understood the compelling urgency of her desire. And, like Lawrence, because I knew I was living with an illness that no doubt would be lifelong, I felt a rage like his, one I now understood could be born from lifelong physical affliction, helplessness, and despair.

5

In the months since my diagnosis, I've met with two counselors specializing in treating people with chronic illnesses. The first suggests that because of all I've lived through recently—the difficult years before my sister's suicide, her death, my mother's long terminal illness, my father's need for help—I must be tired of being the family's caregiver. I've given myself this illness, he suggests, so *I* can be cared for. He urges me to start taking care of myself. He gives me a book to read to prove his point.

I read it. But it strikes me as bullshit. *Sure,* I think, *blame the person who's sick for getting sick.* But I do believe I need to take better care of myself. Focusing on illness, I realize, is different from focusing on wellness. I want to take control over what I can change—my physical fitness, my diet, learning techniques to minimize acute attacks. And I can try to accept what I can't—that I have this illness, and that it might be lifelong.

Over the next few months, I learn that I must avoid these things not to get an asthma attack: Pollution. Exhaust fumes. Smoke. Perfume. Certain foods (tomatoes, cheese, milk). Nail polish remover. Hair spray. Sulfites. Aspirin. Paint fumes. Newsprint. Cleaning fluid. Mold. Any substances used by exterminators. Rushing. Laughing too hard. Fear.

The second counselor, after learning my history, indicates she thinks I have bottled-up grief, rage, and tremendous fear. Could I possibly have posttraumatic stress disorder? She asks whether I've mourned my sister and my mother, whether I've cried about their deaths. Not really, I say. I just continued to do what I had to do and carried on. I tried to live my life as if nothing had happened. But I broke out in hives, felt faint often. What would happen if I started to cry? she asks. Once I start, I say, I won't ever stop.

After our meeting, I have much to ponder. I want to feel free to grieve for my sister. I think that something about the way my breath catches when I have an asthma attack has to do with how my sister died: She stopped her breathing by hanging herself. Perhaps I feel guilt for not having been able to stop her. My breathing disorder might be connected to all the tears I haven't yet shed for her, all the tears I've held inside.

A friend asks if my asthma flared after my sister's death as a way of keeping me connected with her. Though my first impulse is to deny it, I soon admit that this is so. When I was a child, my mother, always depressed, consigned my sister to my care. At first, I hovered over her, trying to keep her out of harm's way. Then, as a teenager, I resented having to take care of her, and I ignored her when I was forced to take her with me. We shared a bed from when I was seven until I left to marry. There was something comforting and troubling in her physical closeness. I wanted my own bed, my own space, yet I worried about her when she wasn't nearby, and I couldn't fall asleep until she had.

In memory, I see myself pulling the bedcovers over my sister's slender shoulders during her fitful sleep, turning my back to her, listening to make sure she is still breathing, that she is still alive.

I reenter therapy to figure out whether my asthma might be related to posttraumatic stress disorder. In time—and this journey takes many years—I discover that this is true. I return to and examine being sent to relatives in Rhode Island when my mother was incapacitated, and then, through all the years we were sent there, being fondled by a relative against my will while I was taking a bath and when I was going to sleep. I remember holding my breath and waiting patiently for it to end and concentrating on the light coming through the blinds. I remember the terror of growing up in wartime, seeing the newsreels, hearing my mother talk about war, and how angry my father was when he came back from the war, and how afraid I was of him, and how, when I was older, he tried to kill me.

Before I began to investigate the link between abuse, terror, and asthma in my life, I'd researched Djuna Barnes's writing of her play *The Antiphon*. Barnes suffered from asthma, and from her letters to her friend Emily Coleman, I'd learned that coughing fits, too, disabled her. Her play graphically depicts how her grandmother (and probably her father, too) sexually abused her, and that her father sold her into sexual slavery with her mother's compliance. Barnes believed this play exposed, and was just payback for, what had happened to her. Working on Barnes's life provided me with information and understanding about the consequences of sexual and physical abuse that I could apply to my own life.

6

Wondering what treatments were available to someone like Barnes in the 1930s, the period during which she wrote *Ryder* (a bestseller) and *Nightwood*, and before modern asthma treatment, I search the archives of the *New York Times*. Throughout the 1930s, doctors debated whether asthma was a disease or a functional disorder. Acquired asthma was thought by some to be a mental maladjustment or a nervous disease, potentially successfully treatable by psychotherapy or hypnosis. By others, it was thought to be caused by an underlying physical susceptibility conjoined with neurosis.

In 1935, doctors used helium therapy experimentally when adrenaline didn't help patients. Though no cure, by supplying "thinner air," it was thought to provide relief for the severely taxed respiratory system, making it more likely that remission would occur.

In 1936, a new treatment, inhaling epinephrine hydrochloride vapor (an unsatisfactory precursor of medicines like Ventolin), was being recommended for childhood asthma.

In 1937, a doctor in Warsaw reported injecting insulin into the bodies of asthma sufferers to induce shock. There were, though, potentially dire side effects: sudden death, destruction of brain tissue. Nonetheless, this treatment became widespread and was used with children at Mount Sinai Hospital in New York City.

In 1942, X-ray treatments were used in New York to try to cure severe cases of asthma. In 1946, an aerosol of hydrogen peroxide, combined with penicillin therapy, was tried. In 1948, an aerosol of isuprel (a beta-blocker, a precursor of Ventolin, but with more cardiac stimulatory effects) was tried. And also in 1948, a professor of surgery at George Washington School of Medicine was reporting success from his procedure of an operation that destroyed the pulmonary plexus of nerves, dividing branches of the vagus nerve to the lung, and denuding the sheaths of the pulmonary artery and veins.

After reading about these treatments, I wonder whether contemporary physicians, certain of their treatment, could be as off the mark as these earlier practitioners. Still, I've been feeling better on this drug regimen, and so I must conclude that it's effective.

7

In the year that it takes my asthma to begin to come under control, I pass through many emotional waystations. Some, I return to and revisit: despair, rage, hopelessness, resentment (of the able), castigation (of myself). And terror, yes, terror, my lifelong companion that I come to know intimately but would like to banish if I could but that is, I come to realize, the warpstring of my existence.

Yet I am learning, too, that change is inevitable, and that the health of my body, like everyone else's and despite much popular mythology, is not completely within my control. I am being taught humility.

My progress—if one can call managing a lifelong ailment progress—comes so slowly that I have no emotional calipers with which to gauge it. I begin to understand how impatient I am, how unable to allow change to happen in its own good time, how much I rush through life, how little room I give myself to breathe.

I return, in my reading, to the wisdom of the sacred books of the East, to the writings of mystics, and Buddhists, and find some solace there. This is the paradoxical lesson I must learn: to give up the expectation that one's actions will produce a desired result; to expect nothing and yet to do everything I can to help myself. Accepting this, I realize, might take me a lifetime.

I learn, though, that I have a particular kid of grit, a stick-to-it-iveness I never realized I possessed—what Winston Churchill called "mettle," what my father told me about so many years before, when I swam across Lake George. I promise that I will do what I can to enable my body to heal, and I keep those promises.

8

Asthma is interrupted breathing. Here is a history of interrupted breathing in my life.

My sister killed herself by hanging. She interrupted her breathing, permanently.

My son was born with his umbilicus over his shoulder. When he was in the birth canal, each contraction cut off his air supply. He was born blue. He almost died.

My mother, near the end of her life, struggled for air. For weeks, I sat next to her as she lay dying, watching her chest, hearing her breathe. Inhale. Long pause. Exhale. Inhale. Longer pause. Exhale.

When I was a baby, my mother fed me on a strict schedule, every four hours. Between feedings, if I was hungry, I cried. But she, as instructed by her doctor, didn't comfort me. During my first seven months, I cried so hard, she said, that I seemed to lose my breath.

In grammar school, during air-raid drills, I always fainted, and no one could figure out why. I was overwhelmed by terror. I imagined low-flying planes strafing our school.

As a child, I spent summers with relatives in Rhode Island. I remember the bathtub where I was washed and fondled, the bed, where my body was invaded, and being so afraid that I dared not move, so afraid that time stood still, so afraid that I was hardly breathing.

I was always afraid because I believed my father would kill me. He was easily enraged, volatile, violent. He beat me, came at me with a knife.

In high school, I drank too much, so much so that I passed out and scared my friends. "We weren't sure," they said, "that you would start breathing again."

As a grownup, I faint. When I'm terrified. When I'm furious but I don't know it.

9

These are the reasons I might have gotten asthma.

When I was an infant, I wasn't taught to control my hyperarousal.

When I was a child, I was afraid of my father.

When I was a child, I was sexually abused.

My father was a heavy smoker. I was a heavy smoker.

We lived downwind from a chemical plant.

We lived downwind from a coal-burning electric plant. The smell of burning was always in the air.

I've lived two houses away from a six-lane highway for years. In my back yard on a fresh spring day, all you can smell is exhaust.

I work in a sealed building. For years, I had an office next to a professor who chain-smoked cigars. I got sick, often. I thought it was bronchitis. He continued to smoke until smoking was banned.

I took birth control pills and later, estrogen replacement therapy. I've read a study connecting the use of estrogens with a higher incidence of asthma.

None of the above? All of the above?

10

Arthur W. Frank, author of *The Wounded Storyteller: Body, Illness, and Ethics*, asks the question: What does it mean to be a writer with a wounded body? Which leads me to ask: What does it mean to be a writer with asthma? I want to learn what writers with asthma suffered, how they described their illness, how they were treated by their doctors, whether having asthma affected their work, whether asthma was the subject of their art, whether their biographers were empathic as to what their subjects endured as people with asthma.

I gather the names of writers with asthma—Djuna Barnes, Marcel Proust, Elizabeth Bishop, Olive Schreiner, John Updike, Edith Wharton, and Dylan Thomas, for starters. Although I know that learning about all of them will take years, beginning to peruse their letters, diaries, and biographies teaches me that they left detailed accounts of their asthma histories, their symptoms, and sufferings, their doctors' treatment protocols. Their letters and diaries are a treasure trove for studying how the disease has been interpreted and treated over time, and the impact of illness on writers' works and lives.

I I

Brett C. Millier's biography *Elizabeth Bishop: Life and the Memory of It*, describes how she wrote a breakthrough work, "The Map"—she called it the first of her mature poems—during an asthma attack. Alone on New Year's Eve in 1935, treating herself with "adrenalin and cough syrup," unable to sleep because of her illness and the effect of her medications, Bishop spent the night gazing at a glass-enclosed map depicting the Canadian Maritime provinces where she was born, and then writing "The Map": "We can stroke these lovely bays," she wrote, "under a glass as if they were expected to blossom, / or as if to provide a clean cage for invisible fish." Bishop would continue to use images of entrapment, like the cage, in her work, to describe her childhood and her asthma.

In a *Paris Review* interview, Bishop described how she wrote her autobiographical "In the Village" when she was treated with cortisone for a severe asthma attack. She'd made notes for the story. But she said she was "given too much cortisone—I have very bad asthma from time to time—and you don't need any sleep [when treated with cortisone]. You feel wonderful while it's going on but to get off it is awful. So I couldn't sleep much and I sat up all night . . . . The story came from a combination of cortisone, I think, and the gin and tonic I drank in the middle of the night. I wrote it in two nights."

"In the Village" explores why Bishop thinks she got asthma, and she locates its cause in her childhood. Bishop's father died when she was five years old. After his death, she was routinely abandoned by her mother and felt terrified by her unpredictability and violence. No relative explained the reasons for her mother's behavior to Bishop, nor why she was institutionalized, nor why she was never able to see her again. Everything in her environment, she wrote, "except the river [that ran close to her home and separated where she lived from the sanatorium housing her mother] holds its breath."

Bishop then lived with her maternal grandparents. But after a brief time, she was removed "against [her] wishes" from that home in Nova Scotia to the repressive, gloomy household of her paternal grandparents in Worcester, Massachusetts. There, she developed severe asthma, eczema, and symptoms of St. Vitus Dance, and almost died.

May Lombardi's "The Closet of Breath" describes how Bishop's "The Country Mouse" links the onset of Bishop's asthma, of her being "trapped forever within her 'scabby body and wheezing lungs,'" with the repressive nature of her paternal grandparents' household, where she was held captive and ignored, and where her behavior was carefully regulated. Her grandfather "smoked thirteen or fourteen cigars a day" and Bishop was forced to breathe the contaminated and polluted air of this house without being allowed to escape its confines. Throughout Bishop's writing life, she transformed her bodily ills into the "images of caging, entrapment, smothering, suffocation, and constriction" she articulated in many poems, including "The Fish," in which she employs the image of a dying mermaid "washed ashore and gasping for breath," and "O Breath," in which the broken lines of the poem imitate the difficulties of an asthmatic's breathing.

Lombardi describes the diaries Bishop kept when she lived in Key West that record and describe her "almost nightly attacks of debilitating asthma" and "her dreams and anxieties." As soon as Bishop moved to a new place, her asthma started to bother her again. She felt as if no place was safe, no place could be home. On a trip to Nova Scotia in 1947, for example, Bishop wrote her doctor, Anny Baumann, asking for advice—Bishop had been having severe asthma attacks for weeks.

> I was taking about 2cc of adrenaline every night. I guess the two nights on the train didn't help much, and it's been getting worse ever since—I have to take about 2cc during the course of the day and 3 or 4 during the night. I stayed in bed yesterday, thinking if I didn't move it might help, but last night was as bad as ever. There is absolutely nothing here that I can think of that might cause it—the boardinghouse is very clean, it's on the ocean, the animals aren't near, etc. . . .
>
> Maybe this will wear off after a while. The only thing I can think of is that maybe you could suggest a change of medicine or something drastic to break it up.

This is one of the most beautiful places I have ever seen. . . . We want to take a lot of trips and long walks, etc., that's what makes asthma so discouraging.

Bishop was fascinated by the figure of St. Sebastian, to whom she compared herself, because she was so often required to inject herself with cortisone or adrenaline (often hourly). "I finally got sick of being stuck with so many things like St. Sebastian," she wrote on January 8, 1952, in a letter to her doctor from Brazil.

Millier's biography records the history of Bishop's asthma treatment from 1934 to 1951, the years during which her suffering was most acute, and the extent to which her life was impeded, not only because of the disease, but also because of the side effects of the medicines she took to enable her to breathe. It recounts, too, the major role of alcoholism in Bishop's life.

According to Millier,

> [She] was treated with multiple doses of injected adrenaline, sometimes three or four cubic centimeters two or three times a night. Later she experimented with nearly every other possible treatment for asthma, including large doses of oral cortisone. The condition . . . fed her sense of homelessness and sent her away from places she would rather have stayed. . . . [She] often traveled specifically in search of air she could breathe. . . .
>
> Asthma is depressing. Not getting enough oxygen in the bloodstream is chemically depressing, and the fear of an attack, anxiety about breathing, and the limitations the disease can place on the asthmatic's activities and destinations, the sleep lost to nighttime ambushes from unseen enemies, the sense of weakness and betrayal by one's body, the manipulation of one's moods by drugs—all conspire to keep the sufferer from rising above her illness.
>
> . . . The major breakthrough in the management of chronic asthma—the introduction of corticosteroids into her therapy in 1952—gave her unprecedented relief from prolonged attacks. . . . Between 1952 and 1954, she took oral and injected cortisone over four extended periods. She was subject to most of the drug's major side effects, including weight gain and extreme nervousness and sleeplessness, but for a time these seemed a reasonable price to pay to breathe freely. Whatever else the cortisone might have done to her, it always cleared her lungs. But . . . in

the spring of 1954, Elizabeth found herself unable to tolerate . . . the "jag" of sleeplessness and nervousness . . . and she began to medicate that nervousness with alcohol. Because she was an alcoholic, she could not control this drinking on her own. . . . [She] began a program . . . using Antabuse, which she maintained, with few lapses, until 1964.

Bishop's testimony illuminates what living with severe asthma was like before contemporary treatment—one that enables someone like me, who carefully follows my doctor's treatment protocol, to lead a relatively normal, though carefully controlled, life. But, despite Bishop's words, it is difficult to understand what it felt like to live with asthma when the only way to breathe freely or to secure temporary relief was through the constant injection of medicines with terrible side effects.

12

So, what have I learned about asthma from what I've read and from reflecting upon my own experience?

I believe asthma is a breathing disorder linked to abuse and that it is probably a manifestation of posttraumatic stress. I believe that asthma tells us that the person who has it is, or once was, so terrified s/he feared s/he would die.

I believe that asthma is difficult to treat because it is necessary to "retrain" the sufferer's state of near-permanent alert. And I believe that there can be no "cure" for asthma, nor a decrease in the number of people afflicted, unless the link between asthma and terror and abuse is recognized.

And I believe that asthma is related, also, to pollution.

13

Leota Lone Dog, one of the founders of Kitchen Table: Women of Color Press, once told me about "Trail of the Otter," a contemporary Native dance performed by Muriel Miguel, a Kuta-Rappahannock Indian, and Floyd Flavel, a Cree Indian. In "Trail of the Otter," which draws from contemporary Native American legends about an otter named "Lola," a cough, followed by heavy breathing—a signal that the oxygen in the Earth's atmosphere is being depleted—is the first sign Lola recognizes of an impending environmental disaster. In the dance, Lola brings the message of her witnessing the breathlessness, sickening, and death of members of her species and its eventual extinction. The dance is both testimony and warning: If one species inhabiting the Earth becomes extinct because its environment has been ravaged, eventually all species inhabiting the Earth, including human beings, will become extinct.

Soon after I hear about this legend, a copy of the *Self-Care Catalog* comes in the mail. It advertises a new product, "a hat that's a portable, wearable air filter." The hat comes with a face screen, a filter, a tiny electric blower, and a battery pack worn on a belt.

Anyone sensitive to airborne contaminants "knows the routine during EPA alerts: Stay inside, avoid activity," the ad reads. "Well, what if gardening sounds like more fun?" Wearing this breakthrough product allows you to go outside "even during . . . pollution alerts."

I sometimes wonder who is more highly evolved. The person who responds adversely to chemical fumes, exhaust fumes, cigarette smoke, and noxious odors, or the person who doesn't. Maybe I'm like the canary in the mineshaft. Maybe my gasping for air is information that other, less sensitive people should heed. Maybe the fate of the planet depends upon people like me whose responsive bodies are telling us there's something very wrong going on. As John Updike, who suffered from asthma, wrote in *Self-Consciousness*, "We move and have our being within a very narrow band of chemical conditions, on a blue-skinned island of a planet from which there is no escape, save for the legendary few who have enjoyed space travel or bodily ascension."

14

It is 11 P.M. I am lying awake in bed alone. My husband is away on business. I think I am going to die. I can't catch my breath. I feel like I'm suffocating, like I'm trying to draw in air through the tiniest of straws, as if I am trying to breathe through a roomful of sodden feathers. I feel I'm drowning, drowning. I have the telephone number of the police plugged into my cellphone so I can get help if I need it.

I try not to panic. Panic will only make it worse. I put on the earphones to my Walkman. Listen to a relaxation tape.

"Lie down, make yourself very comfortable.

"Relax your face. Relax your neck. Relax your shoulders.

"Focus on your breathing."

I listen to the tape three times. By the third go-round, I'm relaxed enough to drift off to sleep. Tonight, I'm lucky. Tonight, it worked. But what about tomorrow?

> *breathless, adjective:* without breath or breathing with difficulty; gasping; panting.

> *breath, noun:* the air inhaled and exhaled in respiration; respiration as necessary to life; vitality.

V AND I

The year is 1975.

I am thirty-two years old, married, the mother of two small children, a Ph.D. candidate, on a charter flight to England with a friend to do research on Virginia Woolf at the University of Sussex in Falmer. This is the first time in my whole life that I am going away without a member of my family. I have no idea where Falmer is, except that it is near Brighton. We have no hotel reservations. We have no idea how we will get to Brighton. But we are gloriously drunk on our third sherry, free from the responsibility of our children for a while. (We have already had enough sherry so that each child can have her or his own little sherry bottle as a souvenir when we return home.) We are, at long last, grownups, going to do *real* research. The next generation of Woolf scholars, in incubation. We are formidable.

⌒

I come from a family, from a cultural heritage, where women simply don't go away to do things separately from men. That is not to say that men don't go away to do things separately from women. They do. And often. But in the land of my forebears, women sit around and wait for their men. Or they work very hard and watch their children and wait for their men. Or they make a sumptuous meal and they work very hard and watch their children and wait for their men. But they don't go anywhere without their men. Or do anything for themselves alone without their men. Except complain. To their children or to anyone else who will listen to them. About their men and about their bad luck in having been born female.

Well, given a background like that, you can imagine the way I felt as we flew high above the Atlantic. There I was, a *puttana*, alone at last.

⌒

Early on in my work on Virginia Woolf, I thought that I would devote the rest of my life to carefully considered scholarly essays and books on every aspect of her life and art. Those were the heroine-worship days when I blanched at the sight of her manuscripts, when I did not dare to think that she had an outhouse, much less that she and her husband, Leonard, used the typescripts of her novels instead of toilet tissue, that she could be hardy enough or human enough to walk across the Downs in her beloved Sussex. I saw her as an earlier generation of critics had painted her for me—frail, weak, crazy, tortured, looking out of windows, vacant, probing the inside of her troubled psyche, like the wistful adolescent she was on the edge of a family picture.

I loved the sight of myself, briefcase in hand, walking up the steps of the New York Public Library, past the lions Patience and Fortitude (I would have preferred lionesses), thinking that the kid who grew up on the streets of Hoboken, New Jersey, was now walking past the painting of Milton's daughters taking down the immortal words of his verse, now walking down the third floor corridor to the Berg Collection, now pressing the buzzer. And they were actually letting me into the sacred recess where I would soon sit next to all those famous literary scholars whose work I had read and do work of my own.

The American Dream.

And as I sat there, beginning my work, I thought that if only I could have the good fortune to be able to sit over a glass of sherry at the Algonquin, or even over a cup of coffee at Tad's Steak House down the block, with someone really famous to talk about Virginia Woolf, life would be so sweet, so very sweet, and I would ask for nothing more in this universe.

⌒

I got into Woolf scholarship quite by accident. (Or so I thought at the time.)

It was a day of torrential rain in April in the early 1970s. That evening, there was a meeting of the graduate class I was attending in Virginia Woolf's novels taught by Mitchell Leaska. Ordinarily, I wouldn't dream of cutting his class, but because of the weather, and a long commute to New York University from suburban New Jersey, and a sick baby at home, I considered staying home. But I decided against it—Leaska's classes were too good to miss. And it's fortunate that I didn't. Because what Leaska taught that evening determined the shape of my life's work.

He was in the throes of his work on *The Pargiters*, his edition of Woolf's early version of *The Years*. In a previous class, he'd told us that earlier versions of the novel were dramatically different from the published text, and he mentioned a few examples—how there were nonfictional interchapters that Woolf later deleted; that the early version was more outspoken about the abuse of children.

I was the first person in my working-class family to attend college, the first (and only) to go to graduate school, and I harbored many misapprehensions about the creative process. When I was an undergraduate, we did close readings of literary works; we never read biography. We were never encouraged to study the process whereby these works had come into being.

Perhaps because of this indoctrination, perhaps because I didn't know anyone who wrote poetry or novels, I came into Leaska's class believing that geniuses like Virginia Woolf never needed to revise their work, that they knew, for the most part, what their work was about from the very beginning, and that they began their work after a moment of great inspiration. I believed that famous writers differed from the rest of us and showed their promise early, that they never needed to undergo a period of apprenticeship during which they learned their craft, that their works were penned pretty much as they appeared in print. I believed that they were convinced of the worth of their work and that they never doubted that what they were writing was worthwhile.

Until that rainy night in April, Leaska had spoken to us only in generalities about Woolf's process of revision, and, compelling as his insights were, and as much as they were changing my view of the composing process, what he taught us hadn't yet inspired me to want to work in the Woolf archive or, even, write a work of my own.

But on this particular evening, Leaska came to class with copies of his transcript of the first page of the earliest draft of *Pointz Hall* for us to contrast with the first page of *Between the Acts*, the novel we were studying. The scene, in draft, is entitled "The Lamp" and it evokes a summer's night: "Oh beautiful and bounteous light on the table; oil lamp; ancient and out-of-date oil lamp; upholding as on a tawny tent the falling grey draperies of the dust . . . ." And on it goes, for a long paragraph of very purple prose, which Woolf later revised to "It was a summer's night . . . ." In that class, we discussed Woolf's change of tone, her excision of much of what she'd written, her playing with a host of images she would omit here but develop elsewhere in the published novel.

Looking at the differences between the drafts, I realized, provided a window into the way Woolf worked, and so provided a way for someone like me to learn how an accomplished writer like Woolf went about the business of working on her craft. And I thought that if Woolf could let herself write this badly at the beginning of her process, and if she needed many drafts to find the right voice for the work, then if I learned how she did it, not only might I understand her process, but I might become a writer too. I could use examples of how she revised to teach myself how to revise. Woolf's process of revision, not her innate talent, though she had that in abundance, held the key to Woolf's genius.

I had never known that earlier versions of literary texts were available. It had never occurred to me before that one could inquire into the process of the creation of a novel and learn about the writing process and the process of revision.

After class, I stopped Leaska and told him that I wanted to do a dissertation on Virginia Woolf, on the earlier versions of one of her novels. He suggested *The Voyage Out* because it was her first novel, and he thought the extant drafts of that novel (of which there were many) might reveal something interesting about that work which puzzled critics.

This sounded like detective work. It was meticulous. It required stamina. Drive. It was exciting. I too would be working with manuscripts. I think I understood that I required a grand consuming passion in a project.

The first day I went to the Berg Collection, where the manuscripts are housed, I dressed for the occasion—long brown skirt, brown boots, brown patterned turtleneck sweater. Anyone, in those days, who pressed the buzzer to summon entrance to that famous collection for the first time will know what I felt that morning: excitement, curiosity, pleasure, desire, terror (there was, after all, Lola Szladits, the formidable curator of the collection, to encounter). The letter of introduction from Mitchell Leaska worked its magic. I was admitted. I filled out a slip of paper. Took my seat at the long wooden table to await the manuscripts. Took out my yellow pad, my array of sharpened pencils, my good eraser. Kept my trembling hands in my lap until the manuscripts of *The Voyage Out*, called *Melymbrosia* in its earliest versions, arrived.

When the manuscripts arrived, I wept. It was early, and I was the first person at work. The assistant who brought me the manuscripts was kind enough to go into the storage room after he saw how moved I was.

How to explain it? It was the smell, the unmistakable smell of smoke that was detectable as soon as I removed the manuscripts from their protective boxes. The smell of smoke that might well have come from their having been in Virginia Woolf's home at 52 Tavistock Square in London that was hit by a bomb during World War II while Woolf and her husband, Leonard, were living in Sussex. It was the sight of that angular, elegant hand—the cross-hatchings, cross-outs, inserts on the page. The false starts, the sure phrase, the faded typewriter ribbon, the circle left by a glass or a cup of—what?—water? tea? coffee? The burn mark where the ash from a cigarette dropped on the page.

All these traces of a life, now gone, though the work lived on. All these traces of a life's work, visible to me, visible to all who toiled over her manuscripts. Her life's work bestowing upon me the privilege of a life's work of understanding her own. And through learning how she wrote, learning, too, how I might work. How I might—and could, one day—write a creative prose work of my very own.

⌒

The Voyage Out is about Rachel Vinrace, a young, inexperienced woman who accompanies her father on a trip to South America. On her father's ship, the *Euphrosyne*, she resumes a relationship with her aunt and uncle, Helen and

Ridley Ambrose, and she meets Richard Dalloway, a former Member of Parliament, and his wife, Clarissa. Rachel becomes involved with two parental surrogates—Helen and Clarissa—but the relationship with Clarissa is complicated because Rachel is sexually attracted to Richard. During a storm at sea, Rachel and he embrace. That night she has a dream that she is being pursued.

Later, when she is at Santa Marina, a fictive South American port city, she meets Terence Hewet, who is spending his holiday there. They fall in love and decide to marry. But both are extremely reluctant lovers. But Rachel dies of a mysterious illness before the couple can marry.

I had no way of knowing that when I decided to work on *The Voyage Out* I would have enormous difficulty keeping the problems I was having in my life separate from the issues Woolf was discussing in the novel. I had reached that moment of sexual reevaluation that often occurs at about thirty. Although I was married, I went through a time when I identified with Rachel so strongly that I believed I shared her distrust of intimacy. It was simpler for me to see myself in terms of Woolf's character than it was to look at my own problems.

I vacillated between thinking that Rachel—and by extension, I—was typical of all women, and thinking that her hesitations—and mine—were pathological. It took many years for me to separate myself from Rachel Vinrace. It took many years for me to understand that part of the reason for Rachel's hesitation was her submerged rage at the misogyny and brutality of the men in her life—all disguised through the artifice of civilization, to be sure, but there nonetheless. In the process of separating myself from Rachel, I learned not to make disparaging judgments about her behavior—or mine—but to look for the causes of that behavior in familial and societal histories. I also saw that I was letting this very close identification with Rachel hold me back, keep me in check, because my work was making me feel very powerful. And I was terrified of feeling powerful.

⌒

I wake up in the middle of the night from a dream. The dream is easy to describe, difficult to comprehend. Ishtar—the many-breasted goddess—with a face vaguely like that of Virginia Woolf but resembling my mother, in profile, has placed her hands under my armpits and has picked me up. Her face is impassive. She does not look at me, does not recognize me, stares past me. She begins shaking me—not violently, but powerfully and rhythmically. As she shakes me, all the things that define me as a woman fall off. They form a pile beneath my feet. As she continues to shake me, still staring beyond me, impassively and without emotion, what is left of me begins to shrivel into the baby doll that I remember having in my childhood. The only openings I have, now, are the hole in the middle of the little red mouth where you put the toy bottle and the one where the water runs out, between the legs. I begin saying, in the doll's voice that I remember, "Mama, mama." Ishtar stares impassively ahead. But she stops shaking me.

⌣

Working on Woolf's composition of *The Voyage Out* was my first long project. One that would take years. It terrified me and it thrilled me. Sometimes I would feel immensely powerful, feel that I, singlehandedly, might change the course of Woolf scholarship. Or I would feel impotent, wondering how I could make any contribution to our knowledge of Woolf.

I learned what it is humanly possible to do in one day; what one cannot do; that one must trust the times when no work is getting done, because it is in those fallow periods that the unconscious mind is working. I had to change the way I thought about time. I had to scale down my expectations to a human level. All of this was very hard for me to do.

Every time I sat down to the project, my infantile power fantasies reared their ugly heads. I always thought I would get more done in one day than it was possible to do. Then my feelings of potency would turn into feelings of powerlessness and despair. I slowly learned that the work could proceed only as quickly as it could proceed. (I have not entirely learned that lesson yet.) I learned that I have the same trouble that anyone else has in working, in writing comprehensible sentences, in revising them, but that if I worked every day, the work would get done. I gradually realized what working on *The Voyage Out* for seven years must have been like for Virginia Woolf. I too was working on a project that was taking a very long time.

There was the temptation, too, to work constantly, without interruption, to get it done more quickly. There was the temptation to work incessantly—

days, nights, weekends—at the mountain of manuscripts, at the letters, diaries, and journals that Woolf had written while composing the novel.

From time to time, my husband reminds me of a moment in the days preceding our marriage. He was at work. I was at our apartment. The place was filthy. I was trying to clean it so that we could move in. All the stores in the neighborhood were closed because of some holiday. I decided that I would clean all the tiles in the bathroom. The only thing I had that would do the job was a toothbrush. So, instead of waiting for him to come back to help me, instead of waiting for the next day to get a scrub brush that would speed the work, I took the toothbrush to the tiles. When he came to pick me up, I was exhausted and miserable, but also triumphant because I had finished.

At the beginning, much of my work on Virginia Woolf's composition of *The Voyage Out* was like that day with the toothbrush.

⌒

One day, after two years of work, I went to the Berg Collection to begin work, as usual, and discovered to my chagrin that the manuscripts of the novel were not now in the order in which Virginia Woolf had written them. Why I had not noticed this before is beyond me. The Berg Catalogue clearly states that each of the manuscript groups was composed of various drafts. On the day I realized that I would have to sort, sequence, and date the thousand or so pages of manuscript, I became slightly sick. I even believed that I was being punished for having been grandiose in my expectations. I knew nothing about dating manuscripts.

I spent that summer taking an inventory of the manuscripts, noting the watermark on each sheet, the color of the ink, how many perforations it had—anything that might help me sort the manuscripts into drafts. Although I read about the dating of modern manuscripts and certainly learned from the experience of experts, I was also secretly grateful that I had voraciously read Nancy Drew detective novels when I was a girl, that I had learned, through her, to be alert to every possible clue. I went back and reread the thousand or so letters that I had read before, searching now for clues to the dating of those sheets.

One night, at about 4:00 in the morning, I awakened from a dream in which I saw Woolf using the pages from earlier drafts of the novel in later drafts. I had overlooked that possibility. I suddenly realized that if I used the watermarks as a guide, assuming that Woolf had used different kinds of paper during the several years the novel was in progress, I might be able to sort the manuscripts into drafts. I also realized that there was a code to the two sets of page numbers that were on several hundred sheets, now scattered throughout the manuscripts. The paginated sheets might represent one draft—one set of page numbers indicating the placement of the sheet within the draft, the other the page number within a given chapter.

There it was, happening to me—my very own "Ah ha" experience. Just like in the textbooks. I rushed upstairs to my desk and in the space of an hour or so, I had figured out the order of four earlier drafts of the novel. Now I could proceed to study the stages of the novel's development, although I still had to date the drafts.

One morning, on the way to the Berg, I discovered that I had forgotten my see-through ruler, the one I used to measure the sheets of the manuscript. I was passing a stationery store, hesitated, but went in and bought another one. On that day, as I was reading Woolf's letters to Violet Dickinson, searching for clues to date the manuscripts I had already sorted, I was fiddling with the ruler. I put it beside the letter I was reading and suddenly realized that the sheet was the same size as the paper Woolf had used in one of the drafts. I quickly checked the watermark. Sure enough. The letter was dated. That accident enabled me to date, to my satisfaction, one of the major drafts of the novel.

Now I was ready to do what I had always wanted to do: analyze the composition of the novel in conjunction with the events that were occurring in Woolf's life.

I remember sitting in the Berg, surrounded by a thousand sheets of paper, while others were on their holidays swimming and sunning themselves, thinking, "This is where I belong. I am in my element."

As I recorded the progress of Virginia Woolf's days to figure out what she was doing as she was writing *The Voyage Out*, I started realizing that this was one hell of a woman, filled with incredible energy, so different from my original impression of her. Reading about her life in London, her visits to

the British Museum, the books she read, the jaunts down to Sussex on weekends, the trips to St. Ives, to Wells, to the Lizard, to Lelant, Cornwall, the
walks, the work, the lived life, fruitful beyond my wildest imaginings, her
engagement with the most important political and social issues of her day,
her teaching of working-class people, I began to revise my picture of her
and my hopes for myself. I decided that it would be foolish of me to spend
endless days alone inside libraries working on Woolf when the great woman
of my dreams had spent no small portion of hers walking around the countryside, cultivating important relationships, particularly with women, taking
tea, learning to bake bread, teaching, getting involved in politics, becoming
an essayist, a novelist, integrating work and pleasure, and having what seemed
to me, in contrast to my confined scholarly life, a hell of a good time.

That's when I bought my first pair of hiking boots and started walking,
first around the lower reaches of New York state and then, at long last,
through Woolf's beloved Sussex and Cornwall and later through Kent,
Cumbria, Northumbria, Yorkshire. I retraced the trips she took while she
was writing *The Voyage Out*; visited the places she visited; read the books
she read; began having important friendships of my own with Woolf
scholars; started teaching; began writing essays, started writing poetry;
wrote a novel.

In 1975 I was on my way to Brighton to Sevenoaks to see Knole, Vita
Sackville-West's ancestral home, delighted by the likelihood that Virginia
Woolf herself had traveled these very roads to see Vita Sackville-West when
she was writing *Orlando*. We had just come through a small stretch of moor
that smelled powerfully of damp and peat when we saw a road sign that
read, simply, "Sevenoaks," the village in which Knole is located. When I
saw that sign, I began weeping, inexplicably and uncontrollably, filled with
a sense of myself newly born, capable of working and having fun, capable
of enjoying my life's work. This was released somehow by that sign and the
sense it inspired of the flesh-and-blood reality of the Virginia Woolf who
had passed, a long time ago, by that very spot to go see a friend, a lover,
another woman.

I thought that I would like to write about these two women, about their
friendship, about their love affair, about their work. I thought about how the
creative act has been misconstrued by many as a solitary and solipsistic act

and how we must correct that misapprehension; we must write about the creative act as it is nurtured by loving friends.

1976

I am sitting outside a speech therapy room, balancing Lyly's *Euphues: The Anatomy of Wit* on one knee and a yellow pad of paper and some note cards on the other. What I am trying to figure out as I sit here, waiting for my four-year-old son, Justin, to finish his session, is whether any part of Virginia Woolf's conception of *The Voyage Out* may have been related to her knowing this work. After all, she *did* say that *Euphues* was the germ of the English novel. Is there any evidence that *Euphues* may have been the germ for hers?

I open the book. I am delighted to find that there is a character called Lucilla in the work and that, for Euphues, she is an inconstant woman (another *puttana*). In Virginia Woolf's 1908 draft of her novel, one of the central characters is called Lucilla, and I become convinced, as I sit here, that the presence of a Lucilla in *Euphues* was no accident.

I glance, occasionally, through the one-way mirror and watch the therapist working with Justin. Every time he sounds a letter correctly, which is virtually impossible for him to do, he gets an M&M candy. Today, because they are working on *s*, the most difficult sound for him to produce because he cannot hear it, he is angry because he hasn't gotten very many M&Ms and he *loves* M&Ms and this is the only place where he is allowed to have them (the therapist's amazingly successful strategy). I know I am going to have my hands full when his session is over. Maybe an ice cream cone will help. Chocolate chip mint, his favorite.

⌣

A while ago we had been told that Justin's hearing is severely impaired. Or rather, *I* had been told. One of the teachers at his nursery school had called and told me that Justin responds to commands only after he sees other kids doing something. I was too unconscious in those days of my own needs to understand that taking your child to a specialist to find out whether he has a hearing impairment is not something you should do by yourself, even if you are a tough woman.

And so there I was, on a rainy day, in the elevator, on the way to the appointment my husband had made with the specialist, by myself, holding Justin's little hand, thinking, maybe he *is* hearing impaired and not emotionally disturbed. I had been secretly afraid that this extraordinarily difficult child, who had been an absolute angel as a baby, who never cried, who slept all night almost from the beginning, had become the way he was because I had gone back to graduate school. I shared my private fantasy with no one, partially because to share it would have been to admit that something might really be terribly wrong, and in admitting that something might be terribly wrong, I might have to confront my fantasy that I had caused it. Sitting in the doctor's office, holding Justin on my lap, I listened as the doctor said, "Yeah, we seem to have a deaf one on hour hands."

I will never forget those words. I will never forgive that doctor his callousness. I will never forget choking back my tears, swallowing my vomit, as I sat holding Justin on my lap, thinking, I must not let this child see me crying about him, not here, and not yet, hating myself, hating the doctor, hating my fate yet again.

But on the way back to the car, we walked, Justin and I, through a rose garden adjacent to the hospital, and, by now, the rain had stopped, and the sun had come out, and the sun was hot, and the roses were so beautiful, and Justin tugged at my hand and looked up at me, as I touched his tangle of red curls, and I thought, "What do I do now? What's to become of him now?" And he said in his garble that only I could understand, "Mommy, mommy, so happy, the sun," and I knelt down, and hugged him, and cried and cried and cried, but I knew he was going to be all right, and I knew that it hadn't been my fault.

What strikes me now, although it did not strike me that day in 1976, is the insane incongruity of my reading *Euphues*, the most esoteric and highly cultivated prose in the English language, while my son struggled to utter his first comprehensible sounds, while a Vietnam veteran, a multiple amputee, struggled, in the room next to Justin, to let go of his rage and speak again, while a woman who had had cancer of the larynx struggled, in the room on the opposite side, to belch up her first sound.

In the acknowledgments to my dissertation (which became my first book), I wrote, in a kind of code, about how Justin had been a model of "persistence and patience for me to emulate," how, during the years when my study was in progress, I had watched "Justin learning to express himself." And printed, in very large letters that he could understand (because by now, in 1980, he was eight years old, and chattering away, and able to read), in his very own copy of my first book (which he insisted that I give him), "Thanksgiving Day, 1980. For Justin—Who was near me while I was writing this whole book and who learned a lot in that time. I love you. Mom."

What I didn't write to him then, but what I write now, is how much I *learned* from him; how, in watching the struggles of a little boy with a voice that no one could understand, I learned to be less angry about the impediments to my own expression. Finding my own voice was, after all, not so difficult a task compared with what I saw him and others experiencing. If he had the guts, surely I did too. After all, he was made out of the same stuff that I was. As he found his voice, so I found mine.

⌣

I finished my dissertation and turned it into a book, *Virginia Woolf's First Voyage: A Novel in the Making.* My next project became the editing of an early version of *The Voyage Out* that Woolf called *Melymbrosia.* An early version of the first novel of one of the greatest literary stylists of the twentieth century might prove useful, I thought, not only to scholars but also to common readers. I had been immensely excited when I first read through the pages of this submerged draft, seeing how different it was from the version that Woolf chose to publish. It was more radical politically, more overtly lesbian in its subject matter, more contemptuous of the patriarchal establishment.

The work of editing the draft went like this: I would go to the Berg Collection and hand-copy pages of Woolf's typescript of the earlier version. (There were 414 pages that had to be copied.) I could copy about 15 or so pages on a good day, but I always expected myself to do better, to do more, as if I were in competition with my own limitations. The work taught me what it was like to be a medieval scribe. I couldn't Xerox or photograph the pages of the manuscript because of the Berg's policy but also because there were many sets of corrections on the sheets in various ink colors (impossible to detect in copies), made at different times, and I was incorporating only the earliest in my transcription.

After I copied a day's pages, I would take my transcription home and type it. Then I would take my pages back to the Berg and proofread them against the original. Again I would take the typescript home, make corrections, then bring the corrected typescript back to the Berg and check that the corrections were correct. (These were the days before computers, so each time there were changes, every page had to be retyped all over again.) Next I would write textual notes. Then I would type the textual notes; proof them against the original; make changes; bring the changes back to make sure they were correct; and so forth. I began to imagine myself in Purgatory.

I come to the breakfast table one morning during this time, trying to shake the effects of a night's work. My twelve-year-old son, Jason (he was six when I began), usually cheerful in the morning, is sitting at the table in a foul, rotten mood. He glares at me. I ask him what's troubling him. He tells me that they had a discussion in his English class about the generation gap. Do I realize he's the only student in the class who sees his mother less than he sees his father? Do I realize my work is killing him? That he hates it? That he can't stand that I'm at my typewriter when he comes home from school? That the sound of the typewriter keeps him up at night? That he needs his sleep?

He begins sobbing. I want to hold him but he won't allow it. I recall that the only time this child has ever had an uncontrollable temper tantrum was on the day he overheard me talking about beginning my second book. He looked at me and said, "Second book?" Then he threw himself off his chair onto the floor, began shrieking and beating his fists against the floor. When I calmed him enough so he could talk, he told me he thought when I finished the first book, he would have me back again.

I understand why he's so angry. My work takes me away from him far more often than he would like; yet at twelve, he's beginning to want to separate himself from me. I ask him if he thinks anything I've done has rubbed off on him. I love his compositions. He writes the most wonderful works of fiction. He says no, emphatically, no. Nothing at all about my work has ever done him any good.

He calms down as quickly as he's flared up. He asks if I'd be interested in hearing the latest composition he's written. I say I am. He pulls a sheet of paper out of his notebook. It is the biography of an imaginary character, John C. Lectica. As Jason reads to me, I think, *A chip off the old block.*

Autumn 1978

I receive a copy of the *Virginia Woolf Miscellany* in the mail. There is an article by Virginia Woolf's nephew, Quentin Bell, who controls her literary estate, entitled "Proposed Policy on Virginia Woolf's Unpublished Material." (An editor later tells me that originally it had been entitled "The Bottom of the Barrel," as in "scraping the bottom of the barrel.")

It reads, in part:

> A short time ago a reputable scholar suggested the publication of an earlier version of one of the novels [Bell is referring to my work on *Melymbrosia*], not only because it would be of interest to other scholars but because it could be offered as—in effect—a new novel to the "generalist Woolf reader." This, I must say, arouses acute misgivings—suppose that the reader agrees with Virginia in condemning the earlier version, suppose that it is below her usual standard? Then, surely it is unfair to give it currency. Some such deflation of values follows any inflation of published matter [and] must surely be apprehended. Scratch the bottom of the barrel and you will come up with impurities.

So here Quentin Bell was, misrepresenting a letter I sent to him asking for permission to publish the earliest extant version of *The Voyage Out.* I argued that publication would enhance our understanding of Woolf's creative process. He suggested that I'd be publishing it as if it were a new novel of Woolf's I'd discovered. But what struck me then—and strikes me now—is his use of the word "apprehended." My desire for a general reader to see Woolf's early work is represented, by Bell, as if it were a crime.

In the past six years of my life, I have probably spent more time working with Virginia Woolf's works than I have doing anything else. My work has become more important than my life. As I face the possibility that *Melymbrosia* might never be published, I must look back over my life to try to salvage something of myself, to try to see clearly what of my past I have tried to bury in my work.

1956

I am thirteen years old. I have begun my adolescence with a vengeance. I am not shaping up to be the young woman I'm supposed to be. I am not docile. I am not sweet. I am certainly not quiet. And, as my father has told me dozens of times, I am not agreeable: If he says something's green, I'm sure to respond it's orange. I have mastered every conceivable method of turning my household into turmoil, or so my father says. I have devised a method of looking up at the ceiling when my father lectures me that drives him into a frenzy.

In the middle of one of these frequent outbursts, I run out of the house, feeling like I'm choking, the tears hot on my cheeks. It's nighttime. I have no place to go. But I keep running. There are welcoming lights a few blocks away. It's the local library. I run up the stairs. I run up to the reading room with its engulfing brown leather chairs, pull an encyclopedia down from the shelf, and pretend to read so I won't be kicked out. It is cool and it is quiet. My rage subsides. I think if there's a heaven, surely it must resemble a library. I think that if there's a God, surely she must be a librarian.

It Is 1957

I am fourteen years old, standing behind the window of the bakery where I work to earn spending money. Inside the bakery, I have to control my appetite or I will eat everything in sight and become grotesque and obese. You can't let yourself do that because boys like only attractive girls, and attractive girls are always slim. What I do inside the bakery is fold paper boxes before I put the pastries and cakes inside. And then I tie up the boxes with red and white string that always tears into my flesh.

Across the street, through the window, I see my friends playing endless games that involve laughing, touching, rolling on the grass. I am behind the plate-glass window, looking at life, looking at them having fun, locked away, earning money by putting buns in bags and cakes in boxes.

On Halloween, children come and paint the plate-glass window. They paint witches and goblins in black and in primary colors. Now I can't even see what's happening in the park. But I still put the buns in bags and the cakes in boxes. It never occurs to me to even fantasize breaking through the window while I'm working or to wash the paint away. Or, more simply, to open the door and cross the street to the playground. Work is work. And work permits no play. I have to work. That is the way it is. Opening the door to let in the sound of laughter while working, crossing the street to the playground after work, learning to enjoy work and learning to be able to play will take many years. And psychoanalysis. And work on Virginia Woolf.

Autumn 1962

I am a senior at Douglass College. In 1962 Douglass College is the kind of school a bright young working-class woman can afford. Douglass is filled with brilliant women, and I've never before been surrounded by so many. I have studied Shakespeare with Doris Falk, the novel with Anna Wells, philosophy with Amelie Rorty. I now have Twentieth-Century Fiction with Carol Smith.

Carol Smith is lecturing on Virginia Woolf's *To the Lighthouse*. She is talking about the relationships between Mr. and Mrs. Ramsay in the "Window" section of the novel. I have never in my life heard such genius. I am taking notes, watching her talk, and watching her belly. She is very pregnant. She is wearing a beige maternity dress. I take down every word, while watching to see when the baby she is pregnant with will kick again.

I learn to love Virginia Woolf. I observe that it is possible to be a woman, to be brilliant, to be working, to be happy, and to be pregnant. And all at the same time.

1982

I am interviewed about how an Italian American woman like me became a Woolf scholar. I search my memory, think of studying with Carol Smith, and suddenly remember my fascination with the figure of Cam Ramsay in *To the Lighthouse*. Cam Ramsay, the child Mrs. Ramsay virtually ignores, so busy is she with her son James; Cam Ramsay, the child who is "wild and fierce." The child who clenches her fist and stamps her feet. The child who is always running away, running away. The child who will not let anyone invade the private space she's created to protect herself in this family with a tyrannical father who strikes out with a beak of brass.

I remember my own adolescence. Could it be that I have seen something of myself in Cam those many years ago and that in trying to understand the relationship between Cam Ramsay and her creator, Virginia Woolf, I am also trying to learn something about my own past? Aren't I now in the middle of a long essay about Virginia Woolf as an adolescent, reading her 1897 diary, a tiny brown gilt leather volume, with a lock and a key, that must be read with a magnifying glass, so tiny and spidery is the hand, an essay that's given me more satisfaction to write than anything I've yet written about Virginia Woolf? And haven't I been stressing Woolf's capacity to cope, rather than her so-called neurosis, in that difficult year? Could it be that in concentrating on Woolf's health, I am also trying to heal myself?

1968

I'm married, and enduring my husband's medical internship as best I can, on next to no money, with a baby who never sleeps and who cries all the time. Although I am twenty-five, I look fifty. I have deep circles under my eyes. I have no figure. I'm still wearing maternity clothes.

I had put my husband through medical school. (According to him, I *helped* put him through medical school—his parents paid his tuition and gave him a small allowance, and I worked as a high school teacher and paid for everything else.) In that internship year, we came very close to divorce. Your basic doctor-in-training-meets-gorgeous-nurse-and-wants-to-leave-his-wife-and-small-baby story.

One day, I look in the bathroom mirror and decide that I will either kill myself or I will go back to graduate school and become economically independent as quickly as I can. I look into the medicine chest, thinking that if my husband leaves me with this baby, I will probably be young, gifted, and on welfare. After wondering whether you could kill yourself by taking a year's supply of birth control pills and fantasizing that, with the way my luck is running, I might grow some hair on my chest, but I probably wouldn't die, I decide that I'll go back to school, get a Ph.D., and teach in a college. I also realize I might buy some time by squelching the young-doctor-leaves-his-young-wife-for-nurse script, at least temporarily, by announcing to my husband that if he leaves me, *he* can have the baby. Then he and his sweet young nurse can contemplate how romantic their life together will be with this baby who cries and throws up all the time.

He tells me he doesn't believe I can part with my child.

I say, "Wanna bet?"

Shortly thereafter, he decides to hang around for a while longer.

⌣

The way I write this now, the "tough broad" tone I take is, of course, a disguise for how hurt I was, for how seriously betrayed I felt. And I really don't know what I would have done if he *had* left me. Unlike many of my friends, my husband *did* stay. I had done everything I was supposed to do. Clipped coupons. Made casseroles from *Woman's Day* with noodles and chopped meat and cream of mushroom soup for all his friends. I had laughed at the story of how Doctor X fucked Nurse Y in the linen room adjacent to the O.R. and how the surgeon couldn't figure out where the grunts and groans were coming from, without paying too much attention to how Mrs. X or Nurse Y might feel about having this sexual conquest the subject of our dinner table conversation. And I didn't think at all then about how the medical profession institutionalized the sexual and economic servitude of women.

I had done everything you were supposed to do, the way you were supposed to do it, and he still wanted to leave me. And that profound disillusionment, that rage at the preposterous hoax that society plays on young women by convincing them that if they do everything right for their men, their men will stay with them forever, I can still feel to this day.

I had been a high school teacher early in our marriage, but that wasn't what I wanted to return to. I now wanted a different career. And my own money. And access to the public world. I wanted to carry a briefcase. I wanted to carry a briefcase while walking down the path at a college, with students to my right and to my left, engaged in serious, important, intellectual discussions about literature. And I never wanted to depend on a man again as long as I lived.

⌣

When I first learned that Virginia Woolf had spent seven years in the creation of *The Voyage Out*, her first novel, I thought that surely she must have been mad for that, if for no other reason. But as I carted off copies of *Melym-brosia*, my reconstruction of the earlier version of that novel, to the Editor's Office of The New York Public Library some seven years after *I* had begun working with her novel, I reflected that I have come to share a great deal with this woman. I have come to be a great deal like her in her attitudes toward the male establishment and art and feminism and politics; I have learned from living for seven years with her to take the very best from her while managing, through the example of her life and her honesty about it, to avoid the depths of her pain.

She has been very good to me, this woman.

In looking back over my life, I realize that my work on Virginia Woolf has helped me make some important changes.

Before I worked on Virginia Woolf, I wasn't a feminist. Before I worked on Virginia Woolf, I didn't know how strong a woman she was. Before I worked on Virginia Woolf, I whined a lot, like my Italian foremothers, about how men got all the breaks and about the ways they abused their women. But I didn't really understand that a social structure had been organized to keep men dominant and women subservient, and I really didn't understand how important it was for women to be economically independent, and the potentially horrifying consequences if they weren't.

Before I worked on Virginia Woolf, I would ask the young doctors who came to our house for dinner if I could get them another cup of coffee, being careful to wait until there was a break in the conversation. Now my husband, Ernie, and our children—Jason and Justin—get up to cook me breakfast. Virginia Woolf has, in many ways, created a monster in me, and I am proud to give her partial credit for it. I like to think that she would have been pleased that my reading *A Room of One's Own* has been a very important part of my emancipation from the tradition of the suffering woman.

Now I am a hell-raiser, a spitfire, and I buy and wear "Mean Mother," "Nurture Yourself," and "I Am a Shameless Agitator" buttons. I have recently started to pump iron (much to the amusement of fifteen-year-old Jason—the would-be writer, the one who used to throw up all the time, who has turned out to be a very nice kid after all—and eleven-year-old Justin, who has something to say about everything I do). But sometimes, when I'm feeling really good and have the time, I still make them bread pudding.

⌒

I think of what Virginia Woolf has done for my generation of women, of Woolf scholars. I think of what she has taught us.

There are the political and feminist messages in *A Room of One's Own* and *Three Guineas*. The anti-authoritarian, anti-patriarchal stance. The exposure of the inequities between the way men are treated and the way women are treated. The difficulty of being a woman and being a creator.

Woolf unleashed our anger. Allowed us to use it constructively. She has taught us the value of work; the necessity of art; the necessity also of a feminist politics. She taught us how to express ourselves as women—in our lives, in our work, in our art.

Woolf was interested in the writer behind the work, in what she or he was like—what kind of house she lived in, what her writing schedule was like, what she ate for breakfast, how she dressed for dinner. She was concerned with what literature and memoirs revealed about the history of the times, its morals and mores. The pages of her essays and her notebooks are filled with questions and answers about the human beings behind the works of art, about the implications of art for humanity. Woolf taught us that writers are human beings, that writing is a human act, that the act of writing is filled with consequences for a society and for its readers. No "art for art's sake." Instead, "art for the sake of life."

She understood that literature, by its very nature, is a powerful didactic instrument and, therefore, as potentially dangerous as it is edifying. Literature teaches us when we are young about the way we are supposed to behave and about the consequences of certain kinds of behavior. Woolf reminds us of how profoundly influential literary texts can be in the formation of character and in the formation of a nation's character.

I imagine Woolf thinking, "What one must do is write a literature of one's own."

28 March 1941

Virginia Woolf commits suicide by walking into the River Ouse with rocks in her pockets. My mother and father are courting. World War II is raging. Many years later I ask my mother if she remembers hearing about Virginia Woolf's death on the radio. She says no. Maybe she read Virginia Woolf some time later when she was pregnant with me? *The Years?* It was a very popular novel. She says no. She'd never heard of Virginia Woolf until I started talking about her.

The fact that Virginia Woolf and my mother were alive at the same time, breathed the same air, so to speak, lived through the same war, is mysteriously significant to me. The fact that my mother was beginning a new life with my father when Woolf was ending hers seems laden with meaning. What can explain the fact that I am devoting a very large part of my life to this woman with whom I have absolutely nothing in common?

She is English, purely and highly bred. I am more Italian than American, rough, tough, a street kid, out of the tenements of Hoboken, New Jersey. We have absolutely nothing in common, except for the fact that we are both women.

And that, I realize, is quite enough.

ADULTERY STORIES

I

Unless you consciously (or unconsciously) want to propel yourself into committing adultery, reading about it isn't such a good idea. Because reading about it, I can assure you, will almost certainly result in your thinking about doing it, and perhaps even in your doing it.

Dante understood this. For in the *Inferno* of his *Divine Comedy*, he recounts the story of the beginning of the adulterous affair between Paolo and Francesca.

Francesca explains to Dante that one day, while she and Paolo are reading about Lancelot and Guinevere, their erotic desire becomes so uncontrollable that they drop the book and yield to impulse. Francesca explains: "He kissed my mouth all trembling: / . . . That day we read no further." And Gustave Flaubert knew this, too. For in his novel *Madame Bovary*, the properly raised Emma's reading about "love, lovers, sweethearts, persecuted ladies fainting in lonely pavilions . . . and . . . gentlemen brave as lions" leads her into clandestine love.

And what was my husband reading before he started *his* first affair, the one that almost ended our marriage when our first son was still an infant? The James Bond novels of Ian Fleming. And how could his life—working every other night and every other weekend as an intern and living on very little money, with a new baby and a depressed wife stuck in the farthest reaches of the New Jersey suburbs—compare with James Bond's?

But if he couldn't be 007, he could, at least, fuck around like 007.

2

The cycle seems to go something like this.

You read a book about adultery. Maybe you stumble into reading it. Maybe you seek it out to juice up your life. The book captures your fancy. You find this curious. You become obsessed by it and can't put it down. You read it whenever you can, ignoring the sexual signals your partner sends your way. ("Not tonight, I have a headache," you say, as you turn your back to her or to him, and continue reading.) Reading about clandestine sex, you're finding, is ever so much more exciting than having sex with a familiar partner.

You tell your friends about the book. You talk about it more than anyone wants to hear about it. If you tell your partner about it, their eyes glaze over, or they look at you strangely. (This should be a warning to them, but they're too wrapped up in their own lives to notice.)

You measure your humdrum life against the passionate and dangerous lives depicted in the novel. The risky phone calls. The clandestine meetings. The intimacy (eyes locking, fingers touching or brushing, tongues licking). The fabulous sex (positions you haven't tried; acts you haven't performed; places you haven't fornicated). And you find your life wanting.

You begin to find your partner boring, and their little endearing habits (the way he sucks his teeth, the way she twirls her hair) revolting. You are unfulfilled. Your job sucks. Your life sucks. Your clothes suck. You need a complete makeover. A lifestyle change.

You realize you've never lived fully, or freely, or erotically (whether or not you have). You've done what you're supposed to have done, what your parents wanted you to do, what your partner wants you to do, what you have to do for your kids. You've never done what *you* want to do. Not once. Not ever.

Unless you begin to find out who you really are soon, you tell yourself, you may as well not bother trying. Life is passing by quickly. You're twenty-five, or thirty-five, or forty-five, or fifty-five, whatever. You don't have that much time left, so you'd better start living life to the fullest. Now. After all, you only have one life to live, and this one isn't a dress rehearsal.

Everything that, a few days before, seemed wonderful (your partner, your home) and meaningful (your life together, your job) and adorable (your kids, the dog, the cats, the guppy—well, maybe not the guppy, who has a terrible habit of shitting long strands while you're having dinner), everything that, at the very least, you thought was bearable and tolerable (the messy house, the state of your marriage) now seems trivial and meaningless. A compromise. A trap, even.

You feel caged. You feel suffocated. You have to to find a way out. Soon. Now. You want romance in your life. You need romance in your life to come alive. Without it, you'll continue to feel dead inside. This is, you tell yourself, the first day of the rest of your life.

⌣

A few days later, you see someone you know, maybe someone you work with, and that person suddenly looks different, has an aura, where previously the person was just someone you worked with or for. And (if you're a woman), you start batting your eyes, and tossing your hair, and making trips past his desk to the bathroom, and you're wagging your ass a lot more than usual on the way there, and he notices you. Or (if you're a man), you're puffing out your chest, you're exaggerating your gestures (and knocking things over as you do so), and you're laughing louder than usual ("Har, har, har," you hear yourself chortling in response to someone's stupid joke at the water cooler, which happens to be close to her workstation), and she notices you.

You meet for lunch. You talk. You pretend you're talking about work. You lock eyes. She patterns your movements, you pattern hers. Soon you're telling each other you've never felt like this before, this has never happened to you before (and you believe it). You tell each other that you don't want to change your lives, that you really respect your husband/wife/partner, and you don't want to hurt them.

You debate the pros and cons of having an affair. You realize you can't shut this off. Still, you tell yourself you can compartmentalize this relationship, tell yourself you'll keep it in its proper place. After all, you're grownups, not kids.

⌣

Finally, you arrange a meeting. At her place (when her partner is away) or at your place (when yours is), even though you know this is risky, or at a motel or hotel about three-quarters of an hour away from where you live—no one will know you there. Or you go to a business conference separately, affecting surprise when you meet—"What are you doing here?"—and you use the stairs instead of the elevator to get to each other's room, and one of you checks the hallway to make sure the coast is clear before you leave.

The sex is fantastic, or great, or good, or not so terrific, it doesn't really matter. Because it's the thrill of what you're doing that you're not supposed to be doing that's really so fantastic.

Soon you realize it's not about sex, not really, it's *the talking about sex*—about whether you want to keep having it, about when you're going to have it, about how good it's going to be when you have it, about how good it was the last time you had it (even if it wasn't), about how you can't stop having it (even though you're not having it all that often), about how you would die without it.

If you're smart, you say these things to each other only face to face (preferably after requesting a full-body search of the other person to look for hidden microphones and cameras, after assuring yourself that all portable devices are turned off and stowed away). You do not leave a message on a phone, whispering these things. You do not e-mail, or write a letter, or text, or send a lascivious photo, or tweet, or post anything on your Facebook page. You do not keep a love diary in which you sound like a moron (as Edith Wharton did after she started her affair with Morton Fullerton). You do not write a memoir (as Louise "Ludovica" Pradier did—she was Gustav Flaubert's sometime lover, and he cribbed parts of it for *Madame Bovary*). In other words, except when you're face to face with that person, you keep your mouth shut.

You do not tell anyone, not one person, not ever. You do not intimate that something transformative has happened in your life when people ask you why you look so good. (Your answer, if you're smart: Weight Watchers, aerobic exercise, and meditation.) Even so, it's likely that many people will learn exactly what you've said to him, to her, exactly what you've done. Your lover, in a moment of boasting, tells one person, and that person tells a few others, and those few tell a few more, and so on, until thousands of people who don't even know you will know. (Remember the lessons you learned about geometric progression. Remember how things go viral on the Internet.)

Or maybe you're the one who starts the ball rolling. Maybe you persuade yourself that it's all right to tell just one person, someone you trust. Because now you have a new and exciting story to tell someone about who you are, a new and startling story to tell yourself about who you are, and you just can't keep it to yourself.

3

Adultery stories take on a life of their own. They are traded like precious baseball cards or stock tips. Other people take possession of the narrative. The narrative then becomes public coin. Although people begin their adulteries to change their lives, to take control of their lives, to author their own existence, people almost always lose control of their adultery stories, and then they lose control of their lives because of their adultery stories. As my husband lost control of his adultery story, because I have written about it, and will continue to do so as long as I choose.

Sometimes adultery stories end tragically—this is common and it entails discovery, disgrace, the breakup of families, the termination of public careers, and possibly even death—murder and/or suicide (as in the suicide of an acquaintance who stabbed himself in the heart and left his lover to find his body and the mess he'd made of the kitchen); tragic adultery stories are the kind most commonly found in fiction—William Styron's *Lie Down in Darkness*, Kate Chopin's *The Awakening*. Some have unforeseen consequences— they seem not to damage the marriage of either party, but years later, after both are dead, the affair is discovered, say, by someone rifling through an ancestor's letters and diaries, and the revelations they contain change everyone's opinion about the lives of the dead. Some end happily enough, as in Sloan Wilson's *The Man in the Gray Flannel Suit*, in which a husband and wife acknowledge the child the husband has sired in Italy during World War II, and the wife understands the circumstances—the brutality witnessed, the terror of impending death—that drove her husband to seek comfort in another woman's bed.

Then there is the retaliatory adultery story. As in Flaubert's *Madame Bovary*, which attacks his lover, Louise Colet. As in Henry Miller's entire life's work, which traduces his wife, June, for abandoning him for her female lover. As in Virginia Woolf's *The Voyage Out*, which satirizes her sister Vanessa's husband, Clive Bell, in the character Mr. Dalloway—Woolf and Bell had a highly charged emotional and possibly erotic relationship after her sister gave birth to her first child.

4

About ten years after my husband told me that he was having an affair and was thinking of leaving me and our infant son, and soon after I learned that he was attracted to, but not sleeping with, another woman (or at least that's what he told me), I awakened in the middle of the night, crept out of bed quietly (so as not to disturb him), went into the kitchen, and started baking corn muffins.

I took up a pad of yellow paper and started to write an adultery story of my own, a retaliatory narrative, although I didn't realize it then. After it was completed and perhaps, published, my husband, if he chose to read it, would never know whether it was a work of the imagination, or whether it was based upon my own experience, whether I, in fact, had had the affair that was described in the narrative.

It was 4:00 in the morning, and an unlikely time for baking, but not an unlikely time for writing about adultery. The house was still, our two sons were sleeping upstairs, and I'd been having the most wonderful erotic dream, and not about my husband.

I will not bother telling you what was happening in this dream. Writing it down would make it seem far more foolish and far less pleasurable than my experience of it. Because you yourself have no doubt had such a dream, you can, therefore, surely imagine what mine was about, so I can spare you the details. All I will say is that what I was very much enjoying took place in an apartment in the meatpacking district of New York City, that I was doing something I don't ordinarily do with my husband, and that, in the dream, it was raining, that I had arrived at that apartment breathless, drenched to the skin, my body luscious and lubricious under my white shirtwaist dress, and that I wasn't wearing any underpants.

In my dream I had forgotten my umbrella, which is why I had gotten wet. This was something that, in waking life, I never would have done. In real life, I would have checked the weather forecast before going into New York, both in the *New York Times* in the morning, and then, again, on WINS 1010 radio just before I left. I would have had my umbrella; I would have had my raincoat; I would have been wearing something dark and sensible; and I most assuredly would have been wearing underpants.

Sometimes (and I was in my mid-thirties at the time), I'd still dream of Roy, the boy I'd loved in high school. In my dreams of him, we never age. We are both still seventeen, the age when last we met, though it was not the last time I saw him. In my dreams he is still my one, my only true love, though in waking life, I surely love my husband, must love him, for now we are married some seventeen years or more and have gone through so much together, and I've never cheated on him, not really, and we'd tried hard, and succeeded, in repairing a marriage that was nearly shattered so soon after it had begun, although now, again, and surprisingly (for these moments always come upon us unexpectedly), it seemed as if our marriage was in danger of ending, yet again.

In my dreams of Roy, we make love, as we once did, out of doors, under harvest moons, and on wet grass. Or in darkened basement spaces adjoining rooms where our friends are having parties. Or in cars in parking lots after basketball away games. Or on a ledge of the New Jersey Palisades overlooking New York City.

On the frequent mornings of these sweet dreams I have about Roy, I linger long in bed while my husband rises to make our coffee, awaken our children, search the kitchen for something for us to share for breakfast, feed the cats, and let the dog outside to shit and pee. In time, when the clatter in the kitchen can no longer be ignored, I rise, reluctantly, and leave my bed, and kiss my husband good morning, and kiss my children good morning.

5

On this night, however, the subject of my dream was not my adolescent lover, Roy, but an unrecognizable Italian man, about my own age or somewhat younger. This dream signaled trouble. So I knew I had to do something domestic quickly. Which is why I started the convection oven. Which is why I dragged out my worn and stained copy of *The Joy of Cooking*. Which is why I started making corn muffins at 4:00 in the morning.

But while the corn muffins were baking (and by now they were browning nicely with perfectly formed little crowns on the top, which meant that, distracted though I may have been, I had mixed them perfectly), I found a pad of yellow lined paper, and picked up my favorite pen, and started writing fiction, something I hadn't done before.

What I found myself writing that night (or morning, actually), while my corn muffins were baking, was this:

> The day before Helen MacIntyre began to have her second affair, she got up in the middle of the night to make her children cornmeal muffins for breakfast. She figured it was the least that she could do for them. Somewhere in the corridors of her memory, she remembered reading a *Woman's Fellowship Cookbook* in which muffins were embarrassingly and fatuously referred to as "love bundles."
>
> Although she wasn't one of those foolish women who would have referred to cornmeal muffins as "love bundles," nonetheless, any time Helen MacIntyre had even begun to contemplate the possibility of having another love affair, she found herself awakening in the middle of the night, unable to resist the impulse to combine a cup of this, a jigger of that, and to sit in the silent kitchen with yesterday's *New York Times*, hearing the reassuring sound of her convection-turbo oven starting up, which always reminded her of a jumbo jet turning on its engines and always gave her a feeling of power and potency, as if she herself could fly here, jet there, on a moment's notice.
>
> She thought about how long it had taken her to appreciate sensation, about how preoccupied she had been for all those long years with all those substitutes for eroticism that women find in women's magazines, substitutes designed to keep their hands occupied with knitting needles and with wool, instead of roving, roving over the silent silken bodies of younger and more sexually active men than their hard-pressed, hard-working, upwardly mobile husbands.
>
> She watched her cornmeal muffins rising, rising, perfectly formed, a solace to her children on the morning of the day when she would put on her hat and coat, grab the express bus into the Port Authority in New York, and meet the younger man who had been described to her some

time ago as sexually voracious. It now sounded very good to her, although she confessed to herself that at the time she had been horrified.

As she walked to the bus station, she saw an old woman in the arms of her daughter being carried—dragged, really—up the stairs into her house. Helen looked away. Not that the image pained her, but for a moment the fact that she was on her way into New York City to see this man at the same time this old woman was just barely managing to negotiate a flight of stairs made her imagine herself 40 years from now, being helped up her own stairs by one of her children. And would she guess then that the younger woman hurrying past with such energy and purpose might be on her way to a day of joy and exquisite bliss? Would she remember?

The last time she had gotten involved, Helen had made sure that it was with a discreet, three piece—wearing tax accountant with a wife and five children in the suburbs, whose idea of infidelity was to drink endless cups of cappuccino opposite her at a fancy midtown restaurant at lunchtime. Nice and safe. Nice and companionate. The illusion of adultery without the risk.

He would talk about his children; she would talk about hers. He would talk about his foreign investments; he would give her advice about starting hers. He would talk about his wife and her sexual inadequacies; she would sigh and stare at the dregs of her coffee and wonder whether he would ever reach slowly, slowly across the table to touch her face and stroke her hair.

The only erotic thing that they had ever done together was to fornicate desperately and quickly one evening on the top of his desk amid tax forms and debentures, but that was largely because he wasn't going to see her for the three months that Helen would be in England that summer, and she had brought a bottle of wine up to his office at closing time.

Now that really was something, she had thought deliciously to herself when it was over. Now that was adultery in the truest sense of the word, and it was wonderful. But it was no harbinger of their future relationship. As soon as Helen returned in September, they resumed their routine of cappuccino and sympathy, a rather banal and boring substitute for what she had come to regard as the real thing.

Actually it had all started this time, she thought, because of John Travolta. For when she saw John Travolta in his white suit, dancing, dancing amid the flashing lights and pulsing sounds, something within her surfaced, and all she could do was smile with imbecility and sink back into her seat, hoping that no one in the movie theater could see her lips part and moisten and her hips thrust forward involuntarily, in the first moment of wantonness and lust that she had experienced in her adult life.

A few days after that Helen made her first lasagna, and served it to her family with a blank smile. The children looked at her puzzled, because she'd told them many times that she didn't like pasta and that she wouldn't cook it for them. They wondered if she was having a midlife crisis because she had also been very generous recently and had taken them to see "Saturday Night Fever" four nights in a row.

But her time had come now. At last.

In her more rational moments—and she was having fewer and fewer of those the closer she was getting to her fortieth birthday—Helen realized that she had been pushed over the brink this time because her son had become a vegetarian. Only another woman would understand that it was this, and not her husband's string of infidelities, that had been the very last straw, the one that broke down her resistance and cast her, once again (but in the real sense this time) into the group of women she'd read about but never, in her earlier years, dreamed of joining—Molly Bloom, Anna Karenina, Hester Prynne—all those interesting, evil, faithless women in fiction, women who'd never been Cub Scout den mothers, who'd never sat through interminable flute recitals, who'd never seen their children portraying roosters in spring pageants.

She would stir the vegetable soup she was cooking and contemplate with some deliberation how she could break out of her circle of misery, of meaninglessness, that was, these days, defined by boxes of bean curd and jugs of foul-smelling protein supplements, remembering the veal stews and the chicken soups of her glorious past.

If you were a woman, Helen thought, *you turned out to be either a Mrs. Portnoy or a Hester Prynne,* and from her current vantage point, she'd rather be up on the scaffold in the sunlight with Hester than in the kitchen cooking eggplant blintzes.

Once, soon after she'd seen "Saturday Night Fever" for the fourth time, when the house was quiet and empty, Helen took off all her clothes, put on the soundtrack from the film, and leaped and pirouetted around the family room in imitation of him, watching her breasts flash and her buttocks gleam in the mirror, until she fell onto the sofa, smashing her face into the pillow, laughing in embarrassment, and then crying hot tears for the profligate she'd never been.

Still, it wasn't the vegetarianism itself that she minded so much but the shelf full of packets of kelp, seaweed, and other vile and nasty bits of detritus from the ocean floor that reminded her of her girlhood. They reminded her, they reminded her of what she would try to avoid in the seawater in those early and idyllic childish days when she had first discovered love, when all the world depended upon a young man's watery kiss, a young man's hand holding yours, and whether or not you could jump higher than the next wave.

6

In the eleventh grade, in American Literature, we read *The Scarlet Letter*. Although we spend much time reading this work, and discussing it, the teacher never mentions sex and never defines adultery, even though we talk about Hester's punishment. But *I* know what all the fuss is about in Salem.

I have a different take on the book from those of my teacher and most of the kids in my class who talk about crime, and suitable punishments for crime, and honesty, and hypocrisy. For I know the novel is a fraud. And I say so. But the teacher ignores my remark.

I have been reading Puritan history for background, and I know that the punishment for adultery in Puritan New England isn't wearing a nicely embroidered *A* on your bosom, standing on a scaffold, enduring the censuring stares of townspeople, and then voluntarily and rather defiantly sticking around the community while you raise your out-of-wedlock child and eventually become an angel of mercy.

I know the least severe punishment for adultery was one or two severe public whippings, potentially life-threatening because of the possibility of subsequent infection. Women convicted of the lesser crime of fornication were whipped and had their children taken from them. So I knew that Hawthorne's novel rewrote history and presented the destiny of an adulteress as far less severe than what actually happened.

Some years ago, I found my high school copy of *The Scarlet Letter*. Leafing through it, I read its underlinings and marginal notes—some, it seems, dictated by the teacher: "Dimmesdale should have confessed his deed so he, like Hester Prynne, could have been joined to the rest of humanity through publicly proclaiming his guilt."

But one comment stood out, revealing the rebel I was. Next to a description of Hester's ennoblement through suffering, I had written in red pen, underlined and with three adolescent exclamation points, the single word "*Fool!!!*" For I didn't think Hester *should* have spoken openly about her relationship with Dimmesdale—I thought it was needlessly self-sacrificing for her to bear the consequences alone. But neither did I think Dimmesdale was wrong to hide his "sin"—I thought that private sexual behavior should remain private. Perhaps it was because I hoped I could keep my intimacy with Roy, the boy I loved through high school, private. (I was too young and naïve then to understand that this was impossible.)

Studying the novel made me angry. I railed at the class discussions about who should or should not have been punished for their sins, about whether their sins should have been openly admitted so punishment could be meted out. Why assume that Hester and Dimmesdale *had* sinned, even according to Puritan standards? I wanted to talk about why women were thought to be fundamentally base. I wanted to discuss whether adultery or infidelity was ever permissible, and under what circumstances. I wanted to discuss the horrific punishments inflicted by Puritans—Hawthorne's own tyrannical forebears had ordered Quaker children into slavery, the starving of Quakers to death, the boring of holes through women's tongues with red-hot irons, the cutting off of men's ears, the hanging of women as witches. But these were never mentioned.

Why, I wondered, were we reading this book? To warn us about the consequences of adultery (but we weren't married yet)? To teach us that if we girls behaved like Hester we might find ourselves with a little Pearl to raise by ourselves?

7

When I was involved with Roy, I wrote poems. A sheaf of them. Penned at the desk my father had built for me, where I was supposed to be studying physics and geometry. I'd carefully filed them, according to date, in an innocuous folder marked "Fragments" that I'd saved through the years.

After I married, I assembled them into a manuscript I called, for want of a better title, *Kinds of Love*. I thought I might submit them for publication, and one or two appeared in small magazines, but then I lost interest in the poems and filed them away.

When I turn forty-five, I realize that if my husband or children find them after my death, they might be taken for poems I've written as a grown woman, as an adulteress. There is so much pain and yearning in them, but also so much ecstasy, that they could signify that I had been involved in an illicit affair.

And so, on an icy winter day when my marriage and my children mean very much to me, and not wanting to cause my family pain, I spend part of a tearful afternoon when I am alone rereading them. I tear the manuscript into tiny little pieces and throw them into my wastebasket without regret.

But not before I memorize a few. Like this one, called "La Mer": "I would like to make love to you just once with our bodies all salty from seawater / so that we could begin by licking the crystals from one another. / You would go first because I can never wait. / And then it would be my turn. / And we would taste each other slowly, pulsating to the rhythm of the sea as it surged outside."

And this one, called "Left Ventricular Fibrillation": "Today I understood for the first time that the heart has parts / and that while one part of the heart has experienced a rent, a fissure that will widen or heal itself / depending upon whether or not you come back to me / the other part of the heart can go on doing things that hearts do / like pump blood from here to there / although I cannot imagine why the heart should want to continue doing these things at this particular time."

That evening, when my husband is collecting the trash, he takes my wastebasket, brings it into the kitchen, and empties it in a flurry onto the remains of our evening meal.

"Are you okay?" he asks. He points to the trash. "Looks like you had a hard day writing," he says, cinching the garbage bag shut.

In fact I'd had a very good writing day. After destroying all my poems, I'd taken out a sheaf of pages of a story I'd started writing a few years before called "Gluttony and Fornication" that began: "The day before Helen MacIntyre began to have her second affair, she got up in the middle of the night to make her children cornmeal muffins for breakfast. She figured it was the least that she could do for them."

8

When I'd begun that story, my husband and I were going through a difficult time. There was, he'd told me, another woman, but I shouldn't worry because he wasn't sleeping with her, he was merely entranced by her. But he said he would never again do anything to jeopardize our marriage, as if by telling me he was only entranced by her and not sleeping with her he wasn't already jeopardizing our marriage.

"Please believe me," he said, which was the tipoff that I shouldn't trust a word he said.

Here we go again, I said to myself. I told him I'd like her telephone number so I could arrange for the three of us to get together to discuss the terms of the dissolution of our marriage, who would get what, who would live where, and the joint custody of our children and our numerous animals (snake, guppy, cats, dog, hamster).

"I want her to know what she's getting herself into," I said. "It's only fair."

"But I'm not leaving you," he said.

"I understand," I said. "Let's just call this a prophylactic encounter."

Was I pissed off? Certainly. Was I worried? Surely. But by this time, I had a good job, a good salary, a house in a joint property state, and, unlike the first time he almost left me, I knew I could take care of myself, and I'd begun to persuade myself I might be better off without him.

A few months later, we hadn't yet had that meeting. I'd called her. And called her. Left messages. But, not surprisingly, she never returned my calls.

But my husband was in therapy, trying, he said, to deal with this crisis. Would I give him some time to resolve this? Of course, I said. I wasn't going anywhere at the moment. My husband told me he was making good progress; he was avoiding her; he was beginning to understand why he behaved this way; I didn't have to worry. It was something about having had an adoring mother, he said. *It's something about your being an asshole*, I thought. And so we planned a conciliatory family trip to Maine.

I can tell you without equivocation that Maine is the wrong place to go on a family holiday if your marriage is in trouble. For aside from eating lobsters, and picking wild blueberries, and looking at the water crash against the rocks, there isn't anything to do but hang out with the people you came with. Which is fine if you're happy. Which we weren't.

I was driving our car along one of those winding Maine roads by the seacoast to our miserable little cabin heated by a wooden stove. We'd had a good enough lunch of lobster; we'd taught the kids how to eat them; we'd pretended to act like an ordinary family on a holiday.

As we came to an especially dangerous stretch of road, Roberta Flack's "The First Time Ever I Saw Your Face" came on the radio, and my husband started gazing out the window with a look I had come to recognize as the *I'm pretending to look at the scenery but I'm thinking about the other woman* kind of look.

"What are you doing?" I asked.

"Oh," he responded after a few seconds, "just looking at the scenery."

I knew he wasn't looking at the scenery, because he didn't look at the scenery ever, not even when, years before, we'd driven through the Alps, or along the French Riviera, or through Provence, or along the Mediterranean coast.

I pulled over to the side of the road.

"Get out of the fucking car," I said.

The kids started crying. They knew us. The knew it would go from bad to worse.

"What do you mean?" he asked, all innocence.

"Don't bullshit me," I said. "You're still seeing her." Whereupon he started shouting. And I started shouting. And the children started crying even harder. And he got out of the car.

So there he was, walking alongside the road, my husband, whom I hated intensely. And there was a cliff. And so I decided to run him over. Or to use the car to ever-so-gently nudge him over that cliff so he'd smash onto the rocks below.

I was very clear about this. I wanted him dead and I had the means to make it happen. I was thinking it through, gauging which would be better—running him over and squashing him, or watching him plummet to his bloody and mangled death below.

If I killed him, it would have been a crime of passion. But, no, it would have been premeditated murder. And so, I reasoned, a capital crime, punishable by life imprisonment or the death penalty if Maine had the death penalty: "Murder aforethought." I realized, too, that if he'd been the one to run me off the road onto the rocks and if I'd died, he'd have had an easier time of it than I would have. A man who kills his wife because she committed adultery gets off easier, you may have noticed, than a woman who kills her husband for the same reason.

I can't say what stopped me because I fully intended to kill him. Perhaps the recognition of the consequences of my crime. Or perhaps my children in the back seat of the car, crying. Perhaps it was the thought that when I returned to that horrible cabin, I would make blueberry muffins with the kids from the gorgeous berries we'd picked earlier in the day.

For throughout that difficult sodden lunch (it had been raining), all I could think about was making those muffins. I hoped that, somehow, they might rescue this disastrous holiday. I saw myself with the kids in that horrible kitchen in that disgusting cabin redeeming the holiday by mixing the muffin ingredients, baking them, smelling their aroma, sharing them with the kids, but not with him.

But perhaps it was this, too. From when we set out on our holiday, as I drove the long stretches of highway heading north, with my husband asleep in the front seat, my kids asleep in the back, I'd started thinking about how one way of my getting through this time was to write something. Something about adultery. But this time, I wouldn't write about him. I would write as if I were writing about me. I'd create a fictional persona, a woman very much like me but not altogether like me, who is on the brink of having her second affair. This, I thought, would be a very good way to make him pay. For he would never know, and I would never tell him, whether this story was based upon my life.

So there he is, my husband, the adulterer, walking along the side of the road, and there I am, the wronged wife at the wheel of our car, pulling up alongside him.

"Get in the car," I say.

"No," he says.

"Get in the fucking car," I say. "I want to go back to the cabin and make blueberry muffins with the kids."

And he got back into the car. And as we drove along the seacoast road, on our way to that godforsaken, disgusting cabin, I did my best to memorize what it looked like here, for I knew I'd never come back, that Maine was forever tainted for me, which wasn't so bad, because I hadn't much liked it to begin with because a gritty city street had always appealed to me more than the beauties of nature. And I wondered, too, whether the cabin had a muffin tin, and whether I'd have to scrub it clean, or, in the more likely event that it didn't, whether there was a general store close by where we could buy one.

OLD FLAME

I saw him once in all these years, walking up the steep hill from the bus stop, past my parents' house, on his way home to the house where he lived with his wife. I was outside on the lawn that day with my two boys, interfering in one of their arguments, this one, about which of them was the faster runner, separating them while they tried to pummel each other, shouting at them to cut it out, telling them if they didn't cut it out we'd go home, they'd have time-outs, they'd lose their TV time for a week, and they'd miss their grand-mother's spaghetti and meatballs.

It was summertime because I remember that he had his suit jacket slung over his shoulder, that the back of his shirt was damp with perspiration so you could see the curve of his spine, the fix of his broad shoulders. It was the first thing I noticed before I recognized him, the jacket, the sweat, the back, the shoulders, then the fingers holding the jacket. Those fingers, that familiar hand.

He was climbing the hill from the bus stop at the bottom, where buses running into and from the city collected people each morning on one side of the street and spewed them forth each evening on the other. He was carrying a tattered briefcase and he was holding his head down as he walked, putting one foot in front of the other slowly, as if he were a kind of Willy Loman in early middle life and he didn't want to be where he was, didn't want to arrive at where he was going. *So he works in New York*, I surmised, later, when I had time to think about it, *and he hates it, and he's none too happy about going*

179

home, conjuring his life the way I wanted it to be—hardworking, bedeviled, anguished, like mine—from the wisp of time it took him to pass us by.

In those nights we spent together all those years ago, we had foretold, for ourselves, independent and unfettered lives, filled more with pleasure than responsibility. Our lives would not wind up being anything like those of our parents. No houses in the suburbs, no boring jobs, no kids to drag us down. We would live abroad, moving from place to place with nothing more than a backpack, changing residence whenever wanderlust overtook us. We would read the great books of the world, watch films, see paintings, hear music. In our future, there would be no thankless work, no problem spouses, no children raging at each other, no ailing parents dependent upon our care, no illness, no dying, no death. But whether we would be together, we discussed but once, and concluded that, no, it probably wouldn't turn out that way.

As he passed, he didn't look up at me, made no indication that he saw me, that he saw us, though he couldn't have missed the three of us, what with my screaming, and my boys shouting and flailing at each other on the lawn. And because he knew it was my parents' house, I knew his not looking my way yet still knowing I was there was deliberate, a repetition of how he'd acted in public toward me through all the time we'd been a furtive couple some twenty years before. I believed I could feel the connection between us still, sensed that if I walked away from my children and up to him and reached out and touched him, it would start all over again as it always had before.

I wanted to believe that it could be like it was before, that he thought about me as much as I still thought about him, dreamed about me as much as I still dreamed about him, even though we were each by now married for more than a decade, he, to his childhood sweetheart, I, to a man I had chosen with both my heart and my mind after I'd realized that freedom terrified me and that what I'd really always wanted was a settled life. Before he married her, I'd pretended he'd considered me a potential lifelong partner, and that I was the one who chose otherwise, even though in our shared dreams of the future we'd scoffed at marriage and never mentioned marrying each other. Our relationship—if you could call it that—was lived in a season out of time, in a liminal space far removed from the small town where we lived, and from the more or less traditional lives each of us would eventually choose.

All that talk of freedom on my part had been a very young woman's bravado, a way of pretending to him and to myself that I was someone I wasn't, someone he needn't fear would try to tie him down or take him away from his real girlfriend, the woman he wound up marrying. I wanted him any way I could have him, which meant I never really had him, only borrowed him from her every once in a while. But I also believed I couldn't marry him or anyone who attracted me as much as he did, for then my lust would eat me alive, leaving room in my life for nothing else, a love of children, a life of the mind, the pleasures of the world. If I'd married him, I would have become one of those women who check their husbands' collars for trails of lipstick, who rifle through their mail looking for suspicious postmarks, who listen in on telephone extensions to their conversations. Still, I'd deceived myself into thinking that I'd had a choice. But I doubt he'd ever considered me anything more than a plaything, someone who'd give him anything he wanted anytime, a conquest to brag about in the locker room.

If someone had asked me who he was, I would have said that we were lovers in high school, not boyfriend and girlfriend, though then, and still, what we were to each other meant everything to me. We didn't date; didn't leave parties together; didn't sit next to each other on school buses to away games; didn't acknowledge each other in the halls of our high school. All those things he did with his real girlfriend, the one he'd started dating in middle school when they were barely teenagers, the one he'd dated all through high school when he was fucking me, the one he'd wound up marrying young, the one he was now living with in the little brown clapboard house with white shutters where she'd grown up, around the corner from my parents' house where I'd grown up, a twenty-minute walk down a steep hill and through the woods and up another, even steeper hill to his back door.

Though we ignored each other whenever our paths crossed in public—and they crossed often, for this was a tiny town, nothing more than those two hills and a valley—we weren't fooling anyone. Everyone—his girlfriend, whichever boy I was pretending to care for at the time, his friends, and mine—all knew what we were up to, screwing each other senseless on lawns, in the backseat of his car or mine once we were old enough to drive, in the musty basements of friends' houses when they were on vacation, and why she put up with it, I don't know, but she did through all those years. For me it was pleasure, yes, but more important, it was the sweet oblivion I needed to forget the grim life I led at home, those times I'd climbed out on the roof to escape my father's blows, hidden in the coal cellar in our basement when he was on a rampage, run down the street with him in hot pursuit, all those nights I'd stayed awake until my father fell asleep, wondering what he would do if I killed myself or ran away, and then slept a fitful sleep filled with nightmares.

Those years with him had been filled with pleasure, yes, but also with a bitter yearning. It was a time marked, not by the moments we spent together, but by the times we were apart. Why I did this to myself I think I know, but who can say. My father had gone to war when I was young, and longing for a man who wasn't there was familiar emotional terrain. As a child, I had spent years never knowing whether or when my father would come home, years yearning for him as I imagined him, years constructing him the way I wanted him to be. And when finally and luckily he reappeared—for he wasn't one of the 60 million people killed in that war—he wasn't, couldn't be, what I wanted and needed. Rather, he came back home that diabolical, altogether unfamiliar beast of a man who had been at war, and I became his enemy, the one he continued to fight throughout his life.

⌣

The last time my father came to dinner at our house, he was barely able to climb the stairs. When I'd invited him, I'd wondered whether it was a good idea. If it was a good idea for him to leave his house, given that he could barely make it up and down his own stairs, couldn't make it to the toilet before wetting himself. If it was a good idea for him to drive, suspecting that his driving was a danger to himself and others, having seen the dents and scratches on the car with far too much horsepower for anyone, much less a man in his nineties, losing his hearing, losing his sight, losing his mind. Wondered whether he still remembered where I lived, whether he'd get lost on the way, whether he'd get into an accident and die, perhaps even hoping he would (as long as he didn't harm anyone else) because that would solve the problem of his care. Wondered whether he and his wife could get themselves organized to get out of the house and to our house by a certain time.

I thought he might be able to, because he wore the same shirt, same pants, same socks, same shoes, every day, changing them only when I went to his house and forced him into clean clothes while I did the wash, though I doubted whether she could because she never knew where anything was, couldn't find anything she needed, and my father spent most of his energy returning her things to where they belonged so she could get them and again put them where they weren't supposed to be.

But we'd invited them, my husband and I, together with the rest of the family—his grandsons, their wives, his great-grandchildren—all of us pretending he was still the man he'd been, the one who'd traversed the Pacific on aircraft carriers in roiling seas, fixed airplanes and sent pilots back into combat, made an old and broken-down house habitable and even beautiful, fought fires, played Frisbee in his eighties, stood on his feet all day doing the hard work of a machinist into his early nineties. Now his life moved from his bedroom to his bathroom, down the stairs to the kitchen, into the sunroom, and back upstairs again, one slow step at a time, after a day of trying to find whatever his wife had lost, staring out the window, staring at the television, staring at a book, staring at his wife when he wasn't yelling at her to do what a good wife was supposed to do—fix his dinner, clean the house, make the bed—even though all his wife could do now was sleep, lose things, and wander the house, and this was driving him crazy, she was driving him crazy.

He'd wanted to come to dinner, was happy he'd been invited. I think we both knew he wouldn't be around for much longer. And I wanted him to come, I really did. This was something new for me, my wanting him to come. For years, I hadn't wanted him anywhere near me, though I'd done my daughterly duty—visiting him, making him supper, taking him on holidays, caring for his household—done it far better than he deserved, I'm told. And did it, I know, not for him but for myself, hoping that by my taking care of him he would one day see that I was better than he thought I was.

But here they were, my father and his wife, looking more or less normal. If you overlooked the stains on the fly of my father's pants, the black-and-blues all over his face and hands, a side effect of one of his medications, her disheveled hair, the terror-stricken look in her eyes: Did she even remember who we were?

My father hauled himself up our back stairs, gripping the railing with both hands, pulling his body up to the next step, pausing, and then pulling his body up again. I stood at the top of the landing, wanting to help, knowing that if I tried to touch him, he'd wave me off, and maybe yell, or worse.

"Goddamn stairs," he said, glaring at me, as if I'd put the stairs there just to bedevil him. "Goddamn it to hell."

I stood there, holding my breath, helpless and afraid, watching him and watching him, hoping he wouldn't fall, as he staggered, then gripped the railing with both hands to pause and rest for a few moments, before hauling his once wiry and strong, but now enfeebled and tortured, body up to the next step, and the next, and the next.

This is the way it so often was. Me, standing and watching him. Me, wanting a different kind of father, a phantom father who'd be happy to see me, who'd climb the stairs with good cheer even if climbing the stairs were difficult for him, a father who wouldn't fly off the handle at me for a good reason or for no reason at all. A father I didn't have to lock into the crosshairs of my sightline every waking moment of my life to try and figure out what he would do next and so what I would do next: exchange a few words; leave him alone; try to ignore him; or run for cover.

He wore his usual khaki trousers, plaid shirt, brown belt, sneakers with Velcro closures, the ones I'd bought him—he'd abandoned his work shoes, couldn't get them on his swollen feet. I was relieved to see his wife had on her jeans and a sweater. I'd worried about what she'd wear because she spent most of her time in a nightgown, and changed only when we insisted—"Why bother getting dressed?" she'd say. "I'm not going to visit the Queen."

⌣

To pass the time until supper, my daughter-in-law proposes a game of charades. The children know the rules and my father and his wife have played with them many times before. I suspect the game will end soon because my father won't remember the directions and his wife will have no idea what is happening though she will pretend to know precisely what is going on.

The children go first. Julia is a purring cat. Steven, a baying dog. My father and his wife say nothing. Their mother guesses both. And then it is my father's turn.

"Think of something you want us to guess, and act it out," my daughter-in-law reminds him. "It can be a book, a movie, a TV show, a saying, an object, an animal, anything, anything at all."

My father pauses. Thinks. Picks up a knife from the dining room table. Hoists himself out of the chair. Hobbles into the living room. Hides himself behind the doorway. *This is a very bad idea,* I think, remembering other mealtimes, other knives. But my grandkids are smiling, my daughter-in-law is smiling, they love games, they love my father, they've never seen him become someone else.

At first, we see the knife in the doorway. Then my father's hand holding the knife. Then his face, eyes wide, peering into the room. His eyes are focused, not on us, but on another time, another place. He's on a mission to survive or to destroy.

He sidles into the room, slices the air, disappears, lunges back into view.

"Zorro?" my grandson shouts. My father shakes his head.

"*Star Wars?*" my granddaughter suggests. *No,* my father motions, pissed now, and exasperated.

"World War II?" I say, thinking, *that goddamned war.* But that isn't the answer either. I want to stop this, stop it right now before he scares the kids.

"Come on," I say, "you win, that was a good one, we can't figure it out, tell us what it is."

My father relaxes. This time I've been lucky, averted catastrophe.

"Couldn't you tell I was flushing out the enemy?" my father asks. I have heard my father's war stories about how, when the Allies landed on that island in the Pacific where he was stationed during the war, there were still Japanese soldiers dug into the beach, hiding in caves, secreted within the interior. You never knew when one might emerge from the jungle at night and lob a hand grenade into your Quonset hut, killing you and all your buddies. When a soldier, who'd tied himself to the top of a tree, would fire on you when you were out on patrol. When one would emerge from the bush under cover of darkness and slit your throat as you slept.

"But what does it mean, 'flushing out the enemy,' and who's the enemy?" my grandson asks.

"You never know," my father answers.

"I'm sorry you had to go to war," I say to my father one day when I'm visiting him. We're on the sun porch, having tea, passing time.

"You're not sorry for me," he says. "You're sorry for yourself."

⏝

The summer day I saw him coming up the hill carrying his briefcase with his jacket slung over his shoulder, he and his wife were living in her parents' house where they'd moved after her parents died so they could care for her younger brother. I'd heard this from a friend of mine who, in high school, had disapproved of us and, in adulthood, made it her business to tell me whatever she knew about the two of them, not because she thought I still cared for him, but to prove how wrong it had been of me to interfere in the lives of these two very good people who were so obviously meant for each other.

Yes, this was a blessed thing they did, giving over their young married life to the care of a difficult teenager, so that it still wasn't just the two of them, as in high school it hadn't been just the two of them because of me. They continued to live in the small town where they'd lived as children, coddled by the familiar, I imagined, when I thought about their life, still living in the town I'd planned to leave as soon as I could, and did, which in the '60s meant marrying, which I did, as much to get out of my parents' house as to begin a life with a man who suited me. So when I saw him walking up the hill on that day, he was well-married, according to my friend, and I would have said that I was well-married, too, although my carefully chosen husband, for a time, had been doing what I had been doing all through high school, living a double life, loving one person and fucking another, and perhaps was doing this still. And so I learned what his girlfriend, now wife, must have felt through all those years—betrayal, impotence, resignation, determination, despair, hope, rage—and after all this time I admitted the wrong I'd done, the pain I'd inflicted on her and on myself too.

It was a way of life I worried I would continue after I married, for I feared I was incapable of fidelity or, rather, I feared I couldn't meet the demands of being a wife and mother without something else, someone else in my life. I never suspected that my husband, a man I chose because I believed him to be solid, loyal, and true, would ever be unfaithful. But he was, and I stayed with him, we stayed together. I thought I understood why he'd done it—that we married too young, that I forced him into marriage, that he needed to take some time away from his responsibility-filled life with me. I didn't condemn him though I felt betrayed. I didn't want to lose him, but even more, I didn't want to lose our life together, didn't want our sons to lose their father. I wanted my marriage, however complicated it turned out to be, just as she must have wanted him.

After I saw him that day, I began to dream of her (and perhaps of myself too). In my dream, she was a red-breasted bird and he had plastered over the entrance to their nest, walling their babies inside while they were crying for food, and when she came back to feed them, she smashed into the place where the entrance to her nest had been, and bloodied herself, and I observed all of this, and found him, and said to him, *Your wife needs help.*

⌐⌐

I'd bumped into his wife once in a health food store one town over from where I lived about ten years before my father came to dinner for the last time. The morning I saw her, she was dressed in a turquoise jogging suit and brand-new sneakers. She was wearing makeup and her hair was coiffed and she looked just like she had in high school, a perfectly-put-together kind of person. I was wearing a faded black sweatsuit and growing out my formerly black-dyed hair to its natural gunmetal gray, and although I often began my day with a smear of lipstick, on this day I wore no makeup and had bags under my eyes from a sleepless night. I was searching for an eggplant for a simple pasta sauce and we met in the aisle between the vegetables and the vitamins. I was holding two eggplants, one in each hand, and she was holding a wire basket full of bottles of vitamins and supplements.

"Hi," she said. "Hi," I said. We smiled at each other the same phony way we had in high school. "So," I said, "I see you're buying vitamins."

"Yes, we try to stay healthy," she said. "We," a locution I'd never used in any conversation about him and me, except when I told my best friend, "Last night we fucked." And there they were before me, she, all blond and tanned and athletic in her royal blue and white cheerleading uniform, cheering for him after he scored a winning basket. And there I was, hunkered down behind a book in a seat in the corner of the bleachers, trying not to witness what was happening.

She motioned toward the eggplants. "I see you cook," she said. "You must spend a lot of time in the kitchen."

"I do," I retorted; "we like to eat well and it takes my mind off writing." I'd been told she knew I had written about her husband, my lover, and I'd heard that it bothered her, although I'd never admitted to any of our mutual friends that he was the boy in my books.

"Oh," she said, "you're still married? We all thought you'd be divorced by now."

She turned away, toward the checkout counter, before I could reply, and I watched her go. I had questions I couldn't ask her, questions she wouldn't know the answers to, about how he was and whether he was happy, and if he ever thought about the time we were together or dreamed about me as I dreamed about him still.

⌒

When I took the call that came in the middle of the night to tell me that my father had died, I said to myself, *I'm glad that's over,* although, of course, it wasn't, because in a way, it had just begun. I struggled back to sleep, into a dream. In the dream, my father is in the bed in the nursing home where he died. His body is covered with a shroud and he has a hood over his head and wrappings around his face.

I stand at the foot of the bed, watching. I don't want to stay, but I can't leave. I say to the body in the bed, *Can I go now? Are you really, really dead?* My father pulls his hands free of the shroud, pushes the hood off his head, unwraps the swaddling from his face, sits up, looks at me, and says, *Not yet.* Then he lies back on the bed, pulls the shroud up around him, and leaves me standing there, knowing that it would start all over again, our life together.

⌒

During the last weeks my father was alive, we spent hours looking at re-productions of his favorite paintings. It was a quiet, pleasant intimacy we'd rarely shared. "Sometimes," a nurse told me, "angry men like your father find their other side for a little while." Though he'd never visited a museum except when my parents took their only trip to Italy, my father loved art, especially the paintings of Leonardo da Vinci, Michelangelo, and Raphael, whose works he studied in the *Time-Life* books he bought. Often, after a long day's work, he would sit and leaf through a volume until my mother called him to supper.

During the last weeks of his life, it was Michelangelo's *Last Judgment* that captured his attention. What can it have been like for him, so close to death, to look at Michelangelo's work, to see the newly buried, the skeletons of the dead, the book of sinners, the hand of Christ committing them to Hell, the devils massed under a fiery sky, Charon's boat ferrying the damned to Hell?

My father pointed to an old, gray-haired, flaccid-breasted sinner whose body was encircled by a snake, its mouth clamped around his genitals. "Death's got him by the balls," my father said.

My father never told me whether he believed in Heaven and Hell, or whether he believed he would be reunited with my mother after his death. He never told me that he was afraid to die, never wondered what would become of him after his death. Instead, he ran his coarse workingman's fingers over the bare flesh of angels, sinners, and saved, as if to touch life one last time.

⌒

On a sunny spring day during the last year of my father's life, I arrive at the nursing home where he lives, am told that he is in the garden, playing Checkers with one of the aides. The garden is his favorite place on a warm day. It's in a courtyard, bounded on all four sides by the brick walls of the buildings where the elders live, some in apartments, and some, like my father, who need more care, in hospital-like rooms. I find him there often, either sitting alone, appreciating the newest blossoms in the garden planted by volunteers, playing Checkers with an aide, or talking war stories with another World War II veteran who always has a map of a significant battle splayed out on the table between them. I've heard my father tell his buddy about the time he rescued a man who'd set himself on fire, who was burned so badly, his penis fell off; the time he saw thousands of men incinerated when a munitions ship exploded because of negligence; the time he was commanded to set a warehouse and its stores on fire after the war was over, and how the toxic fumes felled many men, and how he escaped the worst of it by running upwind, but how he was

affected anyway, and how he started coughing that day and has been coughing ever since.

I pause for a moment, watching through the window as my father plays
Checkers, wanting to go to him but wanting to delay my entrance. I don't
want to interrupt his good time, yes, but I can't tell which father will be
awaiting me.

This aide knows how to handle him. Whenever he won't take his medicine,
struggle with his walker into the dining room, or change his clothes, she's
called, and he does what he's told, just for her, my father says. During our
meetings, she tells me how delightful he is—how he makes other patients
laugh by pretending to jog in place while holding onto his walker; how he
proposes marriage to the nurses; how he is the first to volunteer during
afternoon karaoke sessions.

My father smiles at the aide, shows her how to win. I am baffled by his
joy, wondering what I can do to elicit such a smile. "When you come back
from seeing him," my husband says, "you look like a dog that's been beaten,
but that sidles up to its master trying to win his love."

I walk into the garden, kiss his blotchy cheek.

"Can't you see I'm busy?" he snarls. So I go to his room and she stays with
him, neither of us wanting a scene.

When I see her later, she'll say, "Honey, it's got nothing to do with you;
it's just his disease."

And I'll respond, "It has everything to do with me; it's not his disease,
it's him."

When he returns to his room, my father says, "You still here? I thought
you'd gone home." The aide leaves and I try to help him into bed.

"Don't touch me," he says. "You get out of here. You kidnapped my wife.
You put me in this motel where they're starving me to death. I know what
you want. You want my money."

He grabs me. He's old, he's weak, he's not hurting me. But when I try to
push him away, get away from him, I can't.

"Nurse," I shout, "Nurse."

The nurses know about how my father can turn on me so that it will take
three people to pry him off me, three of them to wrestle him into bed, three
of them to hold him down while another nurse, a very strong woman, evades

whatever he might have in his hand (a pen, a fork, a knife), takes the syringe, plunges the needle into his arm, presses the plunger down, and sends him on another trip to oblivion.

"Has he always been like this?" a nurse once asks. When things don't go his way—and they rarely do—he pulls the sheets off his bed, upsets his tray, throws a framed photograph across the room.

"Worse," I say, remembering smashed crockery, overturned furniture, broken clocks, days of my avoiding him, days of blessed silence, days of his trying, and failing, to patch together whatever he'd destroyed. To the nurses, it's a case of senile dementia. To me, it's more of the rest of my life. "Your father came back after the war, a changed man," my mother had told me.

⌒

On the day my father comes at me after he plays Checkers, I flee the nursing home, run to my car, start it up, drive, not home, but onto the highway, not knowing where I am going, then knowing where I will go, to the town where I used to live.

I want to see my old flame's house even though I know I won't get out of my car to ring his doorbell, won't invade his privacy, won't try to see him. It is something I feel compelled to do, something I've never done before, something I'll never do again. For what I want now, what I want back is not him, but how I felt when I was with him.

His wife and he had moved from her parents' house into his parents' house high on a hill, the house we'd made love in so many times. From his porch, he could see my house; from my porch, I could see his. And we'd talk on the telephone some nights, and I'd look out my window at the light in his window, imagining myself there instead of where I was.

Back then, I told myself, all I wanted, all I needed, was sex with him, and often, but I wanted my independence even more, and I didn't want to be tied down, as if this were a decision I'd made, rather than a condition imposed upon me by his loyalty—if you can call it that—to her, because he wouldn't leave her for me. Yet this, too, his not leaving her because of me, was another kind of gift, a gift from her, who showed me what it was like to be loyal and faithful to someone who was not, who showed me, too, that a good completion takes patience and a very long time. But I do remember a night in a glassed-in porch in his cousin's house, when I asked him whether we could ever be more to each other than what we were, and I think he said, yes, though he might not have, and I think I laughed and said, but then we would spoil this, and then I think he laughed, and said, why the hell would we want to do that, and then I think I said, I don't know anyone who has what we have, and if we became a couple, we'd take each other for granted, just like everyone else, and then I'd be fucking someone else, and you'd be fucking someone else, just like we're doing now, so let's not spoil it.

During the last year we were together, we both said we'd see each other the night before each of us married someone else, and then never again, although that never happened, because by then we'd lost touch.

Sitting in the car outside his house, I remembered one midsummer night when we fled the stifling heat inside his bedroom, went out back, took off our clothes, and lay on the grass, and I was grateful, now, for the time we'd spent together. With him, for the first time, I could unclench my fists and touch, could breathe and inhale summer air, could open my eyes and see the sky above, could feel the breeze on my body and the ground beneath. And I realized that I didn't use him to forget my life at home. For what I had with him, I know, felt more like salvation.

MOVING ON

When our moving company delivers boxes to the house in Teaneck, New Jersey, where I've lived for more than thirty years, and dumps them onto the floor of our living room, the place I sometimes retreat to in late afternoon to drink a cup of tea and gaze out the stained-glass window to the trees beyond our neighbor's house across the street, I begin to live in that liminal space you inhabit when you're moving. After the boxes arrived, I entered what the composer and writer Allen Shawn called the "huge crisis" of moving: "It's actually true," he's said, that when you move, "you are losing a part of yourself and you are going to have to rebuild a sense of where your center is." For that room was transformed into a place I was leaving—it no longer was a cherished space.

I thought of all the good times this room had seen. The family gatherings at Christmas to open presents. The writers meeting to drink tea and talk shop. The friends sitting and enjoying a drink before dinner. But I also thought of all the opportunities for enjoying this room I'd missed. The fires I hadn't made on windswept days. The times I hadn't lingered to see the sun set through the stained-glass window. The journal entries I hadn't made while reclining on the sofa.

On the night of the boxes, I have a dream, one of those heart-pounding dreams from which you awaken in the middle of the night that taint the next day and the day after that. In my dream, the boxes come, and there are so many of them, they fill up the entire living room, floor to ceiling. They are piled everywhere, on top of the furniture, in the spaces behind the furniture.

Inside the room, there is no light, for the windows are covered over. In the dream, I see the boxes from the kitchen, try to walk into the living room, realize this is impossible, know I can never remove the boxes, they'll be here forever. I know I can no longer stay in this house, I must grab my keys, climb into my car, get away. But once I start driving, I have nowhere to go, but I don't want to go back to the place I had, until now, called home. In the dream—and this is when I awaken—I drive and drive and drive.

What will I become in my new home? What will become of me?

Why had this house become so important to me that, unlike my friend who moved from place to place without mourning the life she left behind, I so dreaded leaving it? It was, I knew, the first place that was a true home for me. One where I felt sheltered and comforted rather than threatened and beleagured. There had been that apartment on Fourteenth Street, the one my parents and I lived in during the war where their hopes of making a safe haven for our family were annihilated. The apartment next to my grandparents on Adams Street where my mother and I moved after something terrible happened to her when my father was away, the one my father returned home to, a changed man, the one my sister was born into when my mother couldn't care for one child much less two, the place where my mother's depression deepened. The house in Ridgefield my family moved to after the war, filled with aspiration and pride but also rancor, sorrow, depression, and violence. The apartment I lived in with my new husband after our marriage; there, I thought, we'd build a new life together different from the one I'd lived before; there, though, another kind of violence—a robbery the week we married, me, escaping while the robber hid in the bathroom ("You were lucky you weren't hurt," the policeman said, "lucky you realized he was in there and that you got out the door before he found you"), and then a murder, the body found near the mailboxes, not by me, thank goodness. And then we fled to the apartment deep in the suburbs of New Jersey, where we'd be safe, we thought, but there, a new baby, an unfaithful husband, another place I cried myself to sleep most nights. Next, another apartment, closer to our parents, where we moved at my mother-in-law's insistence ("We can take care of the baby; you can go back to school"), where I lived my life warily, hoping I had, at last, found a home where I felt safe, but then, another war, my husband drafted, but then let go just before he deployed as that terrible war that ruined so many people's lives ended. Last, and finally (or so I thought), this house, the one our parents helped us buy that signified our family had "made it" in this new land to which our grandparents had emigrated with so very little, hoping that, here, they would be safe. And yes, I was happy enough here and felt sheltered and safe, though my husband and I had our crises, but here I learned to strive for tranquility, and we tried, if not entirely successfully, to abandon histrionics in favor of a settled and tranquil life.

⌐

On the day I begin packing, I realize I'll have to pack every single thing I own. And there is so much that I think, "How can I ever do this?"

I am descended from ancestors who had very little, who came to this country carrying the merest of possessions—their papers, a change of clothes, a gift or two to give to those stateside who might help them. As a girl, I had just enough clothing to make it through the week and one good dress, coat, and pair of shoes. When I went to college, all my belongings fit into one small suitcase. How, I ask myself, did I get from there to here, to this abundance, to this accumulation? And so the very thought of packing fills me with a sense of gratitude, yes, but also with a sense of shame.

Stored in our basement and attic, and in the nooks and crannies of several closets around the house, are all the objects that have come into my husband's and my possession after the deaths of his parents and my mother and my sister. Until now, we haven't thrown them away. We have coexisted with all this stuff without giving it too much thought. We've moved a box of his mother's personal effects off an extra chair in the basement and onto the floor when we've needed the chair upstairs to seat another guest at our table. We've kicked aside his father's toolbox in the storeroom when we needed to open an old filing cabinet. We've pushed aside my mother's old clothes in the closet downstairs to get at our winter coats to bring them upstairs. We've moved my father's toolbox containing my family's papers atop a filing cabinet to make sure it would be safe when the basement flooded, which it did, and often. We've lifted my sister's phonograph albums off the reams of paper we stashed down there when we needed another. And each time we've moved something, there has been that moment of recollection, an elegiac pause in the day's passing.

But now, once and for all, I'll have to decide what to keep, what to let go.

Will I keep my mother-in-law's costume jewelry, pack it up, move it to the new house, or throw it away? Keep the three hand-carved Baroque Italian chairs languishing in my basement, a wedding gift to my husband's grandmother by his grandfather? Is this the time to give away my mother's clothing? My sister's handmade doll's dresses kept so carefully by my mother, a reminder that there were good times in my sister's tragic life?

The rusting sieve my grandmother took to America from Italy that I know I'll never use again? The ugly afghan she made me? Do I throw these pieces of my family's past away? My father's tools? The ones he used in order to make the little suitcase for my sister and the triangular desk that fit into a corner at the top of the stairs in our house in Ridgefield, the best present I ever received, the one I cherished during all my difficult times with him, for the making of it proved he loved me? And what about my grandparents' marriage licenses, visas, passports, birth certificates, naturalization papers, work permits, my grandmother's steamship ticket from her long journey from Naples to New York, each item a small, irreplaceable piece of our family's history?

If I decide to throw away any one of these things, they will be gone to me forever. Will I later regret it? For if anything goes, it is irreplaceable; I can never get it back; a piece of my family's past, obliterated, and by me.

And then there are my possessions, and as I pack them, I become ashamed of all the stuff I have because I pride myself on buying only what I need, turning leftover vegetables into soup or into a pasta sauce for another meal, making bread from scratch, saving chicken bones and vegetable parings for stock. The books I own, the ones by and about Virginia Woolf, Henry Miller, Sylvia Plath, Djuna Barnes, the other writers I adore, the art books, the knitting books, the self-help books, the cookbooks. The notes I've taken for the books I've written. The correspondence (many letters from well-known writers). The office stuff, the paper clips, pens, staplers, reams of paper. The knitting needles, the yarn. The clothing. The hand-knit sweaters, needlework, handmade quilts. My father's stained glass. My sister's, my son's pottery. The kitchen equipment, enough to outfit a small restaurant, for cooking is my passion. Packing, I realize, is a full-scale life review.

What shocks me most of all is the pasta, stashed all over the kitchen and in the basement. Forty pounds of it. Bucatini. Ditallini. Orecchiette. Farfalle. Spaghetti. Spaghettini. Orzo. Croxetti. Tubettini. Enough for more than a year. When I tell a friend, she says I'm hoarding it because of my family's history of poverty, starvation, and deprivation in Italy, because as a child, there was often not enough food, not because my parents couldn't afford it, but because of wartime rationing, because of my mother's erratic and eccentric cooking habits, and because, when I was an infant, she didn't or couldn't feed me.

As I survey all the stuff I have, I vow I will never buy another book, not even another cookbook; never buy a hank of yarn, never buy another pound of pasta until I use what I have.

Still, this packing makes me confront all my unrealized desires. The recipes I've wanted to make but haven't. The sweaters I haven't knit. The books I haven't read. The watercolors I haven't painted. The photograph albums I haven't filled. Makes me see the "too-muchness" of my nature. Too many cookbooks; too much wool; too much pasta. Do I accrue all this because of my family's history of poverty? My mother's neglect? My inadequate sense of self? Do I need all this stuff to remind me of who I am or who I hope I might become?

I know that much of what I own, much of what I have—the paintings, the pottery, the art objects, the journals I've kept, the manuscripts—will outlast me. And that, one day, my sons will have to go through my possessions and decide what to keep, what to throw away, too, just as I had to with my parents' personal effects, and that they, too, will have to decide what to keep, what to throw away, just as I must, and that it might pain them as much as it has pained me. Perhaps, like me, they will hang on to a few totemic objects for a while, then, one day, jettison them from their lives. Just as Kathryn Harrison, in *The Mother Knot*, finally divested herself of her mother's "lingerie, old slips and camisoles," intermingled in a bureau drawer with her own possessions; the "pullover; an evening jacket, two cardigan sweaters; a black velvet dress" she'd stored in her closet; and "a compact of rouge, a concealer stick, and three eye pencils" she hadn't parted with. Just as Paul Auster, in *The Invention of Solitude*, describes how he gave "an armful" of his father's ties to Goodwill;

there were "more than a hundred" of them, and Auster describes how he remembered many of them, and how "the patterns, the colors, the shapes . . . had been embedded in my earliest consciousness, as clearly as my father's face had been"; and how this act of disposing of his father's ties made Auster understand, even more than the burial ceremony, "that my father was dead."

⌒

The day we move, I pack my car with my most precious possessions. Everything I don't want to entrust to the moving men. Thirty-five volumes of my writing journals. A framed photo my husband took of me standing in front of the Dome on a trip to Paris when we were chasing Henry Miller's ghost. A few first editions of Virginia Woolf's novels. A stained-glass lampshade made by my father. My son Justin's ceramic pieces; those of my sister. My son Jason's blown-glass pieces; his pastels. My hand-sewn quilt—five years of work there. My most beloved knitted sweaters. A few pieces of my mother's and mother-in-law's heirloom jewelry. Boxes of family photos. My grandparents' papers. The documents from my father's tours of duty in the Navy. My grandkids' paintings—volcanoes and rockets; flowers and fish. A clock that was my grandmother's, then my mother's, now mine—I stopped the clock, wrapped it in towels, found a safe place for the winding key.

I have persuaded my husband it's better if I go ahead, if he handles the move. He knows I'm lying. He knows I'm capable. But he also knows I don't want to watch the house being dismantled, don't want to see it emptied. But I will come back to clean up after the movers are gone, I promise him.

My husband knows I can't bear to see the bed, where I've read myself to sleep every night, where we've made love countless times, disassembled. Can't bear to see the desk where I've written my books wrapped up and carted away from the sun-filled study where I'd pause to look at the little yard out back during a day's writing, or interrupt my work to run into the kitchen to check on a bread rising, a soup cooking. Can't bear to see my kitchen stripped of all my cooking equipment—my "toys." Can't bear to watch the ornately carved antique wooden dining room table we bought at a junk shop for $60, wresting it away from someone who wanted to paint it white, broken down, wrapped in quilts, and removed from the dining room that was too tiny to properly display it. Can't bear to see our Mark Reichert painting of his wife,

Sally, bought with money we didn't have when we were in our thirties, taken off the dining room wall where it has been silent witness to festive dinners and commemorations too numerous to count. Can't bear to see my mother's gilded mirror with its scallop-shell pattern taken off my living room wall: It had hung there since soon after her death, when my father moved into his second wife's home, and getting that mirror assuaged some of my grief, because having it was like having a memorial to her, and, each day, as I passed it to collect the mail, I could remember her standing in front of it when I was a little girl, patting her hair into place before going out, could remember her adjusting the veil on her hat on the day of my wedding, could remember her gazing into it on the day she went into the hospital the last time, and saying, "Mildred, you look like the wrath of God."

And so I'm not there when the men take all the furniture out of the house; not there when they take out all the boxes of books; not there when all the paintings come off the walls; not there when the rugs are rolled up; not there when my husband closes and locks the door to the house. And so I don't see what I don't yet want to see—the old house emptied of everything that has made it our home, the old house, transformed from being my home into a place that has lost its soul.

～

The morning after our move, I have to go back to the old house to await a service man and to clean up for the new owners. The service man is coming to repair a faulty fire alarm before the fire chief comes to inspect the alarm at noon.

I don't want to go back to the old house. I want to remember it as it was before we left. But I have no choice. I have the day off; my husband doesn't. So it isn't until the day after our move that I see our house empty.

I arrive, admire the garden, which has finally matured just as we are leaving. Will the new owners care for it as we have? Will they deadhead the flowers? Prune away the deadwood? Feed the tree out front that seems to be dying? And if they don't, what then? Will they love the garden as I have? Will they enjoy the blooms on the weeping cherry? Sit and take their lunch outside under the giant oak in the heat of summer?

I turn the key in the lock in the side door. Try to open it—it sticks as always. But today I don't kick it open, for today the door will be someone else's and I don't want to risk damaging it. I take a deep breath, walk into the kitchen. And I feel as I once did when I walked down into the earth in Mexico, down into a tomb devoid of light and air and life, a forbidding and claustrophobic place, one I ran from, for it was a dead place, and what I wanted was life, life, life.

But here I can't run, can't leave. I have a job to do, and I am a woman who does what she must regardless of her feelings. And today my job is to wait for the repairman, make sure the alarm is fixed, and tidy up the house.

Uncomfortable as it is to be here, as much as I don't want to be here, still I yearn to stay. I wonder whether I can call the whole thing off, tell the buyers I've changed my mind, that I really don't want to move, rehire the movers, bring back all our furniture, all our treasures, to this, my one true home, set it up exactly as before, and reinhabit the house.

But, of course, I cannot.

I haven't yet bid a proper good-bye to this house, I realize, and I must, even though I don't want to. And even now this is not the place it once was. It has taken but a few hours to change it utterly: an important lesson for me to remember about life's transience. And although this is still my house—in the sense that my husband and I still own it—it is no longer my home.

I start to say good-bye on the second floor in my son Jason's room. And the empty room fills with the sound of Jason's voice as a little boy of five soon after we move here. He is sitting on his bed, arranging his baseball cards, naming players, and he sorts the cards into piles, happy that he no longer has to share a room with his noisy and irritating baby brother. I see him as a teenager, practicing the bass guitar and singing; hear him rehearsing with friends in the rock band he belonged to; see him dressed in one costume, then another, for the musicals he starred in. I see him as a young man packing up the contents of his room to take to college; see him leaving it to marry; see him helping my husband turn it into an office when our family begins a new business in our home.

I move across the hall to my son Justin's room and smile. For there was always something unusual going on in this room—a boy looking for a snake that had escaped its cage or for a ferret that had somehow burrowed into the insulation in the back of the closet or jumped out the window. A young man trying to mop up the mess a leaking waterbed made, or trying to quiet the far too many friends who crowded themselves into this tiny room. A brave young man venturing farther away than any of us had to attend college. A graduate deciding to move into an apartment of his own, then returning to this room to work with his father and his brother.

Between the bedrooms is the bathroom, always more menagerie than a place for washing and showering, which my sons never seemed to do much of until they discovered girls. Here lived schoolhouse pets that needed boarding for the summer—mice, gerbils, species of fish I didn't recognize. Somehow, and no thanks to our haphazard attentions, they managed to live until we returned them (I, with relief) to their proper classroom homes. Here Jason's monstrously ugly goldfish with protruding eyes, called Gloobie, lived in a fishbowl too small for it and survived for years despite our neglect and mismanagement of his (or perhaps her) ecosystem. When Gloobie died, Jason keened for days, insisted on a solemn funeral with a homemade coffin, a tattoo played on a tin can, a family procession to the back yard, and a rock tombstone to mark the final resting place.

I come to the tiny study—a hallway, really—where I wrote for many years, just outside my sons' rooms. I worked here to be near the children, ready to tend to them as they played or through illnesses or after their awakenings from nightmares while I snatched moments at my desk for my work, then minutes, then hours. I kept my study there beyond when I should have, trying to work against the cacophony of my sons' music as one played the bass, the other the drums, or as each listened to recordings of his favorite band played full blast. But the truth is I wanted to be here, near all that energy, all that action, a necessary counterpoint to my writing life.

In the study, a window just beyond where my desk used to be, and I remember one glorious autumn afternoon, the trees all gold and rust, when both my children were playing outside and I was reading and I glanced up and looked at the setting sun, knowing that I was exactly where I wanted to be, doing what I wanted to do.

"I'll never leave this house," I told myself in that moment.

I head down the stairs, the stairs down which my children never walked but clattered, Justin so quickly that we were sure one day he'd tumble to the bottom and crack his skull. And when we had a dog and cats, the ruckus would be unnerving, with Justin, friends, dog, and cats racing down the stairs as fast as they could to goodness-knows-where. Jason never rushed, even at our urging, especially not at our urging, as sure then as now that nothing is to be gained by moving quickly, that moving slowly, purposefully through life garners more joy than rushing.

Always, when the children were growing, the bottom stairs were littered with objects—looseleaf notebooks, games, clothing, sneakers—they were supposed to carry upstairs but never did unless I threatened drastic punishments. "You'll be sorry when we're gone, sorry when this place is as neat as you'd like it to be," one or the other of them would shout from the top of the stairs.

And the truth is that when they left, I was and I wasn't sorry. Oh, I missed them immeasurably, their affectionate roughhousing, their teasing, their boy-growing-into-young-man charm. But I learned to be in this house differently. I grew to like the house quiet, grew to like the time I had there alone.

Besides, they never truly left. After college, after they moved into their own places, they lived close enough to come to dinner a few times a week, and for Sunday gatherings—we are an Italian family, after all. And when they both began the family business with my husband, there they were again, back in the house, back in their rooms, now offices, as working men who turned the kitchen into the company cafeteria, and at that time, I very much wanted them to leave so I could again have my house to myself.

Downstairs, the tiny sunken living room with the cathedral ceiling and stained-glass window, the reason we bought this house. The proportions are perfect, and whenever I spent time here, I felt as though I were in a chapel, in a meditative, sacred space. For this room is the soul of the house, the place I'd retreated to when in pain, when troubled, when confused.

This room could comfort; it could cure; it could turn a bad day good, a good day wondrous. In this room, I spent long, silent, pleasurable moments replenishing my spirit. Once I spent a whole day in front of a fire quilting, leafing through some books, quilting some more, dozing, awakening to the sound of rain on the roof, watching the sky turn pink, then baby blue, then navy after the storm. I always promised myself more days like that one. The years passed. And though I lingered now and again, it remains the only time I devoted myself to its pleasure for an entire day. How often I have taken it for granted through these years, passed through it with hardly a glance to get the mail, greet a visitor, secure a lock, although when we first moved here, I vowed I would spend a little time here each day. But work, and the daily business of life, got in my way, as these things so often do, and now there is this memory of that one perfect day spent here, and, yes, regret, too, that throughout all those years, there was only this one perfect day. But, I tell myself, at least I had that.

The kitchen, the heart of the house. Aside from my study, I have spent most of my time in this room, lingering over breakfast, knitting sweaters, piecing quilts, making daily plans, reading cookbooks, organizing meals, standing at the stove trying out one recipe, then another, then another, eating with my family.

At this table, left behind for the new owners, my husband read drafts of my works in progress, edited them with respect and kindness. Here, my friend and writing partner Edi and I dreamed a book and then made it happen, as we sat together through long days, drinking cappuccino, eating biscotti, editing essays, marking copy.

To make time pass—for the repairman is late for our appointment—I take the worn broom my husband has left behind for me, and I begin sweeping. I go upstairs, sweep the bedrooms, the bathroom, my study. Return downstairs, sweep my kitchen (*the* kitchen, *their* kitchen), the dining room, living room, front hall, and think how curious it is that I am cleaning for someone else, for, although I clean well when I set my mind to it, it is always with great reluctance; I'd much rather be doing something else—making soup, reading, knitting.

And as I sweep, I try to remember that poem of Emily Dickinson's, the one about sweeping up after someone has died, and yes, this feels like that kind of sweeping. It is a leave-taking, a kind of mourning. I am mourning the home I've lost, hoping I can resurrect its spirit in another place.

But when will the new house become a home? When I've organized its rooms, its closets? Hung our paintings, positioned our pottery on the tops of dressers? When I've cleaned it top to bottom for the first time? Or will it take time? Or will it take not time, but instead a bread baked, a soup made, a journey returned from, an illness survived, a few pages written, a sweater knit, to make the house feel like home?

First, though, I must let this house go. But I can't. Not yet. And won't for some time. And when I leave this house today, I fear that I'll be leaving something of myself behind, something of myself that will never be found again, something that will remain here.

Perhaps we haunt the houses we've left, like the characters in Virginia Woolf's story "Haunted House." In her diaries, Woolf spoke of how in memory she still inhabited her old homes—Talland House in St. Ives where she spent summers as a girl, the house in Hyde Park Gate where she spent her childhood. The little girl she used to be, the members of her family, she said, hung about these places "like ghosts in the shade." For Woolf, the past was never past, for it could be relived; our past always exists, she said, "in some dim recess of our brains," awaiting our attention.

⌒

The repairman comes; he does his work. The fire chief comes; he inspects the alarm. All's well. The house is ready to pass into another family's hands. It's time for me to say good-bye.

When I turn to leave, the house is still, save for dust motes dancing through sunbeams in the downstairs study. Have they danced this way each fine day while I was at my desk trying to wrest words from oblivion, ignorant of what was happening behind me? The refrigerator, satisfied that all is well, turns its compressor off. The sink drips, as it has for years, despite all our efforts to fix it.

The house looks forlorn, as if it doesn't know what to do with itself right now. It looks like a girl no one has asked to dance, that girl sitting at the side of the room, folding her hands and settling them into her lap, awaiting someone, anyone, to end her lonely despair.

But perhaps the house is not forlorn. Perhaps it is pausing. Resting, recovering for a few short days. Gathering the sunlight into itself. Yielding to an indolence it hasn't known for years. For soon it will once again be all business and bustle, all noise and occupation. Perhaps it knows it needs this respite from the chaos it has just endured to face the chaos that is yet to come. All those paintings, photographs, mirrors torn off its walls. Carpets ripped off its floors. Furniture shoved this way and that. Doors thrown open, then banged shut, without the least concern for common courtesy. And truth be told, this house has seen more than its share of strife and disorder, though not recently, thank goodness. Coffee cups flung at its windows, fists battering its doors, feet kicking its walls. It has heard oaths and imprecations, for the time that we have spent here has not always been serene.

This house—it could tell stories.

But now there is new life promised this house. New narratives will take place within its walls. And I hope this house will embrace its new family with as much love as it did my own. I wish them as much pleasure from it as I have taken here, but wish them, too, less pain. They seem a far more sensible couple than my husband and I were when we moved here, less prone to histrionics, more likely to talk things out than shout and stalk away. But here too we learned to modulate our rage, learned to appreciate each other, learned to love well and wisely. A rich life is pain, pleasure, hope, disappointment, longing, fulfillment, love, loss, serenity, agitation, all in full measure.

Yes, now it's time to go. Time to close the door one last time. Time to let the house, once full of the din of our existence, ease into the loveliness and stillness of its temporary solitude. Some part of the house will settle more comfortably into the ground, and there will be a creak, a groan, that no one will hear. Above, airplanes will still dip lower than they ought, roaring their way to the ground a few miles away.

Out back, a leaf will detach itself from our neighbor's tree and fall, a prelude to autumn. A bird in flight will lose a feather. It will drift to the ground and will lie there later this day as the new owners enter this house to inspect their new home. On the slate patio, the rusted circle made by our children's wading pool, like a Zen ensō, remains. No human effort has eradicated it. Someday, perhaps—but not, I think, within my lifetime—the force of rain over time may pelt the patio clean and erase this mark that we have left behind. But for now the circle remains. Mute testament to the life we have lived here.

⌒

On the day after our move, I unwrap my grandmother's clock—it had traveled with her to America from Italy. After her death, it was my mother's, and she'd given it to my son Jason. But before our move, he'd given it to me.

"It should have been yours instead of mine in the first place," Jason tells me. But my mother had a special affection for her grandchildren, one that transcended even the special bond most grandparents feel. I was the daughter she couldn't care for; he was the grandson who gave her joy.

I know I will put this clock on top of my mother's china closet. It came to me soon after my mother's death when my father was getting married again. I get the china closet because my father calls me one day to tell me to come and get it if I want it, otherwise he's going to call a hauler to get rid of it and everything else from our family's life together—furniture, photographs, memorabilia. My father is moving on to a new life with a new wife. His new home—the home his new wife lived in for years—has no place for the china closet my mother and he bought used when they moved to the suburbs after World War II, no place for my mother's mirror, my family's photos, none for my sister's pottery, my mother's embroidered samplers.

"What a bastard," my husband says. He, too, is angry that my father wants to dispose of his past. And we hire a U-Haul and collect everything. But in time, I understood. My father needed to leave the past behind. He had lived with sorrow for too long. And this ebullient woman he was marrying gave him the hope of a happy late life, and there was no place in this life for the detritus of his past.

⌣

I had stopped the clock at 1:14, just before wrapping and moving it. The face of the clock was a burnished bronze with ordinal numerals that my father had etched onto it when he refurbished it for my mother after my grandmother died.

I am tired from the move. So when I take up the key to wind the clock, I drop it, and the key skitters over to the heat register, drops into it, drops down, far beyond the reach of any hand.

The key, irreplaceable. The clock, stopped, marking the moment when I left my old home behind and moved into this new place filled with promise and possibility.

ACKNOWLEDGMENTS

Thanks first, and always, to my husband, Ernest J. DeSalvo, who urged these essays along and saved one of them from destruction. And thanks, too, to my sons, Jason and Justin; my daughters-in-law, Deborah and Lynn; and my grandchildren, Steven and Julia, for the love and support that make my writing life possible.

My thanks to Audrey Goldrich, Ph.D.; Lesley A. Fein, M.D.; Tiffany Traina, M.D.; and the staff at Sloan Kettering, for their care throughout the completion of this book.

I wish to thank those who helped me conceptualize and revise the essays collected in this volume: Carol Ascher, Rosemary Ahearn, Alicia A. Beale, Anne Burt, Deborah Chasman, Peter Covino, Gigi Edwards, Hattie Fletcher, Patricia Foster, Edvige Giunta, Jennifer Guglielmo, Lee Gutkind, Kathryn Harrison, Christina Baker Kline, Jan Heller Levi, Mindy Lewis, Mary Ann Vigilante Mannino, John McMillan, the late Sara Ruddick, Salvatore Salerno, Joseph Sciorra, Alan Shepard, Gary Tate, Joe Vallese, Justin Vitiello, and Joanne Wyckoff.

The members of my memoir-writing group, Deborah DeSalvo, Patricia Forbes, Rosanne Guarrara, Susan Herman, Elizabeth Lapin, Elizabeth Lynch, Anastasia Rubis, and Stephanie Urdang, provided stimulation and support during a critical time.

I wish to thank Fredric Nachbaur, director, Fordham University Press, for his support; Will Cerbone, assistant to the director, for his help; Eric Newman, managing editor, and his staff, for their assistance during the final stages of preparing the manuscript for press; Ann-Christine Racette, for the cover design that captures the spirit of the book; Nancy Caronia, for her astute reading of the manuscript; and an anonymous reviewer for reading and responding to the manuscript with great care.

Certain names in these essays have been changed.

Versions of the essays collected here originally appeared in the following publications: "Ghost Writer," revised from "Ghost Writer" in *The Ocean State Review*, 1:1, "Breaking the Jar / Mending the Jar," in *Breaking Open: Reflections on Italian American Women's Writing* (West Lafayette, Ind.: Purdue University Press, 2003), and "Digging Deep," in *Coming to Class: Pedagogy and the Social Class of Teachers* (Portsmouth, N.H.: Boynton/Cook Publishers, 1998); "Lifeboat," in *superstition[review]*, (http://superstitionreview.asu.edu/issue8/nonfiction/louisedesalvo), and in my *Chasing Ghosts: A Memoir of a Father, Gone to War* (New York: Fordham University Press, 2016); "Cutting the Bread," in *The Milk of Almonds: Italian American Women Writers on Food and Culture* (New York: The Feminist Press at The City University of New York, 2002); "Dark White" (published as "Color: White/Complexion: Dark"), in *Are Italians White? How Race Is Made in America* (New York and London: Routledge, 2003); "Passing the Saint" (published as "'Mbriago"), in *True Stories, Well Told* (Pittsburgh: InFACT Books, 2014); "White on Black," in *Embroidered Stories: Interpreting Women's Domestic Needlework from the Italian Diaspora* (Jackson: University Press of Mississippi, 2014); "Fourteenth Street" (published as "Fourteenth Street, Hoboken"), in *What's Your Exit: A Literary Tour Through New Jersey* (Middletown, N.J.: Word Riot Press, 2010); "The House of Early Sorrows" (containing portions of "Faceless"), in *About Face: Women Write About What They See When They Look in the Mirror* (New York: Seal Press, 2008); "My Sister's Suicide," in *Sister to Sister: Women Write About the Unbreakable Bond* (New York: Doubleday, 1995); "breathless, adjective," revised from *Breathless: An Asthma Journal* (Boston: Beacon Press, 1997); "V and I" (published as "A Portrait of the Puttana as a Middle-Aged Woolf Scholar"), in *Between Women: Biographers, Novelists, Critics, Teachers and Artists Write about Their Work on Women* (Boston: Beacon Press, 1984); "Adultery Stories," revised from *Adultery* (Boston: Beacon, 1999); "Old Flame," in *Ploughshares* 35:2; "Moving On" (published as "Transitional Objects"), in *Dirt: The Quirks, Habits, and Passions of Keeping House* (New York: Seal Press, 2009).